'The definitive work on Asia's most vital river, this book
is more than sound scholarship and wise policy. Brian Eyler
shares lyrical and haunting stories, showing how and
why the Mighty Mekong must be saved.'

Ted Osius, Former US Ambassador to Vietnam (2014–17)

'A wonderfully illuminating and beautifully written portrait
of life along the Mekong, and of the forces transforming the
region. Eyler offers the type of insight that can only be
gained from years of on-the-ground experience.'

**Elizabeth Economy, Director for Asia Studies,
Council on Foreign Relations**

'A moving requiem for a complex ecosystem upon
which millions depend for their livelihoods. The book is
an indictment of the failure to treat the Mekong as a single
integrated system or to incorporate the local wisdom of
the communities who best understand the river.'

Judith Shapiro, author of *China's Environmental Challenges*

'Brian Eyler tells the story of a river veiled in mystique.
He sounds a warning about the ominous challenges it now faces:
the encroachment of the state, breakneck hydropower development,
the threats of climate change, and an increasingly powerful China
bent on harnessing the Mekong to power its continued rise. This is
the definitive story of the present and possible future of the
Mekong, and an elegy for one of Asia's great rivers.'

Sebastian Strangio, author of Hun Sen's Cambodia

LAST
DAYS
OF THE
MIGHTY
MEKONG

BRIAN EYLER

ZED

Last Days of the Mighty Mekong was first published in 2019 by
Zed Books Ltd, The Foundry, 17 Oval Way, London SE11 5RR, UK.

www.zedbooks.net

Typeset in Baskerville by seagulls.net
Index by Brian Eyler
Cover design by Alice Marwick

A catalogue record for this book is available from the British Library

ISBN 978-1-78360-720-4 hb
ISBN 978-1-78360-719-8 pb
ISBN 978-1-78360-721-1 pdf
ISBN 978-1-78360-722-8 epub
ISBN 978-1-78360-723-5 mobi

Printed and bound by CPI Group (UK) Ltd, Croydon CR0 4YY

MIX
Paper from
responsible sources
FSC® C020471

To Vicky

CONTENTS

LIST OF MAPS
AND FIGURES

ACKNOWLEDGEMENTS

This book came together over a period of more than 3 years after Zed Books reached out in September 2014 with the suggestion of putting together a book exploring the future of the Mekong region. I am grateful to Paul French for seeking me out and putting his trust in a first-time author. At that time I was living in Kunming, China teaching about China and Southeast Asia to American university students, and writing about happenings in the Mekong region on my website eastbysoutheast.com. I led multiple study tours for these students throughout Yunnan province and into Lower Mekong countries several times a year. These trips to the region showed us the wonders of the Mekong region and built the network of people the reader meets in this book. Later in 2015, I relocated to Washington, D.C. to research Mekong sustainability issues at the Stimson Center, a think tank that promotes pragmatic solutions to traditional nontraditional security issues around the globe. There the tutelage and camaraderie of Dr. Richard Cronin and Courtney Weatherby provided a silver lining to what I previously thought was a doom and gloom future for the Mekong. I am extremely grateful for their contributions to this book both substantive over the years of working together and editorial. The Stimson Mekong team would not have been possible without the longstanding support of Sally Benson and Steve Nichols who also provided integral support for getting this book out of the harbor.

The wisdom and inspiration of several individuals help make this work shine, like Khru Tee who I imagine constantly watching the river from his perch in the Golden Triangle. Ian Baird and Nguyen Huu Thien made significant contributions in correcting contextual issues as well as providing key interviews that set the book on a proper course. I would be nowhere in this venture without the facilitation of Dr. Apisom Intralawan or other people like Brendan Galipeau, Jerry Duckitt, Sorn Pheakdey, Nguyen Thi Thoai Nghi, and Jacqui Chagnon, and the staff at Khiri Travel who all helped introduce me to communities in the Mekong. I'm particularly thankful for the support of Virak Ellis-Rouen in Phnom Penh and Nguyen Minh Quang in Can Tho who set up key visits and were available on social media chat lines at all hours to answer even the most trivial questions in record speed. Mekong River Commission CEO Pham Tuan Phan also was always there to point me in the right direction in times of need.

Early conversations with Jeff Opperman, Jannie Armstrong, David Atwill, Tom Fawthrop, Yu Xiaogang, Jake Brunner, Sean Foley, and Francois Guegan provided insight and direction for the book's conceptual organization. Of course without my Kunming kemosabe Will Feinberg, a.k.a Xiao Fei, my understanding of Zomia and the Mekong's cultural milieu would still be in its primordial stages. Much of this book is inspired by the writing of James C. Scott, David Biggs, Benedict Anderson, Ian Baird, Thongchai Winichakul, John Dore, and Ed Grumbine. Particularly, I found inspiration in the works of John McPhee who makes the world's natural systems come alive on paper. Also we are indebted to Milton Osborne's literary contributions to understanding the Mekong system. Without his seminal book *The Mekong: Turbulent Past, Troublesome Future* this book would have little to rest on.

ACKNOWLEDGEMENTS

Kabir Mansingh Heimsath, Patrick Scally, Colin Flahive, and Ryan Haerer all took deep dives into editing and providing comments on early drafts of the book. Numerous translators assisted with interviews in four languages while collecting primary information in the Mekong region. Many of them will remain anonymous at their request, but those that I am happy to name are Ratana Khumporn, Varin Sutavong, Nguyen Minh Quang, Sorn Pheakdey, and Nem Sopheakpanha. To all of you, I am grateful. I would not have reached success with interviews in China without the productive Mandarin language teaching of Anne Wang Pusey and James Pusey.

Others who influenced parts of this book in some shape or form but did not appear in the text are Yereth Jansen, Li Wensheng, Li Lizhen, Liu Jinxin, Zhou Dequn, Alan Potkin, Fanny Potkin, Mak Sithirith, Somphong Sokdy, Mike Dwyer, Kim Geheb, Stew Motta, Remy Kinna, Sean Foley, Chouly Ou, Tek Vannara, Virak Chan, Pou Souvachana, Le Dinh Tinh, Huy Nguyen, James Borton, Sean Weatheralt, Maureen Harris, Pai Deetes, and Zeb Hogan. To those I've forgotten to mention, please forgive me.

I want to particularly acknowledge the GIS genius of Allison Carr, my former student in Kunming who designed the maps and diagrams for the book. Also, I want to thank the skillful eye and patience of Linda Auld, the book's copy-editor, for making this a much smoother read.

Lastly, and most importantly I want to thank my wonderful wife Vicky for her patience and surrendering of two years' worth of weekends. And I send a special thank you to my parents who planted the seeds of book writing and traveling the world a long time ago.

INTRODUCTION

The Mekong School, located in the Golden Triangle border town of Chiang Khong, Thailand, sits less than twenty meters from the edge of the famed river. The stilted, two-story teak structure was built by the community preservation group Rak Chiang Khong in 2013. Its meeting room is an open-air space on the school's second floor, and local community leaders often gather there on long, woven grass mats to share perspectives on how to preserve local culture, manage community forests, and protect the valuable resources of the Mekong River. The school's main building is only about twenty meters long, and adjacent to it is a small three-walled shack with an open façade facing the river. Three bunches of unripe, green bananas cut down from banana trees along the edge of the school's plot hang from the shack's supporting beams. A store-bought poster of the recently deceased Thai King Bhumibol Adulyadej hangs on the back wall next to large hand-drawn posters of Ho Chi Minh, Che Guevara, and Nelson Mandela. Below these is a painting of the Naga, the serpentine protector spirit of the Mekong. In the painting, the Naga's tail-end is violently hacked into pieces, but its eyes still possess vibrancy.

It is a brisk January morning, and I am sitting on a picnic table between the school and the river speaking with Niwat Roykeaw, the head of Rak Chiang Khong and teacher of all things Mekong. The locals address him as Khru Tee, which translates as teacher or guru, and the Mekong School is his ashram. Over the last few

1

days Khru Tee has shown me how local communities are adapting to changing local conditions. He tells me how local fish catches are in decline and how recently the Mekong's water level will rise unpredictably in the middle of the dry season. Both situations are related to China's dams located hundreds of kilometers upstream from Chiang Khong. His slight figure and long grey hair, tied in a quick tail that ends half-way down his back suggests the Western counter-culture movement of the 1960s must have hit the Golden Triangle decades ago. His main distinguishing feature is a long front tooth that protrudes slightly outward, out of line with the rest of his teeth. A deeper look shows that Khru Tee's eyes contain a flame that holds the stories of the Mekong.

In the 1960s, when Khru Tee was a boy he lived in a stilted teak house on the river side of Chiang Khong's only street. He helped his mother maintain a riverside garden filled with papaya, heirloom chilies, and eggplants, and collect small crabs, snails, and other tasty edibles from the river's banks. He watched fishermen returning to market daily with armloads of fish. On occasion the townspeople would congregate to see a freshly caught Mekong Giant Catfish, which can grow up to three meters long and weigh more than three hundred kilograms. When the cooler winter months came, the family slept on floor mats beside an indoor home fire, a common feature of homes in the Golden Triangle and upland Southeast Asia. The oldest generation always slept closest to the fire, and Khru Tee would compete with his siblings to sleep beside his grandfather's spot to stay warm. To lull him to sleep each night, Khru Tee's grandfather told him tales of the giant Bulaheng, the old man of the Mekong, a protector of the river and its surrounding lands. My personal interpretation of Bulaheng is that of a Paul Bunyan-esque character. Instead of cutting down the forests, however, he was the steward of the

Golden Triangle battling off evil spirits and outside invaders. Mountains and rivers were created from Bulaheng's footprints as he moved through the land. Just as Paul Bunyan raised Babe the Blue Ox to be a giant beast, Bulaheng raised the fish of the Mekong to be plentiful and gigantic and to provide for those who lived near the river. Where Bulaheng rested, he created flat land and taught the people of the Mekong how to plant rice in paddies and build fish traps.

In 2001 Khru Tee, along with a handful of Chiang Khong's residents, occupied exposed rocks in the middle of the Mekong just north of Chiang Khong. A few days before, engineers from China arrived in speedboats and set off explosives on the rocks as part of a development plan to clear the way for the passage of China's trading boats to points downstream. Locals believed the rocks to be a seasonal breeding ground for the Mekong Giant Catfish, and without them, the already endangered species could become extinct. Khru Tee and his friends successfully warded off the Chinese who then settled on building a port structure in Chiang Saen, a city forty km upstream. As Khru Tee told me this story, he said it was the spirit of Bulaheng that guided the protestors forward.

Through programming at the Mekong School, Khru Tee is trying to resurrect the legend of Bulaheng. "If people know of his legend, then they will understand how Bulaheng was a steward of this region's ecosystem. Through Bulaheng, children will learn how the pieces of our ecosystem work together and understand their place in this ecosystem," he tells me. For the past few years during the traditional fishing season for catfish, the Rak Chiang Khong group hosts a kind of festival to commemorate Bulaheng. Each year Khru Tee works with local children to construct a two-story marionette version of Bulaheng they use to parade through town and perform morality plays from the Bulaheng legend.

During our conversation, I make the suggestion that during this year's performance Bulaheng could encounter a dam on the Mekong and kick it down. Khru Tee's eyes light up. "Bulaheng kicks the dam!" he proclaims. "Yes, we will do this!" and proceeds to spread the idea to others sitting around the table. I remind him though that China is regrouping its efforts to destroy the shoals just north of Chiang Khong and canalize the river for the passage of large cargo ships. I ask whether his group is preparing to take action. "This time we will go out there again and stop them. We will have Bulaheng behind us, and if Bulaheng can kick the dam, then Bulaheng can stop the Chinese!" he remarks with assuredness. But given the rapid changes brought by the investment in bridges, highways, dams, and supermarkets in the Golden Triangle, some built by China and some not, keeping the Bulaheng legend alive is proving to be a very difficult task.

The Mekong River is 4300 kilometers long and runs through or forms the borders of China, Myanmar, Laos, Thailand, Cambodia, and Vietnam. Its headwaters originate high in China's Qinghai-Tibetan Plateau, and more than half of its entire length passes through China. In China, it is called the Lancang Jiang or Lancang River. To make it easier for readers of this book, I do not refer to the Mekong in China as the Lancang River. Until recently, most people in China did not know the Lancang and the Mekong were the same river, leading to much confusion in China as to why downstream countries were so critical of how China was treating the Mekong. *Where Have All the Fish Gone*, a documentary by veteran Southeast Asia journalist Tom Fawthrop, shows this disconnect when he films a Chinese diplomat saying that happenings on the Lancang cannot affect the Mekong because they are two different

Map of Mekong Basin

rivers. Chinese media coverage of transboundary events like the brutal 2011 murders of 13 Chinese traders on the Mekong River in the Golden Triangle has done much to grey the dividing line. But to many, the disconnection still exists.

Despite its length, China's portion of the Mekong contributes on average less than twenty percent of all the water in the Mekong Basin. The river originates in the Tibetan Plateau and after it enters Yunnan, its channel falls fast through deep canyons, running parallel to three of Asia's major rivers. In Yunnan, the distance between the Salween, the Irrawaddy, the Mekong, and the mainstream of China's longest river – the Yangtze, is at one point is less than 120 kilometers. In southern Yunnan province, the Mekong also passes close to the Red River, northern Vietnam's most important waterway. Immediately after leaving China, the river is unrivaled in its competition for water. Its basin draws water from all but a tiny northeastern portion of Laos, half of Thailand, and nearly all of Cambodia. South of Phnom Penh, Cambodia's capital, the Mekong branches out into a system of distributaries that deliver water to more than 30,000 kilometers of man-made canals in southern Vietnam's Mekong Delta.

More than sixty-six million people live in the Mekong Basin. This number includes most of the population of Laos and Cambodia, one-third of Thailand's sixty-five million, and one-fifth of Vietnam's ninety million people. China's portion of the river is sparsely populated with the exception of Jinghong, the capital of Xishuangbanna prefecture, the third largest city located along the river's banks with a population of 500,000. A trip down the river would reveal that most people within proximity of the riverbank are settled in small villages and towns with populations in the hundreds or thousands. The average rural person in the Mekong Basin either fishes or farms rice or other cash crops for an income of about $800 per year. The people of the Mekong Basin consume most of their resources directly from the river or the land around it, in addition to what can be purchased at local markets. For instance, the average Cambodian gets about 60 percent of his or her protein from eating fish caught from the Mekong system. On a float down the entire length of the river, which is made physically impossible by waterfalls at the border with Laos and Cambodia, urban areas like the capitals of Vientiane and Phnom Penh would appear as an occasional rarity. Yet cities like Phnom Penh are exploding with new arrivals from rural areas as their urban economies expand. Phnom Penh's population grew from 1.3 million in 2008 to 2 million by 2017. Vientiane's population has nearly quadrupled in the same amount of time from 208,000 to just under 800,000 in 2017.

This pattern of relatively low population density and occasional, yet booming urban development does not apply to Vietnam's Mekong Delta region. As soon as our hypothetical journey down the river enters Vietnam with less than two hundred kilometers to the sea, the once lazy river becomes crowded with traders and farmers. The people of the Mekong Delta transport goods via barges and longtail boats to floating markets located literally in the middle of the river or to large towns and cities like Can Tho, Long Xuyen, or My Tho. In the delta, seemingly unending rows of small one to two-story homes line the grids of man-made canals that were engineered over the last three centuries by the Vietnamese and the colonial powers which failed to dominate Vietnam. Here the population density is 425 persons per square kilometer, more than five times that of the rest of the upstream portions of the basin.

Until recent times, three traits – isolation, the river's unique hydrological cycle, and how these two traits interacted to produce diversity among humans, flora, and fauna – defined ways the river's people interacted with each other, the river, and its surrounding lands. First, the river bisected mainland Southeast Asia, creating a separation between historically Vietnamese and Thai zones of influence. Apart from the Khmer Empire, the river marked the isolated frontiers of kingdoms. To illustrate, a northeast Thai province which borders the Mekong is called Loei, which translates to "the beyond." To the Thai, this was the equivalent of no man's land or a place into which its civilization could not penetrate. Overland travel through the basin has always been difficult. The French explorer Henri Mahout noted how in the mid-19th century it took longer to travel overland from Saigon to the ancient northern Laos capital of Luang Prabang than it did to sail from Saigon to Paris. The Mekong's isolation meant that the great kingdoms and empires of pre-modern Thailand, Vietnam, and Cambodia rarely traded with each other and instead opted to buy goods from Chinese, Indian, and Malay merchants who dominated seafaring trade routes. To be sure overland trade did exist, and this was controlled historically by traders coming in and out of China's Yunnan province. Difficult terrain and relatively low populations determined that the power of these kingdoms rarely extended more than 100 kilometers from their capitals. Because of this problem of geography, modern concepts of borders were not introduced until the late 19th century, and the states that grew from these kingdoms have weak legacies of regional relations. In fact, these states have historically shared better relations with far-flung powers such as China, the Soviet Union, and the United States than with each other. When they did interact, it was to sack each other's capitals or to capture and enslave the subjects of adjacent kingdoms.

The Mekong River is often busy with boat traffic, but it is only navigable in stretches, and this reinforces its isolating characteristic. At its halfway point, exposed rocks and shoals in near the Golden Triangle restrict the passage of large cargo ships. Over the last two decades river trade has picked up between China and Thailand, but hard-to-navigate passes on the 180 kilometer stretch of river require the skills of the most experienced captains. Here the water level often runs so low in the dry season – which lasts from November to June – that China's trading fleet cannot leave dock. Much farther downstream, a natural fault line cuts across the river in Siphandone or Four Thousand Islands area at Laos's border with Cambodia creating an impassable series of waterfalls.

Historically, the challenges provided by mountainous elevation also reinforced the disconnected and remote nature of the Mekong region. A relief map shows that much of mainland Southeast Asia is above an elevation of three hundred meters, and the mountains that define upland Southeast Asia are some of the most difficult to traverse in the world. Kingdoms seeking to expand their reach overland through conquest or commerce all lost steam at the foot-hills of upland Southeast Asia and were easy pickings for the various ethnic minority groups who populated the hills. In wars against the French and Americans, the Vietnamese and Lao communist armies used this elevation to their advantage, hiding out in jungles and caves and taking down the world's strongest militaries by using guerrilla tactics instead of meeting their enemy convention-ally on the field of battle. The Khmer Rouge, a political regime responsible for the killing of over 1 million people in Cambodia from 1975 to 1978 survived in Cambodia's mountains for decades after their ouster by the Vietnamese in 1979. Even today, remote upland parts of the Mekong Basin are centers for opium production because weak states like Laos and Myanmar cannot march their security and drug enforcement agents up the hills to enforce anti-drug laws. At the same time, opium is the only product that fetches a high enough price for villagers or traffickers to be willing to walk it down narrow trails to market.

The river's natural hydrological cycle is its second defining trait. For as long as humans have settled in the Mekong Basin, they have relied on the river's seasonal floods to distribute water throughout the watershed and replenish fields with nourishing sediment flows that encourage high crop yields. Nowhere is the Mekong's unharnessed might more evident and impactful than the Tonle Sap Lake in central Cambodia. During the monsoon season, the hemorrhaging pulse of the Mekong causes the river draining the Tonle Sap Lake to reverse direction, sending so much water back into the lake that its footprint increases by nearly five times in size. This natural phenomenon gave rise to the Khmer Empire, which in the 10th century began to utilize the annual flood cycle to produce three yearly rice yields, enough to support a robust bureaucracy and army so large that the empire grew to cover most of mainland Southeast Asia. Next to the ruins of Angkor Wat near modern-day Siem Reap lie two enormous rectangular reservoirs built at the peak of the Khmer Empire, and these structures were used to retain water through the dry season to irrigate the empire's croplands. Today, Cambodia's modern-day irrigation system is not as sophisticated as it was between the 10th and 13th centuries. Because of this, currently farmers are even more dependent on water delivered by the flooding Mekong and Tonle Sap during the monsoon season. Further downstream in Vietnam's delta, the annual floods also support the livelihoods of the 18 million people who produce 75 percent of the country's rice crop on less than 12 percent of its land.

The two aforementioned characteristics of the Mekong, its remoteness and a robust distribution of water and resources within the river's flow brought forward by its natural hydrological cycle, come together to create the third unifying trait – a high degree of diversity, both among the region's ethnic people and its flora and fauna. Yale scholar James Scott describes the upland parts of the Mekong region as zones of refuge for ethnic groups who have chosen to flee expanding lowland civilizations like the Chinese, Vietnamese, or Thai. In his seminal 2009 work *The Art of Not Being Governed*, Scott gives this upland part of China and Southeast Asia a name – Zomia.[1] The domineering lowland armies could not march their wagons and weapons up the hills to reach those who sought refuge there. Forests filled with natural resources for food and trading sustained the livelihoods and identities of these peoples. This enabled the ethnic groups who lived in Zomia to interact with lowland kingdoms at arm's length on their own terms and in relative isolation. Thus, those who fled to the countless pockets of natural resource abundance were free to pick and choose cultural traits from their previous lowland experience and fill in the remaining blanks with their own invented customs and rituals. For example, China's Yunnan province, which the Mekong bisects, is home to 26 of China's 56 officially recognized ethnic groups and Laos has an astonishing 149 registered ethnic groups spanning 8 different linguistic families. Similar degrees of ethnic diversity are found in the upland areas of Thailand, Cambodia, and Myanmar located in or around the Mekong Basin. Zomia, as defined by the parts of mainland Southeast and China above the elevation of 300 meters, is one of the most culturally diverse regions in the world.

Researchers of the Mekong's fisheries have identified more than 1000 species endemic to the Mekong of which more than 700 are migratory[2]. Only the Amazon outranks the Mekong in terms of fish diversity, but the Amazon is near twice the length and its watershed nearly ten times the Mekong's. No river on earth has more migratory fish than the Mekong. Tropical rivers like the Mekong and the Amazon maintain warm temperatures which provide more opportunities for evolutionary speciation. In other words, fish sleep

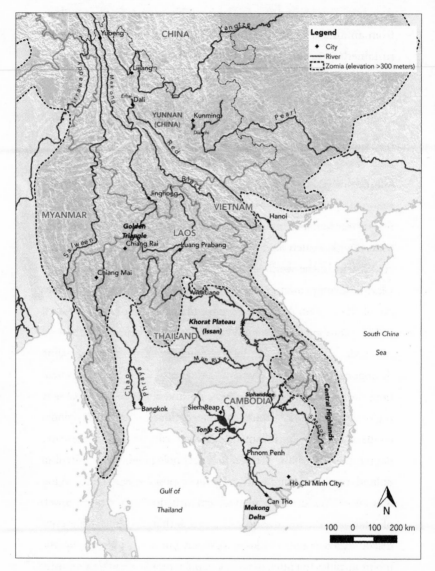

Map of Zomia

less and breed more often, thus speeding up the evolutionary cycle. In flat areas like the Tonle Sap, annual flood pulses send water deep into swamps and forests which enables wandering fish to draw from an almost unlimited nutrient base. The nutrient availability sustained by the annual flood cycle facilitates immense populations of numerous fish species. To illustrate, a typical day's catch on the Tonle Sap will contain more than 20 species of fish of varying sizes. Certain species of fish continue to grow as long as they have food to eat, so the abundance of food produced by the Mekong's floods have produced some of the world's largest fish like the Mekong Giant Catfish and the giant freshwater stingray as well as riverine mammals like the freshwater dolphin. The natural abundance of fish in the Mekong makes it the world's largest inland freshwater fishery, with a catch of more than 2 million tons per year.[3] No other river basin in the world comes close. To provide perspective, the yearly Mekong catch is 13 times more than the catch that comes out of all of North America's rivers and lakes – including the Great Lakes – combined.

Today these three defining and interdependent traits are being dramatically altered by dynamic processes related to modernization, national economic development, and the emergence of new regional frameworks promoting international trade and regional connectivity. Lowland centers of power can, to a much greater degree than the past, use modern technology to seize control of upland resources and hold sway over populations there. What was once a remote and isolated region is now captured in a web of interconnected road and rail projects that not only bring once disconnected countries closer together, but also penetrate up the mountainsides to entice droves of people, mostly young and mostly belonging to ethnic minorities, down to the lowland cities to melt into emerging modern lifestyles.

Countries along the Mekong are now manipulating the productive power of the Mekong ecosystem by harnessing its annual flood pulse and extracting sand from its bed. All of the Mekong countries seek to dam the river and its tributaries. Damming will regulate the river's natural cycle to feed a growing demand for power and distribute water for intense agricultural production. Currently China operates 10 dams on the Upper Mekong with 9 more scheduled for completion before 2030. Laos has plans for 9 dams on the Mekong mainstream and plans for more than 130 tributary dams – all part of its quest to become the "Battery of Southeast Asia." Cambodia will be impacted most by upstream dams, but it too has plans for two mainstream dams and a bevy of tributary dams. Countless studies show damming the Mekong mainstream and its tributaries will have devastating effects on migratory fish patterns and the livelihoods of local fisherman, but few policymakers in the basin heed such warnings. This puts the world's largest inland fishery under threat and subsequently the food security for millions of people who live within a few kilometers of the river and rely on fish catches for most of their protein. To build dams, construction companies clear massive areas of forest and force the resettlement of hundreds of thousands of people. It is said in Laos that population displacement from dam construction is now the top driver of internal migration. Most of these people are ethnic minorities, and upending them from their land and social connections threatens the cultural fabric that makes this region so culturally diverse and unique.

This is not to say that modernization and regional linkages do not bring benefit to the people of the Mekong. Prior to the 1990s, history shows that the region was rarely at peace. In the early 1990s, Southeast Asian governments and the UN joined together to find a diplomatic solution to the decades-long Cambodian conflict, and this coincided with a rapid acceleration of China's economic growth. These two factors delivered a period of relative peace throughout the region that by and large persists to the current day. Today countries like Vietnam, Laos, Cambodia, and Myanmar rank among the world's fastest growing economies. The average person in these countries is under the age of 25. Thailand and China, while moderately better off than the rest of the region, are now struggling with the growing pains of graduating into the ranks of high income countries. In the entirety of the Mekong region, the average person has never been healthier, more educated, or relatively better off than today. But that average person is choosing to engage in a lifestyle less derived from historical and natural traditions of the Mekong and more from the modern West and urbanizing China. Achieving this lifestyle often requires moving out of the basin itself to urban centers like Bangkok and Ho Chi Minh City or promoting trendy lifestyles in the basin's urban areas like Vientiane and Phnom Penh that emulate the consumer based cultures of Bangkok, Ho Chi Minh City, Tokyo, New York, or Beijing. All the while, the Mekong becomes more connected, more harnessed, and much less diverse.

This book demonstrates that the transition, even with the best intentions, is no simple task, for it is a case in point of trying to fit a square peg in a round hole. The machine of economic development that has delivered a relatively peaceful and stable livelihood throughout coastal and lowland Southeast Asia is beginning to now penetrate the inland and remote parts of the region. To keep this machine running, more resources are required. Since the Mekong River and its basin are seen as untapped treasure troves, these resources are being more intensely extracted. There is a common perception among policymakers in all Mekong countries that since the Mekong has provided a bounty of resources in the past, it will continue to do so in the future. Yet limits are beginning to manifest. Downstream countries often accuse Beijing of holding back water with its dams on the Upper Mekong. The Mekong River Commission, established in 1995 with a mandate to promote the scientific study and cooperation over the river's shared resources in Thailand, Laos, Cambodia, and Vietnam is seen inside and outside the basin as a failed institution because it has not established a platform that facilitates a coordinated and equitable distribution of the Mekong's resources. Vietnam and Cambodia continue to oppose Laos's upstream dams, and the rest of the region vehemently opposes Thailand when it diverts massive volumes of water from the Mekong mainstream for irrigation purposes. Thus, even at the national government level, there is recognition that approaches to developing the Mekong Basin are engendering current and future risks.

This book is a journey down the Mekong from the edge of the Himalaya in China's Yunnan province to Vietnam's Mekong Delta. It is the first of its kind to explore four cross-cutting themes that contribute to the dynamic social and environmental change sweeping through the basin: management of natural and cultural resources with a particular focus on water, wetlands, forests; tourism development; rural to urban migration; and climate change impacts. Milton Osborne's 2000 book *The Mekong: Turbulent Past, Uncertain Future*,[4] tells the history of the Mekong from its first settlements at Oc Eo recorded by Chinese traders 2000 years ago, through the Khmer Empire, then to the colonial era and finally to the violence of the 20th century, where the great powers fought proxy wars that brought Main Street USA to the heart of the Mekong. In some ways this book picks up where Milton Osborne's left off with worries of how a rising China would impact Lower Mekong countries. The environmental and social impacts of China's economic expansion into the Lower Mekong is another theme explored throughout this book.

This book, however, by no means is written with a built-in bias against China. I lived and worked in China for 15 years, and my appreciation for Chinese perspectives and development dilemmas is as strong as my appreciation for those of the 5 countries of the Lower Mekong. If this book is anti-anything, it is most critical of the development model that China has appropriated from the West. This model is defined by top-down, investment-led capitalism at the expense of protecting communities and natural biodiversity. Throughout this book I argue that while this model might deliver impressive results for lowland urban areas such as Shanghai, Bangkok, and Ho Chi Minh City, it might not work so well in the remote, upland, and riverine parts of the Mekong Basin.

As much as I can, I explore the history and local cultures of the discussed locales, paying some attention to food and important locations that highlight the Mekong's unique treasures, and I examine how these treasures are threatened. Thus, this book could serve as a companion for the more curious traveler passing through the basin. At the same time, an educated reader, academic scholar, and policymaker should find the book useful because it exposes the risks to the current mode of economic development and discusses pathways forward to improve development practices and protect the core ecology of the river basin.

The first three chapters take place in China's Yunnan province, and the emphasis on China in this book is not without purpose. After all, half the length of the river flows through China, yet most of the existing literature on the Mekong focuses on the portions of the basin downstream from China. Importantly, China is the dominant country in the whole of the Mekong, and its people, investors, and governmental approaches now penetrate deep into the Lower Mekong countries. Chapter 1 takes the reader to the remote Tibetan village of Yubeng, which has been described as the last Shangri-la, and looks at the impact of tourism and climate change on the livelihoods of Tibetan villagers. The second chapter explores the top-down development motivations for China's cascade of dams on the Upper Mekong, and why locals need to participate in bottom-up processes to keep their livelihoods intact. Chapter 3 takes the reader to the ancient capital of Dali and shows how pressures from tourism and agricultural development threaten the viability of Dali's most important resource, Lake Erhai.

The transition into Southeast Asia comes in Chapter 4 through the exploration of why the Akha people who live on mountain-tops in China and Southeast Asia are, after centuries of avoiding lowland cultural dominance, choosing lifestyles that now tie them into trends emerging at the global and national stage. Chapter 5 tells the story of how Chinese business interests – licit and illicit – are dominating the once indomitable Golden Triangle and how local villagers are adapting to change. It is here that we again meet Khru Tee and learn of his actions for local cultural preservation. Chapter 6 travels deep into landlocked Laos and shows how a weak bureaucratic government has little capacity or compelling political interest to improve the lives of tens of thousands of ethnic minority people affected by dams and other development projects, many of which come from China. Chapter 7 discusses from the viewpoint of the entirety of the Lower Mekong, how energy development could be better coordinated and more innovative so that existing plans for more than 180 dams on the mainstream and tributaries could be drastically reduced and result in a better cost-benefit outcome. Chapter 8 explores the destruction of Boeung Kak Lake, an important water resource in Cambodia's capital Phnom Penh, against the backdrop of political developments in Cambodia over the last half-century in Cambodia. Chapter 9 dives deep into the remarkable ecological processes that make Cambodia's Tonle Sap the world's largest inland fishery and explores how communities there are coping with depleting fish catches resulting from over-fishing and upstream dams. Lastly, the book finishes in Vietnam's Mekong Delta and explores options for adaptation in Vietnam's most agriculturally productive region now sandwiched between upstream dams and the rising ocean.

A central inspiration for this book is the theme of personal choice and how the implications of these choices could disrupt and potentially bring an end to the social and ecological nexus that has made the Mekong a vibrant cultural landscape and abundant place of biodiversity. Some of those personal choices are as mundane as the use of a smartphone, while others, like the choice to dam a portion of the Mekong, have much more profound impacts. To be sure, the reader should not get the impression from the book's title that the Mekong River is in its death throes. In February 2017, the CEO of the Mekong River Commission, Dr. Pham Tuan Phan remarked in an interview that "Hydropower development does not kill the Mekong."[5] His words sparked much controversy. If the Mekong is simply viewed as a waterway used simply for power generation, navigation, and irrigation, then certainly dams will not kill the Mekong. But the Mekong is much more than a just a river. Its natural bounty is what makes the river mighty, and its geography along with its natural provisions have given birth to a set of human experiences unique to the rest of the world. In this context, dams, new railways and highways, and the system that brings this new kind of development to the Mekong Basin will without a doubt, unless action is taken in the short term, irrevocably alter the cultural milieu and ecological abundance that still can be found in these last days of the mighty Mekong.

1

YUBENG: THE LAST
SHANGRI-LA

The Tibetan village of Yubeng is hidden halfway up the slopes of sacred Mt. Kawagarbo in China's Yunnan province just a few kilometers from the Tibetan border. Fifty years ago, reaching Yubeng from any nearby major urban area would take months of travel by horseback. No fewer than two decades ago, the only way for someone to reach the trailhead to Yubeng would be to hitch himself and his horse to a line stretching across the Mekong and use a pulley system to traverse the river canyon to the opposite side. Even today, reaching Yubeng is a two-day journey from Yunnan's provincial capital Kunming, 500 kilometers away. A bridge now permits car traffic to reach the opposite shore of the Mekong.

Local lore says Yubeng was "discovered" by itinerant traders leading pack horses along the Mekong in search of food. At the river's edge, a man appeared from the forest, greeting the traders with an offering of barley. In this section of the canyon, no settlements were known to the traders, so the man of the forest caught them by surprise. When they asked the man where he came from, he disappeared into the mountains without an answer. The next time the traders visited the canyon, they came across another man offering barley along the river. This time they were determined to know where the barley was grown. Unbeknownst to the barley seller, the traders poked a hole in his sack and later followed the trail of scattered barley over the mountain. At the end of the trail, in an unknown valley surrounded on three sides by the snow-covered peaks of Mt. Kawagarbo, they discovered the tiny village of Yubeng. The story concludes with a telling of how Yubeng's villagers knew little of the outside world since the surrounding forests and streams provided a bounty of resources and the holy mountain protected their livelihoods. In the hidden valley, all of their needs were met. Yubeng, like many of the remote villages around it, could have easily inspired James Hilton's Shangri-la as he described it in his 1933 novel *The Lost Horizon*.[1]

Even today, Yubeng's residents prefer the isolation of the hidden valley to what the rest of the world has to offer. However, today's Yubeng is also a burgeoning tourist destination for Chinese and foreign travelers willing to spend a few days off the beaten path and away from Yunnan's overcrowded tourist towns. Yubeng's remoteness and sacred pilgrimage sites are a draw for thousands each year. Many make the journey because they find it hard to believe a place like Yubeng could exist. The village still has no road access for wheeled vehicles. A tourist no longer needs to follow a trail of barley to reach Yubeng, but getting there requires a 9 kilometer, high altitude hike from the edge of the Mekong over one of Kawagarbo's low-lying ridges, no simple feat for lowland city dwellers in search of Shangri-la.

When I set out on a morning in June 2015 to make my ascent to Yubeng, I walked among 30 or so Chinese tourists bedecked in hiking fashion's brightest colors. The tourists gave an impression that one could not make the journey if it couldn't be done in style, and recent years of high economic growth in China provided the incomes to invest in pricey outdoor gear. Some who could not endure the climb had already saddled up on mules to be led over the ridge to Yubeng by local Tibetan men. In addition to the hikers, families of Tibetans wearing woolen robes were making their way up the trail to Yubeng. They chanted Buddhist mantras as they spun hand-held prayer wheels. From them I learned of a sacred waterfall located somewhere in the mountains behind Yubeng that was a side stop on the Mt. Kawagarbo's *kora*, a religious hike for Buddhist pilgrims circumambulating the entirety of the mountain. Because Mt. Kawagarbo is known as one of the most sacred Tibetan Buddhist mountains, ranking much higher in local spiritual hierarchy than Mt. Everest, Buddhist pilgrims revere the *kora* around Mt. Kawagarbo as a ritual act. Those who are able-bodied come from all over the Tibetan world to make the journey.

Completing the entire circuit of 240 kilometers takes on average 2 to 3 weeks, and pilgrims stay at local lodges offering basic room and board along the way. In recent years, as Tibetan Buddhist beliefs gain more followers among Han Chinese, more of these new believers are also choosing to make the arduous journey around the mountain. Indeed, some Chinese hikers and even a few Europeans and Americans that I passed on the hike to Yubeng sought to complete this spiritual quest. Many pilgrims were quick to note how completing the *kora* in 2015 was even more auspicious, since this was the mountain's birth year which occurs every 12 years according to the Tibetan zodiac calendar. In the Tibetan world, all inanimate objects, like mountains, trees, and lakes, are possessed or personified by deities or spirits, all deserving of pious worship. Mt. Kawagarbo is the spiritual abode of an eponymous Tibetan warrior deity. The mountain deity grants protection from illness, disasters, and other evils to those to pay their respect. Pilgrims who walk around the mountain are awarded with spiritual merit. Those who violate the mountain and its customs are punished.

At 6800 meters, the highest peak of Mt. Kawagarbo is far from the highest in the Tibetan Himalaya. In fact, it does not even rank among the top 100 highest peaks worldwide, but its 6 peaks covered with permanent snowpack are among the world's most stunning and have long been a major draw for outdoor enthusiasts and mountaineers. At the turn of the new year in 1991, a team of 11 Japanese climbers from Kyoto University and 6 Chinese climbers attempted to be the first to successfully summit Kawagarbo's highest peak. Despite protests from local Tibetan communities claiming the attempt to conquer the mountain was an act of sacrilege and disrespect to local belief, the team embarked for a journey from which none of them would return. Because their bodies were never found, little is known about the fate of the 17 climbers, but locals believe a freak avalanche swallowed the team as they were descending the summit on January 3, 1991. Since the disaster, which ranks as one of the worst in mountaineering history, none of the mountain's 6 major peaks has been summited, and in 2001, the local government banned all future attempts, citing religious and cultural grounds.[2]

After a 3 hour uphill hike through old-growth forests of conifers and rhododendrons, I stopped at an open pass where two of Mt. Kawagarbo's peaks, the fluted Goddess Peak and the broad, Giza-esque General Peak, came into full view. A middle-aged Tibetan man, who introduced himself as Asheng emerged from a shed that served as a rest-stop for hikers and pilgrims. He was holding a bunch of white thistle plants in his hand which he told me were snow lotuses, a rare medicinal herb that grows only in high-altitude areas and is known locally for its anti-inflammatory and youth-preserving qualities. I learned from Asheng that he was a native of Yubeng and had lived in the hidden valley all his life. Asheng disparaged city life, citing bad experiences from visits to Kunming. In the mountains, he could enjoy a life of liberty, maintaining a living selling the highly valued snow lotus and other treasures of the forest like matsutake mushrooms and caterpillar fungus, all of which fetch high prices in the outside world. At the end of a 5-minute conversation, he laid claim to being the happiest man on earth. He encouraged me to drop what I was doing and move to Yubeng to find true freedom. I told him I needed to walk on and see for myself.

As the trail from the pass snaked down a steep ridge, the Yubeng Valley came into view. From above, the sun reflected off the gold-trimmed roof of a Tibetan Buddhist temple nestled in the flat, lower portion of the village. Steep escarpments covered in lush vegetation surrounded the valley and hemmed in manicured fields of barley. Rolling mountain streams fed by the snow-capped peaks of Mt. Kawagarbo formed a cradle of deep valleys before flowing into a small river bisecting the valley center. Two-story Tibetan homes, encircled by plank fences for housing pack mules and other livestock, were more densely concentrated in the lower portion of the village than the upper portion where the homes hugged a ridge alongside a dirt path. A string of multi-colored Tibetan prayer flags several hundred meters long provided a spiritual link between the upper and lower villages. Tibetan prayer flags are commonly found throughout the Tibetan world. Prayers and blessings are printed on the small white, yellow, red, and blue flags. When the wind blows, the prayer flags are believed to bless the areas around them.

In the late 1990s, a slow trickle of outdoor enthusiasts from Japan, Europe, and the United States began making their way to Yubeng. Most were backpackers on their way through Yunnan and Southeast Asia traveling on a shoestring budget. At that time, much of Yunnan was not officially open for foreign tourism, meaning hotels and guesthouses did not have regulatory authority to house

foreigners. So the earliest foreign backpackers offered small donations to whichever local households in Yubeng would take them
in. They were in search of a rustic Tibetan experience in ethnic
Yunnan and had little expectation of comfortable amenities. One
of Yubeng's first guesthouse opened under these circumstances
when a local man named Ahnazhu began hosting foreign tourists
in his home. To start, he offered housing and food to the outsiders
for free in the same way that he would host pilgrims set on the *kora*
around the mountain.

Ahnazhu was the only villager who could speak Chinese
and thus the only villager who could communicate with the few
incoming tourists who could speak Chinese. Though development
of his language skills came from inauspicious circumstances, his
linguistic abilities then landed him in a position later in life which
made him the village's most wealthy and influential resident. Not
having a formal education, Ahnazhu learned to speak Chinese
while serving a prison sentence for accidentally killing a villager
with a rifle while hunting in the surrounding mountains. After
serving his time, he married a local woman and put his newfound
language skills to use. By housing tourists, he became the family's
breadwinner. Through the early 2000s, Han Chinese tourists
started to augment the flow of foreign tourists. These new arrivals
came most frequently during the three Golden Week holidays of
Spring Festival, Labor Day, and National Day, and because of
this, more locals began to convert their homes into guesthouses.
Ahnazhu followed suit, building a six-room guesthouse called
Trekker's Inn. In those early years of low tourist flows, villagers
charged less than a dollar for a night's stay and shared their
income with the rest of the village in a collective fashion. Yubeng's
villagers had always shared their resources, and at first the new
income from tourists was no exception. Ahnazhu managed the

income distribution network, and for a few years the system worked. Even though not all households took in travelers, all of Yubeng's villagers were profiting from tourism.

However, as notions of private property increased and households sought to isolate income from those who had not transitioned to hosting tourists, the villagers introduced a rotation system to reward only those who hosted tourists. Participating households were assigned tourists and then did not receive overnight stays again until the entire pool of households had received an overnight guest. The villagers figured that since such a rotation system had worked for years for transporting tourists over the mountain via mule, it could work for housing tourists as well. But the ballooning number of Chinese tourists, particularly during the Golden Weeks, made the rotation system difficult to manage. Some families had homes that could house 30 guests, while others only could house 10, and some villagers claimed not to be properly compensated for their time and energies. A handful of entrepreneurial villagers spruced up their homes. Some guesthouses were more comfortable than others and offered better scenic views. Tourists complained about how the mandatory rotation system forced them to stay in less appealing quarters for the same price as those with spectacular mountain views.

As business picked up, the villagers then agreed to a new system which allowed tourists to choose their lodgings. Neighboring households banded together in groups of four and pooled income to be distributed evenly among the four households. This way a lite version of the equitable, community-based tourism model could be preserved. But villagers began to lie to each other about how many tourists they were housing. Conflicts flared when neighbors showed up to count the number of tourists staying next door. Mutual distrust and greed – sentiments previously unknown to the villagers according to those who retold the story – caused a system designed with the best of intentions to fall apart. The system was entirely disbanded in 2009 when a state-owned tourism company from Kunming purchased the rights to develop and maintain the village and the valley's scenic hotspots for the price of an admission ticket. The company also required room prices to be set by market demand. Those households with better views and better service charged more. Amongst the villagers, competition for Yubeng's tourists was now in full swing.

Yubeng now receives an average of 100 visitors each day, and during major holidays, these numbers can increase tenfold. Most of these tourists are Han Chinese. A contributing factor to the rapid growth of Han Chinese tourism is the tripling of incomes in China over the last 20 years. More importantly though, Tibetan Buddhism has become increasingly popular throughout China. This new wave of spiritual interest came in the wake of the Global Financial Crisis. Unlike most other parts of the world, the Chinese economy sailed through the 2008 crisis, buoyed by a series of stimulus packages and tight currency controls which awarded government officials, state-owned enterprises, and private export firms with windfall profits. Prior to the Global Financial Crisis, a *nouveau riche* class was emerging in China's urban areas, but the wealthy class really came on the scene after 2008. Among other superlatives, China's fattened upper crust has since become the world's largest consumer of luxury items.

Social status in modern China is conspicuously displayed by the brand name of luxury fashion items you wear and the sticker price of cars you drive. It is also flaunted by the quality of one's political and social connections. Social upward mobility is not determined by what you know, but rather who you know and your ability to make those high-powered connections work to your advantage. When it comes to social customs and gatherings, Han Chinese prefer extravagant banquets and overproduced weddings attended by hundreds to demonstrate status and power. An anthropologist would call this a kind of social performance purposefully orchestrated to separate the "haves" from the "have-nots." One might think that China's newfound interest in Tibetan religion was a reaction against the material excesses of the late aughts, whereas in reality it emerged as a way to further separate the "haves" from the other "haves."

John Osburg, author of *Anxious Wealth: Money and Morality Among China's New Rich* said of the emerging phenomenon in a 2014 New York Times interview, "If you can't [distinguish yourself] from the rest of the herd with luxury consumption, then you look elsewhere."[3] For many Han Chinese, the practice of Tibetan Buddhism, which at its core asks practitioners to relinquish notions of self and social hierarchy, is turned on its head as a mechanism for social climbing in urban China. Historian Jeremiah Jenne, a long-time Beijing resident and witness to this spiritual revitalization calls the new obsession with Tibetan Buddhism a kind of "internal orientalism." He believes the trend is akin to non-Native American's embrace of Native American culture, religion, and aesthetic as a "lifestyle choice" without the internalization of tortured history between whites and Native Americans.[4]

This newly adopted lifestyle choice sends Han Chinese pilgrims to far-flung monasteries in Tibetan areas of Qinghai, Sichuan, and Yunnan provinces where religious restrictions are more relaxed compared to Tibet proper. There they compete for the attention of high lamas called "Living Buddhas" who are the earthly representatives of powerful deities from the Buddhist pantheon. Daniel

Smyer Yu, an anthropologist who specializes in China's post-Mao era religious revitalizations, claims Han Chinese are not attracted to these Living Buddhas for their wisdom or charisma, but rather for the status of the particular buddha that has reincarnated into their bodies – the higher ranking the buddha in the pantheon, the better the social appeal.[5] As a demonstration of status, Han Chinese believers are quick to share their encounters with spiritual ritual and enlightened Living Buddhas through sharing photos and thoughts on social media sites.

This is not to say that within this performance, which is acted out through a combination of tourism and religious pilgrimage, that Tibetan Buddhism does not provide spiritual growth to Han believers. To most Han Chinese, and for that matter to most Westerners who claim to be Tibetan Buddhists, the practice is viewed as an affirming and uplifting experience. Osburg claims that Chinese Buddhism in the post-Mao era is now perceived to be economically and politically corrupt. Comparatively he believes that Han Chinese interpret Tibetan Buddhism as a pre-modern and spiritual experience naturally leading to a well-spring of happiness.[6]

It is important to note that this perception has been formed simultaneously as the Chinese state's economic and political expansion into the Tibetan world has woefully degraded Tibetan society and culture. Paved roads and railways make it easier for Han Chinese to access the Tibetan space; thus, as Smyer Yu claims, the new surge in attention to Tibetan Buddhism has materialistically and spiritually revitalized the religion and its institutions. Due to their proximity to China's urban areas and relatively low altitude which reduces health risks and promotes longer stays, religious sites on the Tibetan periphery get the most attention. Yubeng's recent tourism boom is part of that experience.

Before hiking into Yubeng, most tourists spend the night at Fei Lai Temple, positioned on a mountainside directly across from Kawagarbo. If tourists are lucky to arrive at Fei Lai Temple on a clear day, they can catch a glimpse of Kawagarbo's peak set against the setting sun. There, tourists can choose to pay the exorbitant price of 160 RMB ($25) per person to pose for a photograph on a platform lined with eight white Tibetan stupas, one for each of the holiest Tibetan mountains, with Kawagarbo as a backdrop. Most Chinese tourists choose to buy the ticket, snap a selfie, and immediately send photos to their WeChat or Weibo accounts – all part of the performance.

Once they have made the hike over the mountain into Yubeng, most tourists stay for two nights and are determined to check off Yubeng's major holy sites. They will spend their second day hiking on an 8-hour round trip to the holy ice lake located beneath Kawagarbo's stately General Peak. They rise early on day three to make the 6-hour roundtrip trek to the renowned holy waterfall, Yubeng's most sacred pilgrimage site, before setting off for the 6-hour return hike to their vehicles parked somewhere along the Mekong. For 3 days in Yubeng, paying a visit to the prescribed sites is a rushed task, but to the Han Chinese travelers, the karmic payoff is worth the trouble. Downtime between hikes is typically spent getting a hot footbath, conversing with fellow travelers over a meal to share in the day's discoveries, and making an early bedtime. Some seek out the abbot of Yubeng's monastery for conversation. During the daytime hours, as tourists and pilgrims make way through the mountain trails, villagers and guesthouse workers are mostly free to tend to their farms and make preparations for the evening. Unless it is harvest season, most of this time is spent catching up with family members and neighbors. Most Tibetan locals that I talked to described tourism management as relatively low maintenance.

Before power lines made their way over the mountain to Yubeng in 2012, the afternoon idle time was spent collecting firewood in the mountains. During the peak tourist season at that time, each of the 20 guesthouses required more than 100 kilograms of firewood per day to heat up boilers for showers and cooking stoves. Ahnazhu, who in the mid-aughts was selected as Yubeng's forestry conservation manager, raised awareness of how the need for firewood threatened the surrounding forest. With more villagers scouring the mountains for timber, Ahnazhu noticed a spike in illegal wildlife poaching as well and worked diligently with locals to curb the practice. He warned that if the forests and wildlife disappeared, so would the tourists.

When Yubeng's tourist industry was transferred to the Kunming-based, state-owned tourism company in 2009, the original plan to electrify the village also included a road that would facilitate vehicle transportation. The locals balked at this plan, not because the road would bring in an uncontrollable amount of tourists and threaten Yubeng's pristine conditions, but rather because locals were deeply invested in more than 400 mules that generated income for households and gave the village's able-bodied men a source of employment. If the mules were unemployed, Yubeng's sons and husbands were likely to leave the village to find work in other parts of Yunnan.

Yubeng's villagers, like many Tibetans, practice polyandry, a marriage system in which a wife takes on two or more husbands. When Ahnazhu got married, he became his wife's second husband. In polyandrous societies, which are mostly found in resource-scarce and remote areas of the world, sons are still preferred because of their ability to produce for the family and defend territory. However, one wife marrying many husbands solves the problem of having too many unmarried men. Polyandry also controls population size by creating an incentive to stop wanting a son if your firstborn is a daughter. After all, when that daughter grows up, she will attract many husbands to contribute to your household. Just like many of Yubeng's communal resources, land and property are often shared equally between multiple husbands. A shared and equitable distribution of resources supported by polyandry is arguably what kept Yubeng "hidden" for so many years.

Now with the free market at play, maintaining that harmony, while at the same time managing the increasing need for resources to cater to the tourism boom, requires a constant conversation between villagers, the tourism management company, and a new influx of Han Chinese who now control the village's guest-houses economy by renting the guesthouses from local villagers. Ahnazhu's famous Trekker's Home is now managed by Hua Jie, a forty-something divorcee who pulled the plug on her life in urban, coastal China and moved to Yubeng after a visit in 2014. Wearing trendy, thick-rimmed glasses and camouflage fatigues, Hua Jie struck me more as a cosmopolitan type who sunk in well with a coterie of well-heeled mall-goers rather than a woman who sought out the spartan lifestyle that Yubeng offered. She noted that even after more than a year in Yubeng, caring for the guest-house was much more work than she anticipated, but that life in the village offered the experience of a tight-knit community, one that she had never experienced before. "I've come a long way to find tranquility and have fallen in love with this place. As long as people aren't here to make money, this place will continue to be perfect." She added that if a road is built, then greed will be the only beneficiary. "The government will come in, pave over every-thing, and build cable cars to bring in the tourists and run them up the mountainsides. Look at how cable cars have ruined every other scenic spot in China."

In 2013, Ahbiao, a Han Chinese native of Gansu province, purchased a long-term lease on one of the village's earliest established guesthouses and reinvented it as a luxury boutique hotel called Yubeng Impression. When discussing the ever-increasing influx of tourists, Ahbiao cited how many tourism sites in southwest China are now beginning to limit the number of tourist visits per day. "At the sacred snow mountains in Yading, just over the border in Sichuan, cars are limited to four thousand per day to cut down on emissions. The emissions from cars have an effect on snowmelt and this is a concern. You know, in Beijing, the Forbidden City is limiting eighty thousand visits per day to cut down on the crowds." Personally, having visited both sites numerous times, I felt these limits were set too high. "In 2015, the entry ticket to Yubeng went up from 80 RMB to 230 RMB as a way to limit tourists. But still they keep coming," remarked Ahbiao.

Ahbiao said that when he first arrived in the village, tourists couldn't find a comfortable foam mattress to sleep on. This reminded me of how I was spending my four nights in Yubeng on a thin, straw-stuffed mattress. His guesthouse is now equipped with fourteen well-appointed rooms, each with a view of Kawagarbo's peaks for 280 RMB per night, seven times the price of the room I had chosen. I told Ahbiao of the basic conditions at my guesthouse, and his response was, "This is why more villagers are choosing to lease their homes to outsiders. We [Han Chinese] know how to cater to the needs of Chinese tourists, what food they want, and the services they need. It would take a local a long time to understand this."

I asked whether the influx of Han Chinese operators gave tourists fewer opportunities to interact with local Tibetans, given that mingling with "pure and joyful" Tibetans, as the Han Chinese often describe Tibetans, was a desired part of the overall experience. He noted how all his guesthouses employees are Tibetan and how the Tibetan owner of the guesthouse, Master Arong spends most of his time on the guesthouse stoop chatting with tourists – something he couldn't do if he were managing the day to day duties of the business.

In the last decade, rising incomes and the increase in Han Chinese living and managing Yubeng's properties have changed the ways in which Yubeng's villagers interact with their traditional spaces. This ultimately impacts social relations and one's sense of belonging in the community. Some locals who had leased their homes now lived in smaller buildings behind or beside their large Tibetan homes. Some chose to purchase apartments and live parts of the year in nearby Diqing city. A few did this to stay close to their children enrolled in a boarding school in Diqing. Others bought homes in Kunming and only returned to Yubeng for major festivals and important family gatherings. Yubeng's social coherence was changing.

Later that day I had a long conversation with Master Arong who, after learning I was American, immediately revealed to me that the two people he most admired were the Dalai Lama and Barack Obama. He even suggested it was no coincidence that the two names rhymed. Master Arong also questioned aloud why people chose to settle in large urban areas, explaining that each of the few times he visited a city, a good sleep was hard to come by. He then pointed to the surrounding snow peaks and said, "This is what I see every day." Then looking at me with a mile-wide grin, he said, "And when I close my eyes, the mountains fill my dreams. Why would I ever choose to live in a city?"

On my third day in Yubeng, I set out early for the holy water-fall. I proceeded initially with caution, because the night before, my host spun a few cautionary tales about hikers getting lost in the mountains. Walking up the trail, I soon joined a family of Tibetan pilgrims who had traveled from Amdo in Qinghai province to circumambulate Mt. Kawagarbo. A toddler was strapped into a hand-woven papoose on the back of the eldest man, and later group members would take turns carrying the child up the mountain. We passed minor waterfalls and occasionally stopped at a scenic spot to add rocks to existing cairns created by previous pilgrims and tourists. As a custom, Tibetans build cairns by making vertical piles of smooth stones to make a connection with the spirits embodied in the natural features around them. We also passed near-exhausted groups of Chinese hikers who were taking their time to reach the waterfall, not being adjusted to the thin air at 3500 meters. After 2 hours, we came out of the wooded trail and hiked another 30 minutes up a steep rock path to the waterfall. Its white plume shot out over a brown, granite cliff about 100 meters above. Since I had arrived at the end of the dry season, most of the water transformed into mist before it reached the ground below.

The falls are said to be sacred because a spirit named Bendero lives at its headwaters. Locals must constantly appease Bendero through ritual and prayer. It is said that those who have collected herbs or cut down trees in this area have always fallen ill or died shortly afterward, but those who respect Bendero are rewarded with protection. A few weeks prior, two Chinese tourists were killed at the falls when an avalanche was triggered by their prolonged shouting, a practice which Han Chinese take up in public parks and on mountaintops to cleanse their lungs and release stress, but one that is taboo in the Tibetan world. Similar to the ill-fated Sino-Japanese climbing team, locals claimed that the mountain once again took revenge on those who desecrated it.

Below the falls, prayer flags of every color were draped over wet rocks. Small denominations of currency were stuck to the rock walls as votive offerings to the mountain. After making prostrations before a small white stupa, pilgrims and tourists alike walked in a clockwise fashion underneath the falls to complete a purification ritual. Some completed the circuit three times, and all who walked beneath the falls got thoroughly soaked. Chinese tourists posed for group photos using the falls as a backdrop. Most people approached the cascade in silent reverence.

On my descent, I passed a group of young Tibetan women transferring garbage from the trail's occasional garbage cans into large green bags. Two of the villagers were holding a sign that read in Chinese "Yubeng Village Trash Brigade." I figured they must do this frequently since there was little garbage along the trail, and I had observed no overflowing cans along the way. The women remarked that households are altogether paid 30,000 RMB (roughly $8000) annually to collect garbage only three times a year, a handsome sum in a country where yearly per capita income is roughly the same amount. The income was made possible by a tax on guesthouses. When one of the three garbage days comes around, villagers draw lots assigned to stretches of trail – some only need to collect garbage behind their homes, while others must haul the green bags out of the mountains several kilometers away. In addition to this, three villagers employed by the tourism company sweep the mountain trails once per month to help with upkeep.

In the mid-aughts, garbage collection was apparently not a difficulty, as a grant from The Nature Conservancy (TNC) set up a system which assigned villagers to clean up 50-meter patches of the trail. Family names were written on wastebaskets to demark responsibility for respective patches of trail. Those that helped with forestry management, like Ahnazhu, belonged to the village and encouraged residents to adhere to the household responsibility system. Villagers needed little financial incentive to keep the mountainside and its trails clean, and the TNC grant provided for the removal of 57 tons of garbage.[7] But when management of the national park transferred to the Kunming based firm in 2009, Yubeng's entry price was doubled to 80 RMB, and villagers earned a small portion of the ticket price to clean up garbage. Although money was being made, villagers stopped collecting garbage. They claimed that since the management company accumulated most of the benefits from the ticket (and provided very few services in return), the responsibility for garbage cleanup should have rested with the management company.[8] As a result, the conflict took 4 years to settle, and Yubeng's trails became unsightly and littered with rubbish from Chinese tourists who are globally stereotyped for not being able to put garbage in its proper place. In 2011, Liu Jianqiang, Beijing-based editor of the influential environmental website ChinaDialogue, hiked into Yubeng and remarked how the trail was then littered with garbage – an observation contrary to mine. Stopping at a rest stop, he remarked how stepping just a few meters off the trail led to the "ghastly sight" of garbage piles ridden with disposable ramen bowls, beer bottles, and food containers.[9] Gradually, ticket sales accumulated, and by 2013 the Kunming firm installed green and blue garbage cans which doubled as trail markers. At the same time, the guesthouse tax was levied to support the rotating cleaning crews.

Wang Bo, a Ph.D. candidate at the University of Wisconsin, spent more than a year in Yubeng researching how villagers are adapting to newly introduced waste management systems. He told me the system I observed on the way down from the waterfall is a major improvement but suggested that if tourists were more informed of how villagers interact with the mountains, then they would be less apt to leave garbage along the trails:

Villagers believe the mountains are living beings with the rivers and streams acting as the mountains lungs and arteries. Polluting these streams hurts the mountains. Tourists often hide bottles under rocks alongside streams beds but don't know how the waters expand in the monsoon season and wash garbage downstream creating blockages or permanently lodging garbage in places where trash collectors can't reach.

Wang Bo noted that if tourists interacted more with pilgrims, they would see that most pilgrims haul out the rubbish they take in with them.[10]

Locals told me that most of the garbage gets packed out by mules, but this was a convenient fib. On a walk through a forest grove just outside of Upper Yubeng, I came across a large storage shed overflowing with filled garbage packs. It was later confirmed that most garbage collected since 2013 resided in that shed – mules and horses often raided the shed looking for food and made quite a mess. Now, some villagers prefer installing a cable car from the edge of the Mekong into the village because it can be used to dispose of the garbage created by Yubeng's tourism industry. Pressures were mounting for a more convenient way in and out of the village.

One way to leave Yubeng is to follow a path along the course of Yubeng's central stream, which collects waters from snowmelt and precipitation in the surrounding valleys and cuts a gorge 700 meters deep on its short journey to the Mekong. The stream's crystal-clear effluent gets lost in the Mekong's muddy brown waters upon contact. During the Mekong Basin's dry season, which typically runs from November to May, an average of more than 40 percent of the water in the entire system comes from snowmelt in Yunnan, Sichuan, and Tibet – more than double that of the monsoon season. If global warming trends continue, the earth will likely experience a global temperature rise of 2 degrees Celsius by 2100. But in the Himalaya, a 2 degree rise could happen by 2050. If this happens, small glaciers in the Himalaya will likely disappear altogether and remaining glaciers will experience significant retreat. This means more than one-third of Himalayan glaciers, an area the size of Belgium, could disappear by 2050. Glacial melt will release massive amounts of water previously frozen for millennia into the Mekong, Yangtze, Brahmaputra, Indus, and other rivers whose headwaters rise in the Himalaya. These flows will peak between 2030 and 2050, likely to be followed by a sudden, irreversible period of water shortage if global temperatures continue to rise. Water is already a scarce resource in China, and China's government is rapidly making strides to build resiliency against the coming effects of climate change. One reason China is building hundreds of mega-dams in the headwaters of these Himalayan rivers, one could speculate, is to create a massive battery of reservoirs to store water from glacial melt for future use. This would do much to improve water availability in China, but importantly hold back significant flows of water from downstream countries, many of which also face growing water scarcities.

Barry Baker, a climate change expert at the Conservation Biology Institute in Fort Collins, Colorado, served as lead scientist on a project that studied the retreat of the Mingyong glacier which spills out of Kawagarbo's major peak about 7 kilometers upstream from Yubeng. Local villagers forbade Baker and his team from walking on the glacier or taking core samples, but comparative photography techniques using pictures taken by British explorers long ago compared against recent shots determined that the glacier has receded nearly 3 kilometers since the late 1800s.[11] Recent satellite imagery shows the rate of glacial retreat is accelerating: 1.2 kilometers of the three kilometer recession above has occurred since 2003.

One contributing factor to the speed of Himalayan glacial melt could be linked to the increased thawing of permafrost zones around and below glaciers. This zone covers an area many times larger than those permanently covered in snowpack, and it contains a thick layer of subsurface soil is that is always frozen. Around the Himalaya, global warming is causing lower elevation limits of permafrost zones to move to higher elevations, creating thinner bands of permafrost between snowpack at the tops of mountains and warmer zones below. At the same time, the layer of soil that is always frozen is thinning out. Together these effects introduce more heat around areas impounded by glaciers, and this promotes more permanent glacial melt.

Yubeng's villagers are well aware that Kawagarbo's glaciers are shrinking. Glacial retreat is caused by rising global temperatures and not by local factors, but Yubeng's villagers are so spiritually intertwined with Mt. Kawagarbo that they attribute glacial retreat to lack of proper prayer on behalf of local citizens, disrespectful tourists, and the increase of global material greed.[12] Yubeng's former mayor, Zhang Dafu remarked to me that Spring Festival, an important holiday even to Tibetans, has been notably warmer each year in recent memory. He also noted that Yubeng had no major snowstorms between 2012 and 2015." The lack of snow keeps the tourists coming in, but the snow on the mountain is decreasing. You know, a glacier used to dip into the ice lake, so worshipping the lake also made a connection with the entire mountain. Now that glacier is in retreat."

Yubeng's villagers take great pride in protecting the mountain. In 2005 they successfully lobbied to keep a damaging sawmill off the mountain. They still go to great lengths to lay curses on anyone who tries to climb the mountain and often talk about how the ill-fated mountaineering team got to their just deserts back in 1991. Despite the observable glacial retreat, they do not allow scientists, Chinese nor foreign, to set foot on the mountain's glaciers for further study. From a scientific perspective, as climate change begins to further affect the ecology of Kawagarbo, Yubeng's villagers and its tourists could be at risk from an increase in landslides and instances of drought. But given the deep spiritual connection to Kawagarbo, it is likely that the emotional scarring left as the mountain's snowpack and glaciers melt will have a much more profound impact on the local psyche. To the villager, less snowpack can only mean that the mountain's lifeblood is dying, and this fills them with a sense of grief. Reflecting on Master Arong's comment about his dreams of snow mountains, as Kawagarbo's snow diminishes into the decades of this new century, it is likely that the quality of his dreams, which are the psychological manifestation of his connection to the world around him, and his sleep, will forever be changed.

2

DAMMING THE
UPPER MEKONG

Just south of where the stream draining the Yubeng Valley flows
into the Mekong, the river cuts sharply through a series of steep
S-shaped canyons. A few years ago, the dirt path along the river's
eastern side was paved into a new highway. The road is most
traveled by Tibetans on motorcycles or oversized dump trucks
hauling minerals and sand from local mines and quarries. Small
Tibetan villages of 30 or 40 homes made of stone, wood, and sod
cling to the hospitable parts of the canyon's few terraces. Multi-
colored prayer flags connect each red-roofed home to the local
temple or Buddhist shrine. Sometimes the ends of these lines
disappear high into the mountainside. Halfway up the canyon,
the occasional white stupa keeps watch over these villages. Simple
suspension bridges, sturdy enough only for pedestrian or motorcycle traffic, span the river. Not all villages on the opposite side of
the canyon have bridge access, and their residents must travel a few
kilometers downstream to the next village to reach the paved road.

This pattern of village settlement is broken 40 kilometers downstream from Yubeng in the village of Cizhong where the four-story
steeple of a Catholic cathedral pokes high above the Cizhong's
homes. Eighty percent of Cizhong's 115 Tibetan households are
members of this cathedral, built from local stone in a standard
crucifix form in the late 19th century by French missionaries who

evangelized on China and Myanmar's periphery. Several times a week, ethnic Tibetan women wearing wide purple head wraps and men with cowboy hats file into the stone cathedral to take part in mass led by Yao Fei, the ordained Catholic priest who moved to Cizhong from Inner Mongolia in 2008. Before mass begins, prayers are sung in Chinese language to the cadenced melody of well-known Tibetan Buddhist chants. Frequently on Sundays, European tourists will line the back pews of the nave. They clutch long-lensed digital cameras as they document this uncommon marriage of Tibetan and Western culture.

Cizhong's conversion to Catholicism also made it home to a burgeoning cottage wine industry. Outside of the cathedral, a store sign written in Chinese with English language translation below reads, "One hundred years of French technology, pure handmade. Skilled brewing, white and red wine." Grapes and wine-making techniques were introduced by the French missionaries, but the local wine boom started in the late 1990s with the resurrection of a Rose Honey grape variety found growing on the cathedral grounds. This grape variety was wiped out by a disease in France that killed many grape varieties a century ago.[1] Before northwest Yunnan opened to foreigners in the 1990s, it was long thought to be lost. In the early 2000s, the local Deqin county government intro- duced agricultural assistance programs that brought in other grape varieties to supply a larger winemaking industry in the Shangri-la region. Currently, most villagers sell their grapes to middlemen after each harvest, but some choose to make their own wine to sell by the bottle at Cizhong's local wineries and guesthouses.

An unwelcomed change that threatens not just the local wine and tourism economy but also the unique, inter-faith harmony that enjoins the village's Catholics and Buddhists is coming to Cizhong. In 2018, Yanmen, an upstream community larger than Cizhong with more than 200 households, will be entirely relocated to Cizhong. Unlike Cizhong which is located on a long, narrow plain 100 meters above the Mekong, Yanmen sits low on the banks of the river. It will be completely flooded by the rising reservoir created by the new Wunonglong Dam located 12 kilometers downstream.

"We are most worried about village harmony," says a local wine-maker whose name here is changed to Tashi because of the sensitivity that looms large over relocation and land compensation issues in China. He tells me how the daily routines of Cizhong's Catholics are still deeply entwined with Tibetan Buddhist culture: "It's common for Buddhist monks to give blessings at Catholic weddings and Christmas and Easter. We've achieved this harmony through decades of exchange with our Buddhist neighbors." Combining aspects of dominant religions into a syncretic religious practice, particularly those from lowland areas, is a common trait of upland Zomian communities. But Tashi notes there are only a few towns in Deqin county with Catholic congregations. Yanmen is not one of them. He is worried that despite common ethnic heritage, the influx of more Buddhists, those that have not lived with Catholics, will upset community spirit and social interaction. He brands Yanmen's residents as overly superstitious and tells stories of how they are caught up in a spiteful sectarian feud between the Dalai Lama and Shugden, a local spirit who serves as the protector over the southeast portions of the Tibetan world.

The only place to build the homes to accommodate Yanmen's villagers is on top of Cizhong's rice paddies, which lie between the village and the river's edge. Cizhong's villagers had an emotional reaction when they learned their rice paddies were marked for destruction. The terraced paddies, collectively four or five times larger than the village itself, were carved out of the mountainside in the early 1960s in order to meet increasing grain quotas related to China's Great Leap Forward. Many elders still remember the toil of building the paddies, and today the communal farmland serves as an important space for social interaction since planting rice assembles the collective labor of the entire village. One villager claimed a single rice crop could feed the entire village for 2 years. Although the days of self-sufficiency have long passed in China, these villagers believe the rice harvest provides a blanket of food security and income that other villages in Deqin county do not enjoy. Cizhong is one of only two villages in mountainous Deqin county to have enough flat land for planting rice.

Land compensation is a contentious issue in Cizhong. More than half of Cizhong's agriculturally productive land will be used to either build homes for Yanmen's residents or be redistributed to the newcomers for agricultural use. When news broke of Yanmen's relocation, Cizhong's villagers received offers of 30,000 yuan per *mu* of land (one acre equals 6 *mu*) lost to Yanmen's relocation. Using recent land sale figures from other parts of Deqin county, Cizhong's villagers believe their land value is worth more than 10 times the initial offer. When I visited Cizhong in 2015 the local government's offer had already reached 100,000 yuan per *mu*, but Cizhong's villagers were still holding out.

A faction of Cizhong's former residents who moved away many years prior still owns land in the village. They were persuading those who still lived in Cizhong to take the government's current offer. Tashi told me, "The villagers who left for the city long ago and no longer live here agreed to an offer of 100,000 yuan per *mu*. It's easy for them because they have other jobs and other income, but to us, the taking of our land is taking away our main source of income." Some villagers will lose all of their productive land. Tashi told me how stall tactics make sense since the local government will take 30 percent of the compensation and only dole out the agreed upon compensation in monthly installments over 15 years. At the current offer, with only 3000 **RMB** per *mu* in compensation per month, even the most business savvy individuals will not be able to survive. "We continue to wait," says Tashi, but his lack of confidence is noticeable.

The day I walked through Cizhong was the last day for the 30 or so giant walnut trees that lined the village's only road. These giant trees were felled as part of a road widening project to make way for new traffic patterns introduced after Yanmen's residents moved in. When the trees were standing, they provided a shaded place to meet neighbors on an afternoon stroll. They also produced up to 10,000 yuan ($1500) of walnuts per year. Households throughout China's Zomian upland southwest rely on walnuts as a low-cost source of protein and healthy fats, and wild walnuts are known to fetch high prices in China's urban markets. Now, heaped remains of Cizhong's walnut trees were being scavenged for firewood.

Someone I talked to said one particular villager received 10,000 yuan in compensation, but word around town was that most villagers pocketed only 1000 yuan per tree, a fraction of one year's harvest. When I stopped along a roadside embankment lined above by a fence of grapevines, a local woman emerged to tell me how she lost an entire row of 100 vines to the road widening project. She was only compensated with 40 yuan per vine, approximately the value that one vine will produce in a year. The compensation provided by the dam development company sent a clear signal: you have 1 year to find a way to make up for the damage we've created.

In 2014, Cizhong's former mayor held a meeting with villagers who had filed grievances regarding the construction of the Wunonglong Dam and Yanmen's imminent invasion. Tashi, who attended the meeting said the mayor became enraged at the persistent villagers and said, "This land, this water, these mountains, they are not yours! Stop acting like these are yours! This is the state's land, and these are the state's resources." But to Cizhong's villagers who have lived in the Mekong Valley for centuries, the Chinese state only laid claim to these resources in the past decade, so it is easy to understand how their identity is formed by the landscape around them. "How can a state own a river? The river, like the land and the mountains around us, is part of us," said Tashi.

The struggles faced by Cizhong's residents are commonplace to those affected by hydropower development in China's south-west. At least the people of Cizhong can remain in their homes, unlike Yanmen's residents, but people from both villages demonstrate anxiety toward the challenges of establishing a new sense of community. Yet if the land compensation process does not award the villagers with a package that accounts for both the value of the land and loss of future income, the community's economic security will be put gravely at risk.

From Beijing's perspective, losses in Cizhong's and Yanmen's economic security are of little concern to China's centralized national development plan. Constructing cascades of dams on the Upper Mekong and the Yangtze River and its major tributaries the Dadu, Min, and Yalong, is a means to provide China with massive amounts of electricity to bolster its economic security and energy security. Through 2040, China's energy demand will increase by 90 percent,[2] forcing the country's power generation sector to add an installed capacity equal to that of the entire United States on top of its current generation capacity.[3] Increasing rates of urbanization, a need to remain competitive in the manufacturing export sector, and a rising consumer class drive this increase.

Three decades of intense economic growth have depleted China's energy resource endowment, and remaining deposits of coal, oil, and natural gas are located far from areas of high demand. China's first oil field at Daqing in Heilongjiang province is now nearly depleted. Waning production at Daqing in the early 2000s sent oil extraction industries to Xinjiang on China's western frontier. This also dispatched millions of Han Chinese immigrants to Xinjiang and has partially resulted in restive ethnic tensions between the local Uyghur population and the now dominant Han population. In the early 1990s China became a net oil importer,[4] and today China's overseas oil firms, which rank among the world's wealthiest, operate in every corner of the globe. China has almost always been a net importer of natural gas and now relies on a network of pipelines to deliver gas and oil from its neighbors in Southeast and Central Asia. The high costs of gaining access to and then transporting oil and natural gas to China suggests coal, which China has in relative abundance, will continue to occupy more than half of the country's energy mix.

China is the world's largest user, producer, and importer of coal,[5] which also makes it the world's largest polluter and greenhouse gas emitter. Recognizing the global effect of its carbon footprint, as well as responding to pressures to reduce the health risks related to crippling bouts of air pollution in large swaths of the country, China has made a commitment to peak carbon emissions by 2030. This commitment, announced in 2014, has been met with global enthusiasm and is seen partially as the driving force behind more than 200 countries coming together to sign the Paris climate change agreement in 2015. For China to hit peak carbon emissions by 2030, much of the newly installed capacity must come from renewable energy – including hydropower – generated from inside or within close proximity to its own borders.[6]

Enter the hydropower potential of China's southwestern rivers as a close, clean, and relatively inexpensive solution to this problem. China's plans for hydropower expansion came into view long before reducing its carbon footprint was part of its national agenda. The "Send west electricity east" campaign was conceived in the 1990s as a way to send the power of China's southwestern rivers eastward to fuel China's coastal factory zones and urban areas. In return, interior provinces like Yunnan, which were economically worse off than coastal provinces, would gain revenue that would help them shed their "backward" status. Since Yunnan contained a wealth of natural scenic areas, part of the deal also promised to keep polluting industries out of the province so that tourism dollars would continue to pour in. By 2006, when it became apparent domestic fossil fuel reserves were drying up, Premier Wen Jiabao pledged that by 2020, 20 percent of China's energy would come from renewables with hydropower leading the way.

Blueprints for increasing hydropower capacity on top of existing plans for hydropower cascades on the Mekong, Salween, the Yangtze, and their tributaries were put into effect. In the case of the Upper Mekong, original plans for 9 dams producing 15 gigawatts of power more than doubled to 20 dams producing 30 gigawatts. By 2015, Yunnan's installed hydropower capacity reached 50 gigawatts, enough power to light up 5 cities each with populations of around 10 million. To provide a comparison, the United States which now ranks second to China in hydropower generation has a total installed capacity of 100 gigawatts. Yunnan and surrounding Sichuan and Tibet currently are *each* slated for 100 gigawatts of hydropower. Before the last dam is built, upward of 8 million residents of these remote river valleys, most of them ethnic peoples, will be forced to relocate to lowland settlements far away from their upland homes. Darrin Magee, a Yunnan hydropower specialist, describes this as a transformation of watersheds into "powersheds," a term he coined. Instead of being valued for their multiple uses of water such as irrigation, tourism, or navigation, China's elite see these "powersheds" for the narrow function of producing power. By this logic, regardless of how the people living in these watersheds value their surrounding natural resources, the value of electricity production will always outweigh their needs.

The geology of Yunnan makes it a dam builder's dreamscape. The province's terrain drops 2000 meters from its mountainous northern border with Tibet and Sichuan to the tropical Xishuang-banna in its south. Where there are rivers, this loss in elevation creates long, deep valleys with few to no bends. Yunnan is home to a handful of the world's deepest gorges, like Tiger Leaping Gorge on the Jinsha River, one of Yunnan's most famous tourist draws. For the Mekong or any of Yunnan's numerous rivers, almost any location where the valley narrows makes an ideal setting for a high walled dam. As long as roads can be built to access remote sections of the river and its valley's residents can be cleared, these free-flowing rivers can be converted relatively easily into a cascade of still reservoirs purposed to maximize power generation capacity. Indeed this will be the fate of the entirety of China's Upper Mekong, and by the time all of the planned dams are built, the series of standing reservoirs will hold more water than two times the Chesapeake Bay.

In the eyes of the Chinese state, upland Zomians are consid-ered to be, and often are labeled as "backward," lacking the civilized qualities of the lowland Han Chinese. This prejudice is informed by centuries of treating those on the periphery of the traditional Chinese empire as barbarians, illiterate to Chinese ways and a marginal threat to the state. Imperial policies and expansion projects over the centuries attempted to civilize these peoples into the Chinese cultural tradition. By rule of thumb, the more successful and long-lasting an empire was, the more of the periphery was absorbed into the expanding Chinese state. Those

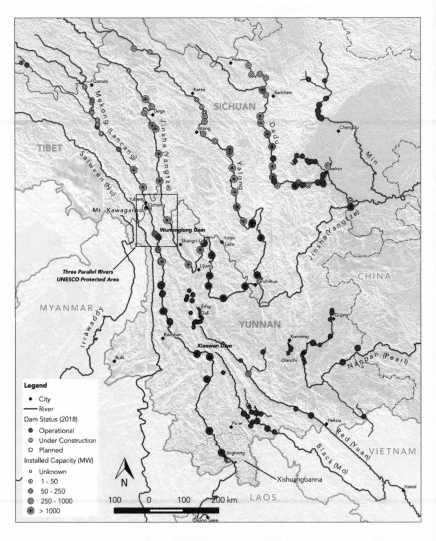

Map of dams of southwest China

who were not converted to the socio-cultural milieu of the civilized Han were either killed or further pushed to the margins. This is the historical process which sent many of these peoples into the remote Zomian upland areas in the first place.

In the 1950s, China's sociologists informed by Marxist theories of social evolution began to study into the upland southwest areas with the purpose of fitting the myriad of peoples living there into common Marxist classifications. Some, like the Wa people, were labeled low on the chain of social evolution as primitive hunter-gatherers, while others who practiced wet-rice agriculture like the Bai who settled around Dali were assessed as more civilized and thus achieved a higher ranking. None ranked as highly as the lowland Han with their millennia of agricultural and technological development. This ranking system converted the people of China's Zomia from barbarians to "backward" peoples requiring development programs from the Chinese government. Since the primitive mountain dwellers used archaic practices similar to those of early humans, then to some degree the cultures and practices must contain insight into early Han cultural DNA. This further supported Marxist theories of socialist evolution.

After 1979 when the Chinese government initiated its reform and opening policies, the method of civilizing remote ethnic peoples shifted from social programming to that of economic development. Now the best way to develop backward peoples was to convert their socio-economic framework to cash-based economies, make them effective laborers, and relocate them within a closer proximity to the national market. After all, the prevailing theory of economic development at that time suggested that it was only a matter of time before a rise in wages pulled these people out of the hills and into lowland towns and cities. These were underdeveloped peoples living in underdeveloped areas. If the state or the state's agents could use technology to optimize the resources of these underdeveloped areas better than those who lived there, this not only increased the general welfare of Chinese economic development, but also provided an opportunity to make these people better off even if it meant physically relocating them to new homes hundreds of kilometers away. To the chauvinistic lowland Chinese, relocating these upland peoples was doing them a favor.

The companies that build and operate dams are responsible for relocating and providing compensation to those affected by dam construction. Local county governments by law are mandated to oversee the entire process. The compensation process is mostly defined by simple accounting procedures. First an accountant takes an inventory of the assets owned by an individual household and then provides compensation. Next, the accountant measures the size of productive land on which the household conducts farming (because farming, to the state accountant, is the only way rural people can generate income) and provides access to comparable land at the relocation site or equivalent value in cash. By and large, this accounting process works in lowland areas because lowland rural people make their living from cash crops and little else. Since cultural values are shared between lowland farming areas and China's cities, adjusting to life in a new place is relatively easy. But in the case of providing compensation and transitional assistance for upland peoples, the accounting process rarely provides an equitable result.

When an accountant comes into a village like Cizhong or Yanmen to evaluate a compensation package for a household, he brings with him a world of assumptions based on years of living in the lowland. For instance, the accountant's livelihood and the livelihoods of all his friends and fellow employees are wholly supported by a monthly cash income. Since he is likely to be the male breadwinner of his household, he searches out the male head of the upland household and asks two questions: "How much income do you generate in one month, and can you identify the assets which generate this income?" The male head of the household responds with an answer somewhere in the range of 2000 yuan per month. For assets, he points to the patch of land adjacent to the home as well as the cows and pigs which will be sold to the local market when they mature. The accountant takes note of the number of marketable animals living within the family compound and then runs off to measure the size of the villager's arable land. The accountant makes a few calculations and then rattles off a number equal to the total value of the villager's assets and income stream. He then abruptly leaves without discussion. After hearing a number that sounds unconscionably low, the villager thinks, "Is that all I'm worth?" But the accountant's initial work is done and the villager now shoulders the burden to struggle for equitable compensation.

To achieve a more realistic outcome for upland villagers, the assessor would be better off augmenting his inquiry with a follow-up inquiry like, "Tell me what you consume every day that you don't buy at the market" because the answer here refers to things not immediately available around the resettlement community. The villager would scratch his head and begin to take inventory of the wood gathered from the surrounding hillsides used for cooking and heating fuel, the quantity of wild fish caught from the river below, the wild herbs collected from the hillsides that fills his household's diet, the local liquor that he distills in his backyard, the wild growing shrubs collected from around his home that are used to feed his pigs and cows. The list would grow and the assessor would scratch his head in frustration because he does not know how to assign a value to these items. After all, the upland economy is alien to him, and most of these items cannot be found in a marketplace. Moreover, if the accountant talks to the villager's wife, who is very likely to be the true manager of household resources, he will produce a higher yet more realistic picture of what is actually used to support the family's livelihood. Women in ethnic groups such as the Tibetan, Lisu, and Mosuo in southwest China often take up a high share of the workload and manage the household. But the accountant fails to understand, because by his own interpretation it goes without saying that males are the heads of the households in China.

The relocation site is never equipped with the abundance of easy resources like access to free water, animal feed and herbs growing alongside the home, and fish in the rivers. The government architects who designed the site do not think in terms of these freely available and shared resources, nor do they think in the terms of the actual space used by the household to produce its livelihood. After all, the government architects live in confined apartments in cities and all their daily goods are bought in a supermarket or department store. When a household moves into its fabricated home at the resettlement site, its members soon discover that the ratio of inside to outside space is turned on its head. Their previous home had small rooms but a large courtyard used for drying crops and keeping the animals at a distance in their pens far across the yard. In resettlement communities, villagers are given large homes with small yards. They often complain of living on top of their livestock with little room for the social interactions previously provided by their outside courtyards. Some communities are resettled in flat lowland areas far away from their mountain homes. Villagers here complain about the loss of fresh mountain air and inspiring views that defined their identity.

When construction began in the mid-1980s on the Manwan Dam, China's first on the Upper Mekong, government officials promised the remote agricultural communities in the surrounding area jobs and prosperity. The dam's developer, a provincial government-owned industry, proclaimed the reservoir created by the Manwan Dam would support fish farms and bring hordes of tourists for yacht cruises beneath the scenic green terraced hills and low peaks of the Upper Mekong Valley. The local government invested in a port behind the dam wall and convinced some wealthier locals to purchase a few large yachts for the incoming tourism boom. The only tradeoff for these villagers was that half of the valley's villages, the ones with the most agriculturally productive land along the riverside, would be relocated 300 meters up the hillsides. This meant that 3400 people, more than half of the Manwan Valley's inhabitants, would lose their homes.

In the early 2000s, Dr. Yu Xiaogang, director of Green Watershed, an environmental NGO based in Kunming, visited the hills above the reservoir and discovered most of the relocated households were living in impoverished situations. The dam began producing electricity in 1993 and nearly a decade after, there were no fish farms in the new reservoir, and zero tourists were taking advantage of the new fleet of boats then rusting at the docks of the Manwan port. He noticed many of the resettled villagers were employed by the dam's owner to clear the reservoir of the flotsam and garbage that accumulated behind the dam's wall – the only new jobs created for villagers. In 2001, Dr. Yu concluded that relocated villagers were shortchanged in the compensation process and sent a report of his disturbing discovery to his contacts in the Beijing government. Shortly afterward, the outgoing premier Zhu Rongji ordered a full reassessment of the social and environmental impacts of the Manwan project which at the time was a showpiece for investment in China's backward regions. Green Watershed was hired to conduct the assessment. At that time it was unprecedented for a national government official at the highest ranks to respond to the appeals of a local NGO. After all, this was seen as an issue for Yunnan province to manage, and the provincial government would not easily come to heel at the request of a small, unknown grassroots organization.

To conduct the assessment Dr. Yu brought in state of the art methods to identify and assign value to what was missed in the original process. Previously, villagers living along the river had access to the river's water for drinking and irrigation purposes, or they could draw water from small streams draining into the river. Dr. Yu's assessment discovered access to clean water was much lower after relocation. Also, the land regranted to villagers after the relocation process was much less fertile than that along the river-side which was naturally replenished by the river's monsoon floods. After relocation, agricultural yields were abysmal in comparison to before, because the villagers had no income to buy fertilizer to keep their fields healthy. He noticed a lack of social cohesion in the relocated communities and took note of the high instance of illness among elderly people as well as a spike in psychological problems and domestic violence. Previously, villagers would plant rice and tend their fields communally since the paddy areas were adjacent to each other. Living in close proximity required villagers to maintain a shared irrigation system that provided water for all. Now, land reassigned to the relocated villagers was spread far apart in the hillsides and poorly terraformed for irrigation. The transitional income given to the villagers did not provide means to create enough flat land for farming. Importantly, Dr. Yu discovered that the dam developer did not move village shrines and burial grounds nor did it provide villagers with the means to re-establish these spaces which are critical to the spiritual experience of these ethnic peoples. Villagers noted that they were never consulted on the importance of their religious shrines. These locally important areas were flooded and destroyed when the dam began to fill in the early 1990s.

When the Manwan reassessment was finished, Dr. Yu's team concluded that in order to restore the livelihoods of relocated peoples, an additional 13000 RMB ($1800) per villager was required. The team determined that the developer needed to provide means for irrigation, terraforming the land, and technical assistance for planting new crops. Also the reassessment found need for the construction of social spaces such as schools and town marketplaces. As was required by the special inquiry from the central government, the developer responded to the needs determined by the reassessment. Livelihoods of resettled peoples began the slow process of recovery. Today, a drive through the hills along the reservoir shows these villages are thriving at a modest level, so much so it is hard to tell the difference between the relocated villages and those that have been there for 100 years. However, other promises did not pan out according to plan. The entire reservoir with a length of 30 kilometers has fewer than 5 fish farms. Even after the construction of a highway with a bridge over the Upper Mekong at the head of the reservoir, few tourists stop to visit the area. Downstream, behind the dam wall, the giant yachts continue to collect rust and garbage accumulation continues to menace the dam.

When I first met Dr. Yu in 2004 he was working on ways to replicate his successful intervention at Manwan on current and future resettlement projects. Foreign foundations saw in Dr. Yu a champion for marginalized peoples and supported his operation with robust funding. His headquarters, then located inside the

Yunnan Academy of Social Sciences was staffed with world-class experts and volunteers rushing to join his cause. That summer, Dr. Yu was so busy that I, as a lowly graduate student researcher, could only get a 20 minute meeting with him. Earlier that year the Chinese government announced plans for a 17 gigawatt cascade of 13 dams on the Nu River which runs parallel to the Mekong on its western side. The western edge of the Nu River Basin forms Yunnan's border with Myanmar, and after flowing out of Yunnan into the heart of Myanmar's Shan and Karen states it is called the Salween. The Nu Basin is home to a number of ethnic groups, and because of its isolated nature, it has more endemic species of plants and animals than any river basin in Asia, making it an important biodiversity hotspot. Any damming of this basin would threaten the basin's ecology and building the 17 dam cascade in Yunnan would force the relocation of 45,000 people.

In early 2004, Huadian, the state-owned dam Upper Mekong developer Hydrolancang, rolled into the Nu Valley to promote the so-called benefits of dams to local communities there. Soon after, Dr. Yu's team sprang into action to hit the Nu Valley villagers with a dose of reality. His tactic was to transport groups of villagers from the Nu to the Manwan site along the Mekong. There he arranged for resettled villagers at Manwan to share the story of how their livelihoods were trammeled by the relocation process. The Nu villagers were so enraged when they learned that Huadian's false promises were merely a propaganda campaign that instead of returning home, they continued on to the provincial capital at Kunming to launch a surprise protest outside the government headquarters. This demonstration once again prompted a response from the highest ranks of government. Days after the protest in Kunming, Chinese Premier Wen Jiabao announced a suspension of the entire cascade until further assessments were made. Dr. Yu and his team had again struck victory. With dual successes under his belt and a tested formula for success in fighting for the rights of Yunnan's upland people, his achievement brought him international accolades. In 2006 he was awarded the Goldman Environmental Prize, and in 2009 he won the Ramon Magsaysay award, which is considered by many the equivalent of the Asian Nobel Prize.

But the suspension of the Nu River cascade in 2004 marked the beginning of a risky uphill battle for grassroots organizations like Green Watershed in securing rights and adequate compensation for relocated peoples. Hydropower developers like Huadian and Hydrolancang linked up with provincial and county governments in China's southwest to increase intimidation tactics and apply pressure on local communities to quickly accept relocation packages. As Dr. Yu tried to unroll his procedures for equitable environmental and social impact assessments, without warning Green Watershed lost its office leases and the organization was barred from taking foreign funding. After receiving the Magsaysay award in 2009, Dr. Yu's passport was pulled by the provincial government, prohibiting him from international travel.

The government stimulus packages released after the 2008 Global Financial Crisis gave China's powerful state-owned hydropower developers more cash and resources to ensure that their dam-building dreams were protected from further disruptions. In 2012 when Dr. Yu and a consortium of environmentalists entered the Yalong River valley, a long tributary of the Yangzi River to meet with representatives of the more than 100,000 people to be evicted from the Valley, they discovered most villagers were in a state of fear and shock over the relocation process. The local security bureau used intimidation tactics and told people that any resistance to dam construction would be met with the full force of the law. No one informed villagers in the Yalong Valley of their legal rights. Because of the increased security presence, Dr. Yu and his team were unable to produce similar results in negotiating with the dam's construction company or the local government. Most attempts at grassroots mobilization were thwarted at every angle. Since then, Dr. Yu has shifted to more arms-length techniques to impact hydropower development in southwest China.

"The hydropower lobby has nearly unlimited power at the local level, and it's become too strong in Beijing," Dr. Yu shared with me during a recent visit to Kunming. "This special interest group can easily influence the top ranks of government in Beijing and circumvent policymaking institutions such as the National Reform and Development Commission or the Ministry of Environmental Protection." He told me how the lobby promotes a discourse of clean energy to support China's economic development while generating fake news campaigns suggesting dam opposition is a plot by foreign interests seeking to thwart China's advancement.

As the power of the hydropower lobby increases, the space for organizations like Green Watershed to function at a grassroots level in China is shrinking. When he took power in 2012, Xi Jinping openly acknowledged the need for increased civil society partici- pation in solving the country's problems, particularly those related to environmental degradation and rural livelihood concerns. However in 2014, his administration issued a new registration law placing tight restrictions on the actions and funding channels for non-government organizations. But in a surprising turn, in 2016 the Yunnan provincial government announced a moratorium on damming the mainstream of the Nu River and unveiled a plan to develop the Nu Valley for mass tourism.[7] Apparently the Beijing government became concerned about the high instance of earth- quakes in the Nu Valley and forced the Yunnan government to change plans for damming the Nu. The Nu Basin runs adjacent to the Mekong, but an argument over seismic concerns is not stopping damming there. Many dam critics saw the Nu moratorium as a sign that the hydropower lobby is losing sway in Beijing. But if this is the case, fears of Beijing's tightening future regulation of dams could lead powerful developers like Hydrolancang to get started on the remaining proposed dams.

Today, Yunnan's Upper Mekong cascade of six mega-dams is fully operational. The 1350 megawatt Dachaoshan Dam opened in 2003 a decade after Manwan. Then in 2008 came the cascade's southernmost dam at Jinghong just a few kilometers upstream from the capital of Xishuangbanna prefecture. Shortly after this 1750 megawatt dam opened, its flood discharge channel was twice severely damaged by intense releases during the monsoon season. In 2011, a 4200 megawatt Xiaowan Dam went online. A behemoth with a 292 meter wall, Xiaowan was once the second highest dam in the world (at of the time of this book's publishing, it ranks third). Its reservoir holds the equivalent volume of half the Chesapeake Bay. Two hundred kilometers upstream, the 900 megawatt Gong-guoqiao Dam opened in 2011 and finally the Upper Mekong's other behemoth, the Nuozhadu Dam with a capacity of a whopping 5800 megawatts began filling its reservoir in 2014 and was not ready for full operation until 2 years later. The Nuozhadu reservoir also holds half the equivalent of the Chesapeake Bay, and its reservoir is more than 100 kilometers long. More than 43,000 people were relocated during the decade of Nuozhadu's construction. Above these dams, Hydrolancang has completed or is in the process of building 13 more dams of comparatively smaller capacities than the Upper Mekong cascade, but still capable of holding a massive amount of water. In 2012, plans for the Guonian Dam located at the foot of Mt. Kawagarpo were cancelled because of its proximity to the Mingyong glacier.

Construction on China's Upper Mekong dams continues, but the generation capacity of its existing dams on the Mekong is highly underutilized. Yunnan province currently wastes much of its hydropower due to congestion in China's national grid and a political economy that still favors coal as a main source of power generation in coastal provinces. Powerful interests in Guangdong, where 22 percent of Yunnan's power is sold, would rather buy power from coal plants in Guangdong than from Yunnan's dams. Despite recent reductions, coal will still account for more than 60 percent of China's power generation into the coming decades. It employs magnitudes more people than hydropower plants. If too much power from Yunnan is transmitted to Guangdong, this will put tens of thousands of unemployed laborers on the streets. Moreover, Guangdong stands to gain the most from new government policies promoting energy efficiency standards. So as Yunnan's hydropower capacity increases, Guangdong's energy needs are reaching a plateau.

This translates into wasted economic benefits for Yunnan province and dams that make little commercial sense for their owners. To illustrate, between 2013 and 2015, wasted hydropower capacity in Yunnan province rose tenfold. During 2014's monsoon season, because China's power grid could not absorb all hydropower generated from the battery of Yunnan's dams, hydropower firms like Hydrolancang were losing more than 100 million yuan ($12mn) per day.[8] In 2016, Yunnan's dams reportedly wasted 300 terawatt hours of electricity. In the same year, Thailand consumed half that amount. The glut of power is attracting new customers to plug directly into power generated by these underperforming dams. Recently crypto-currency miners have set up facilities in the Upper Mekong to take advantage of the dirt cheap electricity. Of greater concern, however, is the breaking of the decades-old pact between Yunnan and the coastal provinces that kept Yunnan clean and green. Now, heavy industries are relocating from the coastal provinces to Yunnan where they can access cheap power, and lax regulations in Yunnan province allow them to pollute freely

China's dam developers have now joined the ranks of China's off-shore oil companies as some of the world's most powerful and wealthiest energy firms. These developers are rapidly expanding their activities abroad, driven by the global demand for "green" energy and access to cheap financing from China's government-sponsored banks. Because of widely documented detrimental environmental and social impacts of large dams, multilateral financing institutions like the World Bank and Asian Development Bank have set a high bar for issuing loans to support dam projects around the world. This has created a space for Chinese financial institutions which have lower standards and often issue loans to curry political favor, particularly in the developing world. As is discussed in later chapters, Chinese dam developers are not the only game in town for damming the Lower Mekong, but they are certainly leaders among a pack of developers whose projects are slowly strangling the Mekong ecosystem and displacing hundreds of thousands of people.

· Owen's River

· not really a sense of place

3

THE ERHAI VALLEY

The 4200 megawatt Xiaowan Dam sits just downstream from the confluence of the Mekong and the Yangbi River which drains from Dali's Erhai Lake. In 1946 a group of American and Chinese engineers built one of China's first hydropower dams at a location between Erhai and the Yangbi's confluence with the Mekong to generate electricity for the city of Dali, but that dam was decommissioned in the late aughts when Xiaowan's giant reservoir began to fill. Today the name's Dali and Erhai are well-known among the Chinese populace as these locales are featured in a hugely popular historical fiction series written by Hong Kong author Jin Yong in the late 1950s and early 1960s.[1] But few in China and the rest of the region know the Erhai Lake is part of the Mekong Basin.

Prior to the 20th century, the Erhai Valley, like most of Yunnan, was isolated from the rest of China. It could only be reached by winding through high and dangerous mountain passes easily defended by the valley's inhabitants. This relative isolation coupled with a long and wide fertile plain on the west side of Erhai contributed to the rise of several independent kingdoms that not only, at times, challenged the expansion of the Chinese Empire, and at their peak created conditions for an empire whose control reached deep into Southeast Asia. In the 8th century, the dominant ethnic groups living around the Erhai Valley banded together to form the Nanzhao Kingdom and established a city-state near modern-day Dali. The success of these upland people in forming a thriving state structure certainly pokes holes in James Scott's theory that Zomians tend to avoid state formation, but we can assume a critical factor of the upland people's success was their settlement along the flat plain of the Erhai Valley to cultivate paddy rice. This would have produced a bumper crop that gave the Nanzhao the ability to build the foundation of a wider-reaching governance structure. Historical records from the Nanzhao era are sparse and difficult to decipher, but the records of surrounding kingdoms show that into the 9th century, the Nanzhao expanded deep into what is modern-day Myanmar, then into Laos and Thailand. Eventually, the Nanzhao expanded northward to conquer Chengdu, the capital of Sichuan province.

Positioned at the crossroads of trade routes between China and India, the Nanzhao emerged as a regional center for the study of Tantric Buddhism, the most sophisticated form of Buddhism at the time. Tantric Buddhism was likely delivered through intermittent alliances with neighboring Tibet, where the religion was widely institutionalized. In the early 10th century the Nanzhao overextended itself and eventually imploded when top members of its ruling family were murdered. This sent an exodus of people out of the Erhai valley. Today, scholars argue that the founders of kingdoms which over time would comprise the national identities of modern-day Thailand, Laos, and Myanmar were founded by those fleeing the Erhai Valley as the Nanzhao fell apart.

As Nanzhao was in decline, Duan Siping, a Nanzhao descendant, established the Dali Kingdom in 937 bestowing the area with its modern-day namesake, Dali. The Dali Kingdom was never as far reaching as the Nanzhao, but its dominance over most of Yunnan allowed it to flourish for three centuries as an independent kingdom and emerge as Asia's leading center for Buddhist teaching. Scholars from as far as Persia and India cloistered in Dali's highly reputed Chongsheng Monastery to study Tantric Buddhism. Religious pilgrims journeyed from afar to the Erhai Valley to worship at sites commemorating the life and times of the historical Buddha, Siddhartha Gautama, located along the lake's 140 kilometer shoreline. Today Dali's three pagodas which sit at the base of a replication of the Chongsheng Monastery, along with the ancient city wall, are the only standing structures remaining in the city from this time. In the last decade, Dali's tourism bureau has built recreations of commemorative Buddhist sites along Erhai's coastline in addition to Chongsheng Monastery.

In the 13th century, Kublai Khan's Mongolian armies overthrew the Dali Kingdom to establish an official administrative unit of the Mongol Empire called Yunnan. This was the first time the name Yunnan appeared on a map. Legend says that the invading Mongols were led through a secret path over Mount Cangshan by a traitor and put an end to the Dali Kingdom. However, it is more likely that the last Duan king directly surrendered to the cosmopolitan Mongol Horde, as he was rewarded with the title of Yunnan's first governor.

Dali's first Mongol ruler was Prince Hugeshi, a practitioner of Islam who garrisoned an army in Dali composed mostly of soldiers from Muslim parts of the Mongolian Empire. This demographic shift marked a transition from Buddhism to Islam in the Erhai Valley. Waves of Muslim immigrants began to dominate the region's trade routes. Dali's most famous Muslim governor was Sayyid Ajall Shams Din-Omar, who served in various positions in the Persian territories of the Mongol Empire and is thought to have been born in Cairo. By 1257, Sayyid Ajall successfully transformed Yunnan's agriculture economy and despite his Islamic heritage, introduced institutions of Confucian education and worship from Han China into Yunnan. Myanmar scholar Thant Myint U in his

2011 book *Where China Meets India*, describes Dali's Mongol period as the start of Dali's slow integration process into Han China.[2] Today, Yunnan's Muslims revere Sayyid Ajall as a founding father.

The center of political control in Yunnan shifted from Dali to Kunming with the fall of the Mongolian Empire and the rise of the Ming court in the 13th century. However, its isolation would again prove Dali to be a prickly locality when in the late 19th century, a local Muslim trader name Du Wenxiu led the Panthay Rebellion against the crumbling Qing dynasty and established an independent Muslim sultanate. Du Wenxiu's rule over the Erhai Valley and a large swath of Yunnan province went uncontested for nearly two decades. When the French explorers De Lagree and Garnier, who traveled up the Mekong on a failed expedition to find a navigable river route into China, neared the gates of Dali in 1868, they found themselves in the middle of a cosmopolitan regional capital, bustling with commerce and functioning governance structures.

The Panthay Rebellion was eventually put down when the Qing army marched on Dali in 1872. British soldiers allied with the Qing to put down the Taiping Rebellion in central China joined the Qing artillery ranks and surrounded the city walls. Du surrendered hoping that the Qing would show mercy to those loyal to him, but not before he consumed a fatal dose of poison. The Qing army removed Du's head from his corpse and shipped it to Beijing in a vat of honey to prove the rebellion was quashed. Then the Qing turned their guns on the city and drove its residents out of the valley. Thousands who could not escape were forced into the lake where they drowned. The crushing defeat of the Panthay Rebellion, and the larger Taiping Rebellion, along with a handful of other minor rebellions in southern China during the 19th century sent waves of migrants to seek refuge deeper into Zomia. Many of them fled through the Mekong's deep valleys into the Southeast Asian peninsula. Others fled westward to Myanmar where today Chinese Muslims are called the Panthay. Today Du's courtyard home is a popular site on Dali Old Town's tourism circuit, and a plaque at the entrance describes Du as an officially recognized hero who struggled against the Manchurian Qing invaders, who were themselves a foreign challenge to Han civilization. But the plaque underplays Dali's historical tendency to break away from the Chinese state.

Dali's rich historical legacy, the scenic backdrop of verdant Mount Cangshan which forms the western border of the Erhai Valley, and the blue water of Erhai Lake now draw more than 20 million tourist visits per year to Dali Old Town. By comparison, Angkor Wat, by most accounts the most famous attraction in the Mekong, receives less than 3 million visitors per year. By many magnitudes, Dali Old Town is the most visited tourism destination in the Mekong Basin. Similar to Yubeng, the influx of outsiders is driving a change in the local identity and puts the waters of Erhai, the Mekong's second largest lake, at risk.

In 1999, when I first visited into the Erhai Valley after a 10-hour bus ride from Kunming over tortuous mountain roads, Dali was a sleepy town mostly visited by wanderlust travelers who marked the city as the northernmost stop on backpacking tours of Southeast Asia. At that time, China still ranked as one of the world's poorest economies, with a per capita GDP of $800, eight times smaller than what it is today, and few Han Chinese could afford the time and money for a trip to Yunnan province. Many of the Chinese that did venture to Dali were young artists seeking refuge from China's rapidly urbanizing areas in the north and looking for inspiration in Dali's fantasyland. After all, Jin Yong's novels paint the region as filled with magic and natural wonders. These Han transplants set up art studios, cafés and guesthouses in their search for an alternative lifestyle inside the walled Old Town.

Tourism was far from the only game in town. The Old Town had all the functionalities one would expect in a Yunnanese town: schools, hospitals, several markets, the headquarters of a local military division, functioning Buddhist temples, and even a Catholic cathedral. Local companies quarried valuable marble from Mount Cangshan, and several women-led cooperatives produced tie-dye fabrics. Both products were sold in markets throughout China, and the tie-dye coops often won regional and global awards as model examples of small enterprises. Dali's silversmithing techniques were also well-known throughout China. In the late 1990s and early 2000s, on the cobblestone streets of Old Town, you could still see middle-aged Bai women wearing white blouses with intricately quilted wool aprons, their heads wrapped with black headdresses. They were bringing wares home from market or they were sitting outside their shops sharing the latest news of the town. Many of these women also took advantage of the freewheeling nature of the Western backpackers and began to peddle marijuana up and down "Foreigner's Street." When sipping coffee at an outdoor café, inevitably an old grannie would approach you and whisper "ganja ganja" in your ear. An outsider visiting Yunnan during this era would invariably run into a local somewhere along their travels who would remind the traveler that in Yunnan "the mountains are high, and the emperor is far away," and the local recreational drug trade was a reminder of the lack of control that Beijing held over China's periphery. At that time, most middle-aged and elderly men still wore the blue woolen *zhongshan* outfits popularly known as Mao suits. This fashion had already passed in most other parts of China. Some young women wore a moon shaped headdress made of white yarn with an embroidered crest – a tassel hanging to the right signified to potential suitors that they had yet to marry. Vendors selling *rushan*, a local delicacy of deep-fried cheese wrapped around a stick, marked the corners of major intersections.

One of my fondest memories of Dali was meeting Mr. He Liyi, an elderly Dali resident who spoke English and had recently completed a book in English called *Mr. China's Son* which detailed on his interactions with the Flying Tigers, a group of American airmen stationed throughout the eastern British Raj and China's southwest during the Second World War.[3] The book also detailed how he and Dali survived China's Cultural Revolution. Through a few publishing runs, *Mr. China's Son* attracted more foreign tourists to Dali. Dali's inspirational culture inspired American writer and entrepreneur Colin Flahive to move there in 2002. Although he did not stay long and chose to set up the successful Salvador's Coffee House in Kunming with a group of friends, Flahive recalled Dali's charm in his memoir *Great Leaps*. He writes, "Dali has the kind of charm that makes you want to spend each day at a different café and write the novel you never had time to work on. It's also a good place to settle down, buy a dog, grow some dreadlocks and spend each day stoned strumming the guitar."[4]

In 1999, on an afternoon walk just outside the old town's south gate, I came across some young laborers building row after row of monotonously designed storefronts that extended for several hundred yards into the distance. As a student at the time curious to know how China's future would play out in the new century, I couldn't help but want Dali to stay as it was forever. Since still so few people were coming to Dali, I asked one of the laborers for what purpose were the buildings being constructed, given they were so unlike the unique stone structures inside the ancient city wall. "Maybe shops, maybe guesthouses, maybe restaurants," he said. I countered with an observation that the few tourists that did visit Dali preferred to stay inside of the walls of the Old Town, the young man's reply was similar to one that I was to hear repeatedly from almost everyone I met over the next decade in China. "China's economy is speeding up – everything is going to change."

In 1999 a rail link from Kunming to Dali was completed. In the early 2000s a new expressway opened from Kunming, cutting my 1999 10 hour ride time in half. The added convenience made it easy to return to Dali. I took my closest friends from the US there, then I took my future wife, several groups of American college students, and finally in 2009, I took my parents to Dali on their first trip outside the United States. Into the decade, as disposable incomes continued to rise, tourist visits to tranquil Dali rose quickly year after year. In 2003, Fang Lijun, one of China's most prominent modern artists whose artwork now sells at record prices globally, purchased a small plot of land inside the southwest edge of Dali Old Town. There he constructed a studio and guesthouse using design styles which synthesized ancient Bai architecture with a modern, industrial feel. In the center of the courtyard was a koi pond covered partially by a glass structure with a transparent floor. The architectural style was daringly unique. When I first stayed there in 2004, like many who were awed by what China's *nouveau riche* were doing with their money, I had never seen anything like it in China.

Fang hired a local Bai man, Shi Laoshan to assist in building the guesthouse and has kept him on to the present day. I have visited the guesthouse nearly every year since then, caught up with Fang Lijun a few times, but more importantly established a long-standing friendship with Shi Laoshan who is now middle-aged. Like a true man of Dali Old Town, Shi's favorite hobby is perfecting body positions related to his afternoon nap which is known to extend into the early evening. Napping became more difficult for Shi around 2007 when tourism developers began knocking down entire blocks of Old Town to construct replicas of ancient structures like the Wu Temple just down the street from Fang's guesthouse.

The Wu Temple and many buildings like it were destroyed in the 1960s during the Cultural Revolution. But as tourists' tastes for re-experiencing China's past, particularly Dali's ancient history were piqued, replicas like the Wu Temple and Chongsheng Monastery were recreated throughout the valley. Nowadays the Chinese tourist frequenting Dali is not one looking for respite in cafés and art studios. Rather, these day trippers are often bussed in to be ushered around the Old Town in stretch golf carts. Tour guides espouse watered down versions of Dali history through loudspeakers attached to the golf carts. Or the tour groups are led on quick pedestrian tours through Dali's alleyways *en masse* by loudspeaker equipped guides. They visit sites like Du Wenxiu's home for a few minutes and pose for a photo before being ushered on to the next site. Restored Nanzhao temples in Dali Old Town and the Buddhist pilgrimage sites around the lake satiate the tourist needs of these day trippers. However, the clamoring lines of tourists which now pass directly by Fang's guesthouse interfere with Shi's notorious hobby and the desire for relaxation by his vacationers. In the evening, a raucous cacophony of noise from a row of 20 nightclubs in the adjacent alleyway each blaring live music penetrates into the guesthouse grounds. Shi Laoshan says the guesthouse still has plenty of customers but "those that come year after year say that the old feeling of freedom is gone. There are too many people in the Old Town. Many now choose to stay in guesthouses along Lake Erhai's shores. They want a quiet place."

The tourism business has brought much new wealth to Dali and lifted nearly all of Dali's residents out of poverty. Many have left Old Town, leasing their properties to outsiders like Fang Lijun. On my last visit to Dali in 2015, I caught up with an old friend, Ahzhao, a Dali native who has ridden the wave of Dali's tourism success. Ahzhao is ethnically Bai, and he got his start in tourism in 2005 as a middleman selling bus tickets and rides on a mountain scaling gondola just south of old town. In 2009 he and his wife borrowed money from relatives and purchased one of those nondescript concrete buildings I observed just outside of the city wall in 1999. The family converted it into a guesthouse and restaurant now famous for soup made of wild-caught carp from Lake Erhai and a braised pork knuckle dish renowned throughout the Erhai Valley. Local regulations required him to paint the building white and decorate upper parts of exterior walls with painted scenes of Old Town, Lake Erhai, and Mount Cangshan. Proud of the Bai tradition, Ahzhao also incorporated traditional Bai architectural designs throughout the guesthouse.

On that visit, Ahzhao and I sat down for some tea to discuss tourism's impact on Dali. He noted that many business proprietors from outside provinces who control a large majority of Dali's tourism industry only adhere to the minimum requirements for preserving the appearances of Bai architecture. This does much to dilute local cultural values. "We can't find a good Bai restaurant in the Old Town anymore," he said, an observation with which I agreed. "Ten years ago, we welcomed all of these new things because we had never seen them before, but now we need to be proud of our heritage and tradition." He laments how the flood of substandard restaurants, noisy bars and clubs lining Dali's streets, and throngs of shops selling congo drums and other random tchotchkes crowd out the handicrafts unique to Bai culture. To be sure, the silversmiths and local hawkers of quilted tie-dye clothing and wall-hangings are still to be found, but they often get lost in the flood of stores selling cheap souvenirs made in factories in faraway Guangdong province.

"If we lose our heritage, then Dali will only be a place famous for its scenic views," says Ahzhao. Like Shi Laoshan, he cites how more tourists are choosing to stay in guesthouses lining the lakeside several kilometers from Old Town. He tells me how some of the waterfront guesthouses rent rooms at exorbitant prices. Some rooms on the opposite side of the lake that have full views of the lake and snow-capped Mount Cangshan now sell for more than 3000 yuan per night ($500). He notes how a constant stream of well-heeled urban tourists now keeps those rooms constantly booked.

Before I left Ahzhao, he noted another challenge to the future of Dali Old Town, one that looms larger than any other: water management. "Every March and April the city runs out of water. You won't see this advertised online, but tourists who show up in the spring often go for days without washing. Needless to stay, they don't stay for long." He remarks how Dali's spring seasons are warmer than ususal and now the valley receives less rainfall. "When Mount Cangshan's snowmelt is gone, and its streams dry up, water is pumped in from the lake to irrigate lakeside fields, but it's not fit for human use." Ahzhao told me of when he was a child, how the streams flowing from Cangshan through the Old Town were filled with water year-round. Now a facility for processing drinking water bottles up much of that water for sale in local markets before it reaches the Old Town. Also the unfettered development of luxury real estate compounds offering lakeside views from the lower heights of Mount Cangshan divert water previously sent to the Old Town and lower areas. "Most hotels now are drawing groundwater from wells, but this is beginning to run out. Some hotels even have saunas! When we were young, we never saw saunas in Dali," said Ahzhao.

The 40 kilometer long fertile plain that sits between Erhai Lake and the 18 peaks of Cangshan mountain could feed an ancient empire, but meeting the current demand required by the mouths of tens of millions of tourists each year requires massive amounts of fertilizer, pesticides, and water. The volume of tourists creates incredible amounts of wastewater. This, along with fertilizers, pesticides, and animal waste, all runs downhill into the lake, creating a menace for the Erhai's ecosystem. After decades of poor prioritization and billions of yuan poured into failed water management policies, the lake's future sits on a razor's edge.

In 2001, Dali's local government realized it had a problem when it took more than 2 years to rid the lake of a persistent algae bloom. During the summer months, this algae bloom threatened water quality and the aquatic life in the lake. A previous decade of intense agricultural practices on the fertile plain between the lake and Mount Cangshan and a lack of water treatment for the flows coming from surrounding areas of human population created the conditions for algae to cover more than half of the lake's surface. The creeping volumes of tourists exacerbated this problem. Algae thrive in water with high levels of nitrogen and phosphorus, elements commonly found in fertilizer and untreated wastewater. These elements are critical to sustaining life in any lake, but when volumes spike, an algal bloom can spread at an uncontrollable speed and cover large portions of a still body of water. The algae then prevent sunlight from reaching the bottom of the lake, impacting on plant growth. Subsequently, fish and animals living in affected areas have less to feed on. Algae is a fast-reproducing but short-lived plant. When it dies, the decay process consumes a disproportionate amount of oxygen from a still body of water, robbing a lake of oxygen and threatening the viability of the lake's ecosystem to sustain life. This process is called eutrophication, and if left unattended, it can kill a lake.

Lessons from Yunnan's capital, Kunming, showed the stewards of Erhai Lake that a dead or dying lake would threaten incoming tourism. In the early 2000s, Lake Dianchi, which sits on the southern edge of Kunming was rendered useless by an irrepressible series of algae blooms. Local Kunmingers who grew up swimming and fishing along the lake, China's eleventh largest in area, lost faith in its municipal government's ability to rein in the lake's pollution problem. In addition to the algae bloom, unfettered dumping of industrial and public waste into the lake left Dianchi's water unusable for even the most basic purposes. In 2003, all fishing, boating, and swimming in the lake were prohibited and this prohibition exists to the current day. Tourism was only a small part of Kunming's local economy and not all tourists visiting Kunming would utilize or appreciate scenic views of the lake. In contrast, local government officials in Dali knew its tourism future depended on keeping the lake clean.

On Erhai Lake, early improvement measures were targeted at managing and cleaning water at a few key polluting points along the shore. The prevailing approach was to build water treatment infrastructures where water enters the lake to catch pollutants and restore the lake's natural nutrient balance. The local government built facilities to filter and treat water coming from Dali Old Town and other rapidly growing communities around the lake. In its northern, upstream reaches, the government created man-made wetlands filled with plants to naturally filter the nutrients out of the incoming water and to slow the pace of water flowing into the lake. The government toyed with replicating Kunming's use of water hyacinths on the lake to cut down on pollutants. Water hyacinths are an invasive species found floating in lakes and streams worldwide, and their root system can effectively consume and sequester large amounts of nitrogen and phosphor. However, Dali quickly abandoned this plan when neighboring Kunming introduced water hyacinths at such a rapid rate that the fast-reproducing plant quickly covered the entirety of Lake Dianchi, delivering the same devastating effect as an algal bloom.[5]

The summers of 2004 and 2005 passed with no signs of algae returning to Lake Erhai. But in 2006, following a particularly warm spring, another algal bloom, this time the worst to date, forced another round of infrastructure investment. This time, the approach once again plowed money into physical infrastructures by once again increasing the number of lakeside water treatment plants and artificial wetlands to control point source pollution. An additional measure removed all practices which would directly introduce fertilizers and waste into the lake. At the wave of a hand, lakeside fish ponds and rice paddies managed by local communities were converted to wetlands. The grazing of animals along the lake was made forbidden and rural shoreline homes were demolished. Little compensation was given to households to alleviate the impact to their livelihoods, and many locals had to sell or lease their land to outside investors.

These measures have kept major algae blooms at bay for the last 10 years with only sporadic occurrences in a few spots along the lake's shoreline, but evidence suggests the lake's ecosystem is still at risk. Professor Zhou Jun from the faculty of Natural Resource Management at Dali University has been researching Erhai's water quality for the last decade. On a trip to Erhai's shore-line, he noted that fish biodiversity is dropping at an alarming rate. "Ten years ago, the water was clear enough to see much of the lake's bottom, but now because the water is filled with pollutants, sunlight penetrates less than two meters of water," he noted. He said this increased turbidity, or cloudiness in the water, means that less of the lake bottom is covered with grass. In turn, there are fewer plants to absorb and filter nutrients flushed into the lake. Those plants also take up a critical position on the lake's food chain. "Only about 10 percent of the lake's deeper reaches can now support life. This is changing the structure of the lake." Historical records show Erhai to be one of Yunnan's major fishing grounds, but poor water quality and the introduction of invasive species have culled the lake's diverse fish populatoin.[6]

"Dali was once known for its fishing sailboats, and people came from far and wide to see them. Now Dali's fishing fleets are side-lined for much of the year and can only operate if the water quality reaches level two. Even then, they can only fish for a few weeks of the year," said Professor Zhou. Water quality at level two is a designation set by the Chinese government. The quality of water worsens as the numbered ranking system increases. Water rated at level one can be directly consumed as drinking water without treatment. Level two water is potable with treatment. Level three is suitable for agricultural use, and level four is suitable only for industrial use. Level five is deemed too toxic for use. Kunming's Dianchi Lake has fluctuated between the fourth and fifth levels for the last two decades.

Economic development and the tourism boom has created the need for new food supplies, and this, in turn, has introduced new streams of pollutants into the lake's ecosystem. While milk, cheese, and yogurt have only within the last 10 years become a coveted part of the mainstream Chinese consumer's diet, processed dairy products have long been part of ethnic Chinese cuisines. This is particularly found in Tibet, Mongolia, Qinghai, Sichuan, and northwest Yunnan province where pastoral livelihoods were a key part of the traditional economy. *Rushan*, the deep fried cheese dish, and pan-fried or steamed white slices of cheese often served with local salted ham are integral parts of Bai cuisine. Large patches of grasslands hidden atop Mount Cangshan served as the traditional grazing grounds for cattle and goats. But Dali's tourism boom and the greater region's new infatuation with fresh milk has refocused the dairy industry to Dengchuan, a town on the northern edge of the lake. There the cumulative manure footprint produced by Dengchuan's 100,000 dairy cattle equals more than 14 million pounds of nitrogen per year. During the summer monsoon months, much of that nitrogen is washed downstream into the lake. Some of the manure is marketed to farmers as fertilizer for use on Erhai's fertile plain. This, in turn, sends these nutrients into the lake. To date, no market opportunity has arisen to transport the fertilizer out of the valley.

Recent economic growth in Southeast Asia and India has caused a surge in the price of garlic, and the Erhai Valley has responded to fill that rising demand. Historically farmers at the north end of Erhai only produced rice and beans to serve their subsistence diets, but in the last decade, 90 percent of farmers there planted garlic during the non-rice seasons. Garlic, which is produced for export, requires large amounts of artificial fertilizer. Previously farmers were wary of the amounts of chemicals spread on their fields because they consumed what they planted. Now the consumer market is out of their sight, so farmers tend to pile on the fertilizer.

The same can be said for pesticide use. A local restaurant owner once warned me not to eat the fresh arugula often served in local Bai salads because local farmers who grow it use more than ten times the recommended application of pesticide. The heavy use of pesticides, which are cheaply purchased in local village markets, guarantee a timely crop yield and a visually appealing product. This helps guarantee a sale. When driving or riding a bicycle along lakeside fields, one will invariably see countless farmers with portable pesticide packs strapped to their backs spraying away at that season's crops. When the summer monsoons come, excess pesticide and fertilizer from agricultural production are washed through treatment plants ill-equipped for proper filtration. During the summer months, the color of the lake turns a greyish blue.

In 2014, the Dali government launched its "2333 Plan" which sets a goal for Erhai to reach level two quality in 3 years using 3 billion RMB spread over 3 project designations. What looks like more of the same approach is exactly that: throwing money at the problem and relying on government action for change.[7] The plan would convert another 20 square kilometers to wetlands, build wastewater treatment plants in every village, and end point-source pollution from each of the 117 streams that feed into the lake. After describing the 2333 plan, Professor Zhou Jun noted his worry that these efforts might not be enough. "What we need to do is focus on restoring the lake's ecosystem, change locals minds about agricultural practices, and not encourage the Erhai Valley's big industries to cheat. Long term improvement is brought about by behavioral change, not by government funding." Professor Zhou also noted how the proliferation of lakeside guesthouses which without exception sent 100 percent of wastewater into the lake posed a new threat to Erhai's water quality. To observe the impacts the new lakeside guesthouses, he recommended I visit Shuanglang, a new tourism destination sitting across the lake from Dali Old Town.

I had been to Shuanglang in 2009 before tourism really took off there. On that visit, I considered buying one of four newly constructed lakeside residences in Shuanglang that had just hit the market. Dali and Mt. Cangshan across the way would make the perfect view for a Yunnan vacation home. Similar to Fang Lijun's guesthouse, this building was designed with a mix of modern and Bai architectural styles, the fusion of which was an emerging trend in the late aughts. I quickly decided against it because Shuanglang was too remote for my liking, and I actually worried that the Beijingers who constructed the buildings would not recoup their investments. Part of the draw to Shuanglang in 2009 was a small island no bigger than a soccer pitch, populated by a handful of traditional Bai homes built centuries ago. These homes opened into large courtyards surrounded on three sides by a two-story wooden structure. Hand-carved wooden window panes and transoms displaying traditional Bai motifs decorated the interior walls. A fourth side to each courtyard was formed by a white and grey wall, also two stories high, made of stone and concrete. The wall's interior was positioned to reflect sunlight into the home and warm it on cold days. Large Chinese characters painted on the fourth walls of these courtyard homes gave them an air of sophistication.

On the tip of the small island were two large modern structures which stood in contrast to the traditional Bai homes. These were the twin vacation homes of Yang Liping, China's most famous dancer. Yang helped put Yunnan on China's cultural map by staging her trademark peacock dance during a mid-1990s performance on China's annual Spring Festival Gala, an annual not-to-be-missed television event. To most Han Chinese, Yang's dance is a manifestation of Yunnan's place in China's nation-building narrative – an ethnic, feminized match to Han China's dominant, masculinized culture. Her dance uses the peacock theme to represent an untamed and exotic aesthetic that fixes Yunnan as a diverse, uncivilized province on China's periphery. Yang's two mansions, one called the Palace of the Sun and the other Palace of the Moon are vermillion marble structures built into the rocky shore. Inside, ceiling-to-floor windows offer a total view of snow-capped Cangshan across the lake.

Over the years, the combination of Yang Liping's celebrity draw and Shuanglang's scenic views have brought a tourism explosion to Shuanglang. In 2010 Shuanglang was awarded an exit from a new highway running along Erhai's eastern shore connecting Kunming to Lijiang, another major tourist destination to the northeast of Dali. The highway entirely bypassed Dali's Old Town. Those tourists headed to Lijiang who did not have time to visit Dali, all began to stop in Shuanglang for a day trip.

After wrapping up my interview with Professor Zhou, I rented a motorbike to make my way around Erhai to Shuanglang. Before parting, Professor Zhou warned me that Shuanglang was now the worst that Yunnan tourism had to offer and predicted overdevelopment of tourism in Shuanglang would soon bring some kind of crisis to Erhai's eastern shore. As I approached Shuanglang, car traffic had already backed up more than 2 kilometers outside of the town's entrance due to a lack of parking. Impatient drivers chucked half-consumed plastic bowls of ramen noodles along the roadside. The lakeside building I had considered purchasing six years ago was now a coffee shop. The building beside it was now a bar that apparently, at least according to the signs outside the building, was a famous matching ground for one-night-stands, a new fad among single Han Chinese tourists to Yunnan.

The Han Chinese have long viewed the female side of Yunnan's "barbaric" and "backward" ethnic peoples as sexually promiscuous. In art galleries throughout China, Han artists often depict ethnic Dai women from southern Yunnan's, Xishuangbanna bathing nude in the waters of the Mekong. In another example, the "walking marriage" tradition of the Yunnan's Mosuo people is often interpreted by Han Chinese as one where married Mosuo women could engage in sexual relations outside of their marriage at will. I first heard of the walking marriage from a Beijinger who told me Mosuo women were polygamous and could "walk" with any men they wanted. Male Han Chinese tourists now flock to Lugu Lake, the traditional home of the Musuo people, 200 kilometers northeast of Dali, looking for a good time with Mosuo women.

Reality tells a very different story about the "walking marriage." The Musuo are a matriarchal society which developed in relative isolation in the mountains along the border of Yunnan and Sichuan. In the Mosuo walking marriage tradition, a husband must physically move into his wife's household, but custom requires him to return to his mother's home during the daylight hours to conduct household chores. As in Yubeng, this arrangement promoted the role of women as household leaders and encouraged gender balance among offspring. Prior to motorized travel, after completing his daytime chores, a husband had to walk to his wife's home each evening and then walk back to his mother's home every morning. The custom was labeled as a walking marriage by Chinese anthropologists. But as early tales of the Mosuo people, who were "discovered" in the 1980s, spread through mainstream Chinese culture, the walking marriage tradition was interpreted as one which gave Mosuo women the right to engage in free sexual relations with whomever they please. On visits to Lugu Lake, male Han tourists are often impressed with the charisma of the Mosuo women, but they do not find what they are looking for. To compensate, the tourism town of Lijiang, not far from Lugu Lake, has capitalized on such unmet expectations and over the last decade has turned into China's capital for one-night-stands. The new highway from Kunming to Lijiang has caused this practice to seep into Shuanglang.

Shuanglang had expanded to four or five times the size I remembered from my visit in 2009. All around was the smell of acetone and glues being used to build new guesthouses, each trying to outcompete the other for views of Cangshan. I asked an owner when the guesthouse building frenzy began. He did not know since he had only arrived from Jiangsu province a few months prior, but he boasted how Shuanglang had more guesthouses than Dali Old Town, a statement I found hard to believe. In the middle of town, a blue metal fence encircled a patch of land containing the jack-hammered remains of the village's three-story schoolhouse, which was soon to be replaced by a five-star hotel. The village's open-air marketplace with its carved and ornate platform for holding local opera performances and town meetings was now the only public space remaining that villagers could use to congregate. Every other inch of the town had been colonized by guesthouses, coffee shops, restaurants, and brand-named retail stores.

When I approached the pedestrian bridge to Shuanglang's island, a ticket seller appeared and made me purchase a 10-yuan admission to the island. I asked whether revenue from ticket sales would go toward preserving the island against the onslaught of guesthouse construction. She refused to tell me how ticket revenues were used. On the island, the traditional Bai courtyards I had remembered were nowhere to be found. They too had been knocked down and replaced by guesthouses, some of which were five or six stories high. Without exception, all of these new struc-tures sent wastewater directly into the lake. The pathways through the small island had turned into narrow canyons which never saw the sun. Because of a lack of space, workers were welding window fixtures together as tourists tried to squeeze their luggage around the makeshift construction sites. I could not imagine who would want to spend a few hours here, let alone a few days. As I rounded a corner by a half-built guesthouse, a pound of wet cement fell from above onto my head and shirt. I looked up at the workers who care-lessly caused this minor accident to happen and shouted for them to take greater caution. They did little to acknowledge that they had ruined my clothes, nor did they offer an apology. I washed off the cement at a public bathroom and decided to get back to my motorbike as fast as I could. Before leaving the island, I did find one of the old courtyard homes, however, now converted into the kitchen of an adjacent guesthouse. I made a pact with myself never to return to Shuanglang.

Some think awarding Dali with UNESCO World Heritage status could be a way to introduce a more stringent set of standards for protecting the Old Town's historical legacy and the lake's ecology. This scope of the UNESCO Heritage designation could reach as far as to provide a restorative umbrella over Shuanglang. But if neighboring Lijiang Old Town serves as an indication, UNESCO World Heritage designation status could make the situation even worse. After winning World Heritage status in 1997, Lijiang's tourism flows boomed, and today the city receives almost 40 million tourists per year, nearly twice as many tourists as Dali. In 2007, UNESCO threatened to remove Lijiang from the list of World Heritage sites because overcommercialization there had all but erased the educational and historical value of the local Naxi culture. Today Lijiang enjoys an infamous reputation among most Han Chinese as a den of tourist traps and sleaze bars, and the city struggles to maintain its image of one of Asia's top tourism destinations.

In Dali and the surrounding Erhai Valley, as is true in all other parts of modern day China, local government officials sit at the top of the economy. Their political success is measured by their ability to continue to drive economic growth within their locality. In their eyes, better roads bring more tourists and more tourists bring more guesthouses, restaurants, and retailers. The seemingly endless cycle of growth brings huge tax revenue to localities like the

Erhai Valley and also many opportunities for officials to engage in corruption and graft. Thus, the political futures of local officials are secure as long as tourists' visits increase year on year and officials are able to sign off on tax and income generating projects like hotels and luxury real estate complexes. Additionally, officials in China are known to skim funds off the top of these investments for personal benefit, and this practice continues despite Xi Jinping's wide-reaching anti-corruption campaign.

To solve problems associated with sustaining economic development, officials inside and outside China's portion of the Mekong Basin are incentivized to add more physical infrastructure to a landscape. They are incentivized to work this way rather than to engage with a broad set of stakeholders to identify root causes and build a shared market-based or community-based approach to find innovative and efficient ways to manage problems. This misalignment of incentives and lack of participation of local stakeholders to identify needs and sustainable solutions creates a vicious cycle in China that has careened out of control and is wrecking local ecologies and communities. Unlike other communities in the Lower Mekong explored later in this book which act at the community level to improve their livelihoods and the environment around them, most individuals in Yunnan lack the agency and opportunity to take action to solve environmental issues affecting them and their surrounding community. These individuals passively expect the government to take care of the social and environmental issues fomenting around them. Today, Dali's tourism industry and Lake Erhai's ecology are now approaching a tipping point, and sooner or later this will elicit another top-down response from the local government, continuing the vicious cycle.

4

THE AKHA AS
MODERN ZOMIANS

China's most popular meat is pork, but the industry that brings 1.5 million pigs to market per day is often dogged by disease and scandal, subjecting pork prices to major volatility and raising concerns over food safety. In 2013, 900 people were arrested in northern China for the crimes of passing off rat, fox, and mink meat for pork.[1] In 2015, even more were arrested in a meat smuggling plot in Yunnan province after school children became ill from eating tainted pork. A follow-up investigation revealed that the school's pork was frozen more than 40 years ago and had traces of E Coli bacteria.[2] However, China's pork crisis has brought an unexpected economic boon to Nanpenzhong, a small village of 130 households located high above the Mekong on a mountaintop in Yunnan's Xishuangbanna prefecture. After the road that connects Nanpenzhong to the valley below was paved in 2014, the village's mayor, Ren San, began to raise black "small-eared" pigs using an organic homegrown feed and water from surrounding springs. As demand for organic meat took off in China, he gradually taught the rest of the villagers how to raise pigs, and now three other adjacent villages are following suit. Twice a week, a cargo plane filled with freshly butchered pigs from Nanpenzhong is flown out of Xishuangbanna's airport to points east. Soon after, the pork is served at high-end restaurants in Shanghai, Beijing, and Guangzhou. Nanpenzhong's pork sells for more than twice the average price of pork in China, and its high demand has put the village, which only a decade ago would have easily ranked as one of China's poorest, on the verge of affluence.

"Half of the villagers now have cars, every household has a motorcycle or two, and some of our children are now going to college," says Ren San, who has a slight paunch and the outline of a butterfly crudely tattooed on his right forearm. He was first elected in 1998, and since then has introduced tea, coffee, rubber, and now pigs into the local economy. He learned how to produce these cash crops by enrolling in rural development and agricultural extension training programs sponsored by the local government offices in Xishuangbanna's capital of Jinghong. Ren San and all of Nanpenzhong's 400 villagers are of the Akha minority, a group once labeled by Chinese anthropologists during the Mao era as one of China's most "primitive" and "backward" ethnic groups. More than 2 million Akha live high in the mountains of southern Yunnan, eastern Myanmar, and the northern hills of Thailand, Laos, and Vietnam. Anthropologist Patricia Pelley says that from an Asian lowlander's point of view "the higher the elevation, the greater the degree of savagery,"[3] and no one lives higher than the Akha.

"In the 1990s, the Chinese government required us to get personal identification cards. I had to find Chinese characters to match my name, because before the IDs, I never had the need to write my name out. The Akha people never had a written language. We did a long time ago, but one day when our people were looking for a new place to settle, we got hungry and ate our language!" says Ren San with a laugh. He continues to tell the legend of how long ago the Akha people were once literate, but when their fertile homeland was invaded, they were forced to flee. To stave off starvation, they ate the buffalo hides on which their texts were recorded.

Innovations like written language, hierarchical power structures, and wet rice agriculture were components that produced successful, long-lasting empires in Asia. However, for the Akha, it was the escape from these inventions that has kept their common identity intact, preserved an egalitarian cultural milieu, and promoted a sustainable use of natural resources. Ethnic groups common to the upland areas of the Mekong Basin like the Akha have been constantly migrating both southward and up mountainsides for centuries. It is hard to pinpoint exactly how long ago the Akha left the lowlands and headed for the hills. They have only in the last few decades begun to write down their history through the construction of a new written language system. Before, Akha history was orally transmitted through storytelling and songs.

Ren San tells me of how the people in his village came from the north and eventually settled near the top of the mountains in southern Yunnan. We sit on the covered rooftop patio of the newly built village headquarters of three stories which houses the village kitchen, his office, the local Communist party headquarters, and a few spaces for village gatherings. The headquarters is an anomalous structure among the collection of traditional Akha homes. He points to a mountain top off to the north. "My father told me about how we came over that mountain in the 1950s." He repositions his finger, "then the village moved over there in the 1960s. But we ran out of water, so the village moved here in 1971."

By referencing stories in Akha traditional lore with events recorded in the annals of southwest China's history, today Akha historians claim that the Akha once established a wet-rice civilization in lowland areas of Sichuan. They eventually moved southward to settle around Kunming, more than 2000 years ago.

93

Ren San's rendering of Akha history says conflict with newly arrived groups from the north dislodged them from Kunming in the first century BC, and then they were pushed farther south to the Red River Valley. There they established a city-state called Jadae. To maintain its viability, Jadae allied with the Nanzhao and Dali Kingdom and began to flourish. One of the most well-known Akha stories tells how things began to fall apart when a powerful Akha king mimicked practices of the surrounding kingdoms and began to tax his subjects. A band of mutinous Akha assassinated the king for his greedy ways, and this experience built an aversion to taxation into the Akha way of life. Without a king, the Jadae state fell easy prey to Mongol invaders in the 13th century and was destroyed. The Akha once again sought refuge to the south, deeper into the Mekong Basin. Now they were on a path to permanent exile. Anthropologists suggest that the southward expansion of the Dai people happened at roughly the same time. The Dai possessed greater military prowess and pushed Akha further to the margins.[4] Today the Akha in Xishuangbanna's mountains are surrounded by Dai villages along the Mekong tributaries below. Because of their exodus from the north, elements of Taoism and Confucianism inform their cultural practices, and they have largely avoided the influence of Dai culture and its Buddhist elements.[5]

Oral tradition exalts the Jadae state as the high watermark of Akha political development and laments the loss of civilization by memorializing the Akha's long-lost culture of wet-rice cultivation. The planting and worship of rice sit at the center of a complex system of Akha rituals, the practice of which is passed down through storytelling and the grooming of religious leaders. Akha stories also warn against becoming enslaved or conquered by expanding governments. Dutch anthropologist Leo Alting Von

Geusau, who lived in an Akha village for the latter half of his life, observed how the Akha surround themselves with a "heritage of defeat" and see themselves as a relatively powerless group which must live by its wits and stay well clear of lowland power centers.[6]

The Akha are known for their impressive oral recitation of more than sixty generations of descendants that traces back to one common ancestor. The chronology of the Akha's great migration is also woven into this oral family tree. Recently, study of the recitations has helped modern Akha scholars attach events in Akha lore to recorded history. A new name is added to the line of descendants shortly after the child is born through a naming ritual. Traditionally, the family is responsible for teaching newborns to remember the family line and other stories from Akha history, although this practice has waned in recent years. Twelve times a year, the Akha worship their ancestors at an altar in their home and then congregate collectively as a village to celebrate. These rituals define the Akha calendar. They also guide the Akha through rice cultivation practices such as plowing fields, planting seedlings, and harvesting rice to guarantee a good yield. This calendar denotes which days of the year are auspicious and which are unlucky. Observing these rituals assures that all villagers continue to revere their ancestors and guarantees they will engage in similar activities on the same days throughout the year. This helps to maintain village solidarity. To break the ritual cycle would bring disrespect to ancestors, bad fortune, and also break down village ties.

These rituals are performed by village religious leaders who then teach their sons or other talented males how to conduct them. The rituals also require the sacrifice of chickens, pigs, or buffaloes and the drinking of grain alcohol made from the village's sacred spring. When an Akha person dies, the family will sacrifice up to three buffalo to give the departed spirit a respectable sendoff on his or her way to the ancestral realm. Over a mourning period of 7 days, the meat of the sacrificed buffalo is shared with all the villagers and consumed at village celebrations. Since throughout history the Akha people have been constantly on the move, their cemeteries have no tombstones or markings to identify the location of the dead. This way, when it is time for the Akha to move, the spirits migrate along with them. The Akha believe that the spirits of their ancestors are always around them and must constantly be revered.

Another factor which kept the Akha constantly in "flight mode" and moving farther southward was the search for food resources. They, like many of the Zomian ethnic groups occupying the slopes in upland southwest China and mainland Southeast Asia, practiced swiddening agriculture. This practice is often derogatorily labeled as "slash and burn" by lowlanders who believe their wet-rice cultivating practices to be far more superior. Yet swiddening, like lowland wet-rice cultivation, is a millennia-old practice that when practiced by a small community, can sustainably develop and conserve a landscape. Most lowlanders claim swiddening creates an unending pattern of denuded mountainsides, but this is unfounded. Swiddening agriculture most often used a rotation of fixed plots of land to produce low yields of rice, yams, or other subsistence crops. At the community's periphery, land for planting is chosen for its soil quality, location, and thickness of vegetation.[7] The slope is then cleared of trees and bushes and burned to create a natural fertilizer before producing a crop. Depending on the quality of the slope's soil, it could be used for a period ranging from 2 to 10 years before rainfall and growing crops stole away its nutrients. Once depleted of nutrients, the field is set aside to fallow for about a decade while it regenerated and the process would be repeated on an adjacent slope. The smaller the community, the fewer slopes are used.

This practice, which is now banned in China, Thailand, and Vietnam, created a patchwork of barren plots among the lush vegetation of tropical forests in upland Southeast Asia. Lowlanders, past and present, were quick to note how the reduction of forest cover left a negative environmental footprint and thus labeled the process as "backward." Despite the ban, some ethnic groups still swidden the slopes of Zomia. Most detractors do not observe the process over a long period of time and fail to realize how swiddening prioritizes a fixed series of land plots. At the same time, large swaths of forested space surrounding the planted areas are conserved and protected. Conversely, lowland rice paddies and agricultural plains used for monocropping expand by clear-cutting surrounding lowland forests. Lowlanders are rarely critical of this practice since it satisfies their own food security and market demands. Clearing lowland forests for monocropping reduces shade cover which increases temperatures. Without forests' root systems to hold the land together, these areas are more susceptible to natural disasters like floods and landslides. The lack of forest cover has caused an unprecedented loss of biodiversity in the lowland areas. Swiddening, when properly managed, also maintains lines of forests in zones between planting areas. This promotes wildlife habitation and mobility, keeps the mountainsides humid and cool, and prevents landslides.

James Scott and other Zomia scholars argue that engaging in swiddening agriculture is the critical action which enables uplanders like the Akha to maintain a distinct identity and separation from the domineering mechanisms of the lowland state.[8] Because the uplands historically have been easily defended from lowland military invasion, expanding states traditionally left the upland peoples to develop in relative seclusion. Roads did not exist in the mountains for wheeled transport, and armies literally could not carry enough rations on their backs to sustain meaningful military actions in upland areas. Further, getting the yams, cassava, and upland rice to the lowland markets made little economic sense because these low-value goods were too heavy to transport and fetched low prices. No lowland tax collector was willing to make the journey to tax upland people for their agricultural production. Swiddening agriculture was a "state preventing characteristic" that provided an ample subsistence diet and prevented uplanders like the Akha from being enslaved or taxed as royal subjects. Moreover, swiddening, when combined with the rice planting rituals of the Akha calendar, promoted open and equal access to subsistence resources, common property land tenure, and open frontiers as the material conditions that form the foundation of Akha egalitarianism.[9] Thus upland geography, underpinned by swiddening, provided for a relative isolation or "encapsulation", a term used by anthropologist Leo Alting Von Geusau.[10]

The yields from swiddening were typically not enough to sustain a livelihood, so those who lived in the upland areas also needed to forage the surrounding forests for fruits, animals, and other non-timber forest products like mushrooms and bamboo shoots to supplement their diets. Keeping this balance between farming and foraging meant that maintaining forests was paramount to survival, and in the Akha tradition, this is done through the strict enforcement of cultural taboos. Akha culture describes forested areas outside a village as the realm of free-roaming spirits and powerful wild animals possessed by those spirits. The Akha can only access this space for the hunting of "safe" and common wildlife like boar, deer, and bear. To even see, let alone kill, rare wildlife like wild buffalo, leopards, or rhinoceros, would bring great misfortune to an individual and his family. Likewise, trees from the forbidden forest were not be cut down because they too could be possessed by spirits. Timber for building homes and firewood could only be collected from community forests located close to the village. The community forests acted as a buffer enabling the sustainability of a manageable stock of resources between the village interior and the forbidden exterior surrounding the village.

Those community forests also produced mushrooms, bamboo shoots, and medicinal herbs – high value, low mass products which fetched high prices at lowland markets and were well worth the schlep down the mountain. This is one way that the Akha and other upland Zomian groups maintained contact with lowland areas. If community forests were not managed, these valuable non-timber forest products could not keep critical cash flows coming in. Later in the 19th and early 20th centuries, the Akha in Xishuangbanna began to harvest rattan from these forests and alongside swidden rice, they grew opium – both products fetching high prices in lowland markets. As a way to display their earnings, the Akha women often tie coins to their traditional headdresses. I person-ally have seen coins more than 100 years old displayed as jewelry on Akha women. James Scott categorizes the lowland dependence on such high-value upland products as a kind of "weapon of the weak."[11] This further enabled uplanders to maintain and defend distance from the state. Nanpenzhong village's burgeoning organic pork industry, another high value/low mass product, is an inno-vative extension of this process. But the establishment of roads, forward military bases, and market development have allowed the Chinese state, and many of the downstream Mekong states, to gradually wrest control over mountaintops from those who have occupied them for centuries.

To the Akha, the encroaching Han Chinese, whose political machinery began to penetrate the mountains after the establish-ment of the People's Republic of China in 1949, were the most dangerous kind of free roaming spirits populating the forbidden frontiers of Akha space. In the 1960s, during China's Cultural Revolution, Communist work brigades were assigned to Akha villages and banned the traditional rituals of the ancestral planting cycle. They forced Akha villagers to remove the ancestral altars from their homes, banned the wearing of traditional costumes, and carried out campaigns to "Launch a Battle Against Ghost Mountains." A decade before, Mao Zedong banned ancestral worship among the Han Chinese in order to build a population of loyal, Communist followers dedicated to building the Chinese state. Akha villagers who remember the Cultural Revolution say they were not afraid of retribution from their ancestors over breaking ancient traditions because "Chairman Mao Zedong was the super powerful god governing over all spirits."[12] The forbidden forests were declared state lands and mountainsides were logged bare. Chinese mapmakers labeled the mountains as zones for resource extraction, and this clashed with the traditional interpretation of Akha space. During China's post-1979 reform era led by Deng Xiaoping, the Akha and other ethnic groups in China were once again allowed and encouraged to resume the wearing of traditional costumes and to carry out ancestral rituals, but land use patterns remained to be determined by the Chinese government.

Nanpenzhong's village gate serves as a kind of airlock to keep the forbidden, outside spirits away from the heart of the village. Akha tradition requires the gate to be dismantled and rebuilt with freshly cut trees each year during a protection ritual led by the village's religious head. In China, this practice ended in 1998 due to a nationwide logging ban which also put an end to swiddening agriculture. When I made my first 90 minute ride up the 16 kilometer mud track to Nanpengzhong in 2009, I was leading a group of American college students to conduct a few days of field study with the Akha. Village mayor Ren San greeted us at the village gate, now a permanent structure made of steel piping. A red cloth banner with "Welcome All Euro-American Students to Nanpenzhong" was stretched across the top of the gate. Many villagers dressed in full Akha regalia lined both sides of the gate. They sang us a welcome song which I later learned told the tale of their ancient migration from the north. My group of twenty-somethings all lined up to clap along with the song, and each person was invited to down a small cup of grain alcohol made in the village and blessed by local religious leaders. Most of the college students jumped at the chance, but some approached the ritual with apprehension. The ritual was required by village elders as a way to appease these new outside spirits who were entering the village.

Previously, the elders, who had little knowledge of world geography, asked Ren San, who arranged the visit, where the "Euro-Americans" came from. Since we had flown in from Kunming, he pointed to the sky. For years, this suggestion reinforced the idea that this group of Americans of various colors, shapes, and sizes were indeed spirits visiting from afar. It was not until after the completion of cement road in 2014 that Ren San piled the village elders in a bus and drove them to the outskirts of Jinghong's airport to prove that these American's were flesh and blood, just like them, but they traveled the world in airplanes.

On another occasion late in the evening in October 2014 Nanpenzhong's constable, who was always around to ensure the group's safety, invited me and a few of the American students to attend what he described as a "party for real Akha culture." On our way through the village, a few of the village's male youth who were drinking and singing karaoke at a small convenience store, dragged the students and me aside and pleaded for us not to join the gathering. "They practice superstition! You shouldn't go! It's dangerous!" they all warned. I found their remarks odd. I was not sure if they were serious or just trying to encourage the students to join them in their own merriment. Against their warning, we forged ahead. After a short walk on a dirt path, the constable led us into a home filled with more than 100 villagers drinking and feasting around low squat tables. As guests of honor, or perhaps as powerful outside spirits that must be appeased, we were asked to sit with the elders and receive blessings from them. They tied black threads around our wrists, symbolizing the connected nature of the Akha people, and wrapped a stem of rice blooming with purple flowers around our left ears. Everyone there was adorned with purple rice flowers. An elder turned to me and said, "You have come at a good time. The rice is flowering." The celebration continued until dawn.

The encounter with the village youth who tried to dissuade us from attending the party was a worrisome experience because by my understanding, the rice flowering festival was a critical cele-bration of Akha culture. Despite the brief interlude of the Cultural Revolution, the Akha in Nanpenzhong village were still carrying out the full suite of rituals related to the planting calendar and ancestral worship. Compared to other ethnic groups in Yunnan province, much of their ethnic heritage seemed to remain vital to community members' identities and daily lives. Whether the rejection of the celebration was a matter of youthful rebellion or a cognizant rejection of Akha culture is unknown, but a recent change has done much to separate Akha youth from their culture in China.

In 2013, all Akha parents were required by law to send their children to consolidated boarding schools in lowland areas. This decree effectively removed the villages of all children age 6 to 15 from the village from Monday to Friday for most weeks of the year.

Parents welcomed the move because it put their children in contact with better teachers and innovative educational technologies. The larger schools built in lowland areas also helped to maintain cohorts of Han Chinese teachers who eschewed life in difficult terrain. Previously the village's children were educated in a simple schoolhouse located a few kilometers down the mountain road in an adjacent community. However, under the new arrangement, the only way for the village's youth to observe and participate in Akha ritual culture, whether a wedding, funeral, or planting ritual, was if it happened to fall on a weekend. The strict Akha calendar gives no preference to weekends. Ren San told me how his son cannot recite the ancestral line and now such practices are only taken up by the few "geniuses" of the village. To counter the potential loss of contact with this living culture, Ren San has established a small museum to Akha culture and memorabilia in the village headquarters, but this room is mostly visited by outside visitors and rarely by the village's children.

The banning of swiddening in 1998 and the introduction of replacement cash crops also challenged the egalitarian distribution of resources in the village. The forests surrounding Nanpenzhong, with the exception of a few large communally shared patches, were long ago cleared and are now lined with rubber trees. Rubber made its way up the mountainside as a preferred cash crop in the early 2000s and today rubber plantations cover more than 20 percent of Xishuangbanna's land.[13] Rounds of land redistribution in the early 1980s gave each household in Nanpenzhong (and the rest of China) land parcels the size of which was determined by the number of household members. This legal requirement broke the Akha's timeless tradition of common land tenure. Akha historian Wang Jianhua claims that local leaders also took advantage of the land redistribution process to personally seize control of land in the village's common forests, making them instantaneously better endowed than others.[14] When the Chinese economy was taking off in the early 2000s, those villagers with more land planted more rubber trees. Poorer families with fewer resources had to lease land to generate income to purchase rubber saplings. Through the late 2000s income disparity began to grow in Nanpenzhong. A few villagers who earned higher incomes pulled down their homes made of wood and bamboo and replaced them with concrete structures like the ones they had seen in the lowland. Others bought automobiles which provided for more economic activity than those who did not own cars.

Ren San thinks the cottage organic pig industry is a way to combat growing income inequality in Nanpenzhong. He first used state funds to introduce a shareholder system for the village's coffee and tea crops to evenly distribute the proceeds of these goods to all villagers, as long as they all pitched in to maintain the fields and bring in the crops during harvest season. Rubber cannot be grown at elevations higher than 800 meters, and about half of the village's agricultural land is higher than this. In the aughts, tea and coffee helped to some extent, but when the price of rubber peaked in 2011, the subsequent sharp drop in prices hit household incomes hard. Ren San sought out other forms of income generation to provide the village with stability and build resilience against global price fluctuations and found his preferred weapon of the weak – organic pigs.

Today, national and global market fluctuations now determine the village's economic gains and losses, whereas with swiddening agriculture decades before, Nanpenzhong's economic viability was relatively independent from what was happening in other parts of the world. The free time that cash cropping provides allows for village women to engage in long-respected community activities like quilting ethnic costumes and gives men time to share the stories of Akha tradition. Nanpenzhong is now host to several Akha festivals that attract Akha people from as far as Thailand to celebrate Akha culture. Without cash cropping, roads, and cars such pan-Akha celebrations would be much less frequent. But free time and extra income has introduced gambling and higher rates of alcohol consumption. I had firsthand exposure to this unfortunate consequence when one morning I woke in the village to learn that one of the local youth was killed in a road accident the previous night as he drove his motorcycle up the mountain road after a long night of drinking.

The mandated move away from swiddening has come at a large ecological cost and has also shifted how the Akha in Nanpenzhong interpret and use the land around them. Lands managed by the Chinese state, much of which is used to produce rubber, now entirely surround the village instead of protected, forbidden forests. Xishuangbanna's forests were once known for producing a ubiquitous morning fog that kept lowland tropical areas cool throughout the year. Today less than 20 percent of Xishuangbanna is covered by natural forest. Vast rubber plantations are blamed for making Xishuangbanna dry and arid. Nanpenzhong's villagers continue to cope with outside change as globalization has come to their door ste. No longer are the Akha "encapsulated" on the mountaintops.

At the end of December 2014, I caught up with a 22 year old Akha woman named Meepu in Maesalong, and upland town in northern Thailand's Chiang Rai province - not far from the site of the daring June 2018 cave rescue of a youth soccer team. She and her friends were selling organic tea at Mae Salong's annual Akha New Year's Festival. Booths selling other agricultural products like honey and wine were arranged around a dirt square at the western end of the town. At one end of the square, several felled trees were assembled like a tall tripod, and Akha youth and tourists took turns on a swing attached to a vine fixed to the tripod's central axis.

"That's our Akha swing!" Meepu remarked. "All of the Akha have a yearly swing festival. Since we're celebrating New Year, we put our swing up the other day." I discovered that Akha youth look forward to riding on swings at the annual festival like Western children look forward to opening presents on Christmas day. The smiles on the swing riders' faces confirmed this. I later learned of an Akha song that paid tribute both the "heritage of defeat" and to the annual swing festival. Its chorus line went "When you don't have your country anymore you can still feel free swinging in the air."[15]

Meepu was not born in Mae Salong. She, like all the Akha in northern Thailand at one point in history, came from China. While most of the estimated 75,000 Akha in the hills of northern Thailand migrated there in the 20th century, Meepu and her family arrived in 2004. Before the move, Meepu's uncle in Thailand contacted the family and told Meepu's parents how she and her two sisters could receive a better education in Mae Salong. Her mother was 8 months pregnant with a 4th child when the family made the 2 day journey through eastern Myanmar's Shan State. The morning of their departure from Mangang village in Xishuang-banna, just over the mountain from Nanpenzhong, the entire village gathered for a send-off feast, and the family received blessings from the village elders. At the Mae Sai, a border town with Myanmar, her uncle produced a document that claimed the family had been living on his land in Mae Salong for a few years. After paying a small bribe, the family was let through immigration.

Prior to the 1950s, the Akha and other upland ethnic groups could just walk across China's borders into Myanmar, Laos, and

Vietnam. Some eventually ended up in Thailand. Borders at the periphery of these countries were only regulated at a few checkpoints. This permitted a somewhat free flow of goods and people through the hills and mountains of the Golden Triangle. During the decades of the Cold War, the rise of the "Bamboo Curtain" isolated Communist China from non-aligned Burma, and US-backed Thailand made cross-border contact more difficult. However, borders remained relatively porous as China actively supported Communist led insurgencies in Thailand and Myanmar and successful Communist revolutions in Laos and Vietnam.

A ride up the windy roads to Mae Salong feels like a quick journey from lowland Thailand to upland Yunnan province. Above an elevation of 1000 meters, the language of roadside signs changes from the Thai alphabet to traditional Chinese characters. Mae Salong is a one-road town, and that road stretches for 3 kilometers on the top of a high mountain ridge. Most of the homes that crowd the road are occupied by descendants of Chinese Nationalist Kuomintang (KMT) soldiers who fled Yunnan after the People's Republic of China was established in 1949. These KMT regiments first fled to Burma and tried to launch CIA-backed counterinsurgencies into Yunnan to try and retake the homeland. To support themselves, the refugee KMT forced other Chinese who had fled Yunnan into conscription and put the Golden Triangle on the map as the center of the global opium trade. In the early 1960s, the KMT were evicted from Burma and settled in the hills of northern Thailand. Mae Salong was the location of the KMT's largest regiment. The Thai government saw the KMT and their lucrative opium trade as a potentially destabilizing force, but instead of evicting the KMT or forcing them to repatriate to Taiwan, the US-backed Thai regime employed the KMT to fight against Communist insurgencies flowing out of China into Thailand,

Myanmar, and Laos. To the Thai, these KMT units served as a buffer to what they perceived as a growing Communist threat.

Yang Congguang, who is ethnic Chinese, serves as the pastor of a Baptist church in Mae Salong. His family fled Yunnan to Burma in 1958 and converted to Christianity after they settled in a peaceful ethnic Lisu village in the hills of what is now Eastern Shan State. In the 1960s, the borderlands between Yunnan and Southeast Asia were rife with conflict, and the family was surprised to find a community where people lived to high moral standards, did not gamble, drink or smoke. All the Lisu in the village converted to Christianity during the pre-war era. As a teenager, Yang was forced into KMT conscription despite his aversion to war. He fought for a few years as a reluctant soldier and eventually escaped. He was pursued as a deserter, and when the KMT visited his family but found no trace of Yang, they shot and killed his father as a form of punishment. Yang continued to evade the KMT as a trader and eventually made his way to a seminary in Bangkok to become accredited as a pastor. In the early 1990s, with the end of the Cold War, the KMT handed in their weapons in exchange for citizenship. Yang and his wife built a one-room church at the west end of Mae Salong. Their congregation was mostly Akha, and during the weekdays, the couple ran a free school that taught Chinese language to stateless Akha children who could not gain access to the local Thai-language school. After a few years of Chinese language schooling, the Akha children could enroll in a bilingual Thai-Chinese primary school sponsored by the Taiwanese government. There they could learn to write and read in Thai and test into a Thai high school with the potential to go on to university.

More than a decade later, Meepu's uncle would recommend her and her sisters to enroll in Pastor Yang's school as a pathway to higher education. Upon arrival in Mae Salong, Meepu and her family converted to Christianity, and the subsequent schooling with Pastor Yang opened pathways for eventual matriculation into the local Thai education system. Meepu graduated from a high school funded by Thailand's royal family, also in Mae Salong, at the age of 20, and after graduation, she taught Chinese language classes for Pastor Yang for 3 years to save up for college tuition. To help with her university aspirations, the church occasionally takes occasional donations to support her savings.

"My parents make just enough income to support the six of us, so it's impossible for them to support my college education," Meepu shared after I asked her about her family's current economic situation. "At the church I meet people from all over the world who give me advice on how to follow my dreams. Someday, I want to become a Chinese language professor." She admitted that she is not a fan of the Thai language, but she learned it because of its convenience. "My Chinese language is better than my Akha. I don't understand the Akha songs that the elders sing."

Christianity came to the upland border areas of China and Southeast Asia via British and French missionaries during the colonial era. As the buffer zones between China and Southeast Asia were forming into the 20th century, ethnic uplanders saw Christianity as a way to link themselves with the broader world system and also form enclaves isolating them from the violence emanating from lowland anti-colonial, nationalist movements. In the early days of the Cold War, foreign proselytizers were banned in Burma, China, and Vietnam and eventually Laos, but by the time missionaries were expelled from Zomia their roots were already deeply laid. Ethnic upland peoples like the Lisu, Karen, Kachin, and the demobilized

Chinese KMT, continued the evangelizing missions. Missionaries in Thailand remained continuously active and maintained contact with groups through upland stations in northern Thailand.

Prior to the 1980s the Akha in upland Thailand and Myanmar strongly resisted conversion to Christianity. Replacing swiddening rice cultivation with swiddening opium production was a means of to keep the Akha traditions alive. But as rebel groups like the KMT grew more isolated, they demanded higher rents from opium growers like the Akha and squeezed the Akha's economic livelihood. This meant less cash income for Akha villagers and put pressure on village resources. The Thai state, with help from the royal family, instituted crop substitution programs sponsored by the United Nations. These programs tried to wean upland ethnic people from producing opium, but poor road access and an already crowded lowland market set these programs up for failure. With fewer resources, the animal sacrifices required by Akha tradition were harder to afford and began to be abandoned.[16] Opium cultivation produced high rates of addiction among village youth, and young people were emptying Akha villages for jobs in lowland urban areas. Many young Akha women were trafficked into the sex trade, and Akha villages that were once remote and isolated saw a rise in sexually transmitted diseases when young people came home. In addition to introducing pressures for the Akha to produce a basic livelihood that pushed the Akha out of their traditional space, these factors caused a breakdown in tradition. Conversion to Christianity offered ways for the Akha to navigate the changing world and re-establish a moral code in ways that their traditional Akha culture could not.

Conversion to Christianity also provided a pathway to citizenship for stateless Akha. In China, ethnic groups are welcomed as part of the national populace as long as they do not cause trouble for the Chinese state by forming separatist movements. The

Han Chinese built in buffer zones populated by ethnic peoples in western reaches when the PRC was established in 1949. To a degree, this was also a practice during the imperial era. Thus, China's nation-building narrative is inclusive of ethnic groups and their members are citizens of the state. Thailand requires loyalty to "Nation, Religion, and King" which implies a singular preference towards the Thai Buddhist nation. This notion is exclusive and tacitly discriminatory toward other ethnic groups. In Thailand, the Akha are officially labeled with other groups like the Karen, Lahu, and Hmong as "hill tribes." The lowland Thai often refer to these hill tribes as "living ancestors" – backward peoples of the mountains from which the Thai nation grew out of over centuries. When the Cold War ended, the Thai government granted most upland ethnic people the status of illegal alien immigrants. Some, like the KMT who had fought to put down Communist insurgencies, were quickly given legal alien status and put on the pathway to citizenship, but most upland ethnic peoples maintained illegal alien status and were restricted to living in the hills. Avoiding Thai border security forces who were notorious for taking advantage of illegal aliens or running illicit human trafficking rings was therefore an imperative for the Akha.

Currently there are more than 17,000 Akha citizenship applicants in Mae Fah Luang district, where Mae Salong is located. Today only 50 percent of Akha have legal status as residents or citizens. Local Thai-funded NGOs provide some support to upland ethnic peoples in Thailand to apply for citizenship, but Christian churches – many of which are regionally and globally connected – provide stable flows of financial and legal support to help parishioners along their pathway to citizenship. Christian Akha can easily access these services. In addition, conversion to Christianity offers access to faith-based hospitals and financial assistance for education.[17]

Many Akha who live in Thailand's upland areas see greater
benefit in encouraging their children to learn Chinese and English
than Thai. They interpret Chinese and English as global languages
that offer more opportunities for upward mobility. The globally
networked Christian church is a vehicle for facilitating broader
advancement. To illustrate, Meepu told me how many of her Akha
classmates from Pastor Yang's church were now working in China
and Korea. Also on previous visits to Mae Salong, I met with Ashi,
a young Akha man who graduated at the top of his class in Pastor
Yang's church. He went on to finish an English language BA at a
private university in Chiang Rai and then an MBA in Beijing's
Tsinghua University. Ashi now manages a tech startup in Chiang
Rai. Recently, Meepu's plan has also paid off. In September 2016,
she enrolled as a first-year student in a teaching curriculum at a
public university in Chiang Rai.

However, Christianity is also dividing the Akha community.
Since the 1980s, converted Christians have been establishing
smaller, exclusive communities within villages. This divides social
space and undermines the traditional egalitarianism that once
pervaded Akha culture. Akha Christians often look down on
non-converts with disdain. Akha scholar Li Haiying observed how
non-converts no longer ask Akha Christians to join them to work
together in the fields because Akha Christians often boast of how
they are now free and how their love lives are much better now that
their husbands do not drink or smoke.[18] Akha Christians are known
to accuse Akha non-Christians of being primitive, backward,
demon worshippers. Some Christian pastors force Akha converts
to burn their ancestral altars and renounce ritual ways that define
Akha culture.[19] For example, the traditional naming ceremony
which connects a newborn's name into the long ancestral line is
banned. Christian Akha are also forbidden to seek help from tradi-

tional leaders or use traditional medicine practices. The practice of elders tying blessed strings around villager's wrists to demonstrate the connectedness of community has been replaced with the Christian handshake. When I asked Meepu about traditional Akha culture she described it as something alien to her where elders kill chickens and worship ghosts.

Traditionally, an Akha person was positioned in an internally controlled community governed by common beliefs and values. Connecting to social and economic systems, such as Christianity or the capitalist market, shifts the individual Akha toward that of an outwardly controlled system which emphasizes individual achievement and the linking into globally managed systems introduced by national governments and missionary influences.[20]

Akha scholar Wang Jianhua, who was born in a village not far from Nanpenzhong in China and now lives in Thailand, is leading a pan-Akha movement to promote and preserve Akha culture. He is worried that traditional Akha oral storytelling is dying because young people are not learning to speak Akha. "They have begun to think of themselves as Burmans, Chinese, Lao, or Thai first and Akha second." He claims that Christianity's mission of sending the Akha out into the world is a threat to Akha identity. "Once ties to home and the ancestors are lost, they will lose their identity."[21]

Akha scholar Li Haiying relates a story where a Christian family with a sick relative was not permitted to see a traditional Akha healer for medical help. The family's pastor said this would be a violation of their faith. As a result, the family abandoned the church and returned to the old Akha ways. After seeing the Akha healer, the family member got better.[22] Anecdotes like this are helping the neo-traditionalist movement gain ground in northern Thailand and eastern Myanmar and encourage "return conversions" to Akha traditions.

Where Christian Akha claim their heritage is preserved through speaking the Akha language and wearing traditional dress at festivals, neo-traditionalists say that Akha identity is inseparable from ritual observance. For instance, neo-traditionalists point to the Akha ritual for the adoption of outsiders, which simply requires an outsider to be given an Akha name during the traditional naming ceremony. The newcomer can become Akha by being tied into the ancestral lineage long before he or she gains fluency in the Akha language. To neo-traditionalists, ritual ancestor worship comes first before blood ties or language abilities. Central to the debate is the question of whether religion and culture can be separated.

The neo-traditional revival started in 2008 with a series of cross-border conferences promoting Akha identity throughout upland China and Southeast Asia. New Akha élites, many of whom were empowered by agricultural success, are now promoting a pan-Akha culture. These university professors, businessmen, government officials, and NGO workers are encouraging an Akha revival. They inspire and train village elders, ritual specialists, artists, and musicians. While the oral tradition is still emphasized, these élite stakeholders agree that the future of Akha culture is threatened and therefore must be recorded for younger generations. Over the last decade, they have agreed upon a common written language system and now promote a standardized Akha culture. The oral historical narrative tying back to the Jadae state and common ancestor varies across the Akha world to some degree. But a consensus on main points is being distilled into a mainstream saga now written in books and told graphically through artistic renderings. These documents are now easily passed around the Akha world via social media. Indeed, Ren San has them on display in his Nanpenzhong's Akha heritage museum. Many returned converts are constructing grave markers with pictures of individuals and personal information. This practice was picked up during their Christian experience and is anathema to the former practice of unmarked graves. The Christian exposure also results in the overemphasis of kings and a supreme creator who sits at the center of standardized Akha mythology. Previously, the Akha were described as a people who eschewed hierarchy and bowed their head to no one.[23] In many ways, these methods act in direct opposition of the "state-avoiding techniques" that previously kept the culture intact, but they also represent the flexibility of Akha people to adapt to modern practices while making strides to preserve core traditions.

Scholar Micah Morton is critical of the neo-traditionalist approach. He claims that certain Akha are composing their own theories of culture that in part challenge and incorporate dominant models of nationalism and globalization, all the while reproducing and claiming a distinct Akha way of being in the world.[24] He also observes how the standardized Akha culture promoted by neo-traditionalists approves of three ancestral observances instead of twelve. This simplification of Akha ritual is a way for traditions to compete with various cultural systems vying for the attention of Akha. In the 1990s, to encourage return converts, practices such as twin infanticide and sending divorced women into exile were abolished. Also, the burden of animal sacrifice for Akha ritual was reduced. Anthropologist Deborah Tooker claims that the simplification of Akha culture as promoted by the neo-traditionalists relegates ancestral practices to a few spheres such as birth, death, and marriage, instead of permeating everyday life.[25] But to the neo-traditionalists, reduction of Akha traditional rituals is more preferred to the wholesale abandonment of tradition by the Christian Akha.

I recently reached out to Ren San for a follow-up chat and update on Nanpenzhong's cottage organic pig industry. I contacted him via the Chinese social media platform WeChat from my home in the US, and we talked for an hour using the app's video platform. He spent most of the time chatting about his recent efforts to teach the village's youth the importance of Akha culture. While we talked he sent me photos and a few PDFs that displayed the work of neo-traditionalists. He also sent videos of recent Akha gatherings, photos of Akha genealogy lines, group pictures of attendees at recent Akha conferences. He could not have been prouder to tell me how Akha today are working across borders to preserve their culture. After we signed off, I reflected on how the penetration of state and market forces enabled me to communicate with Ren San high in the hills and interact with Akha culture from the other side of the world. I could now under-stand Akha culture in ways I could not during my previous visits to Nanpenzhong.

Because of their historical adoption of "state-preventing practices," the Akha have been able to maintain an arms-length relationship with dominant, state-led systems. Through their millennia-long migration through Asia, they have adapted aspects of Chinese culture into their own belief system. The Akha trans-formed their "heritage of defeat" into a vibrant identity, and when threatened with slavery and taxation, still maintained economic contact with the lowland by selling off valuable goods of the forest. This practice continues today. The technologies and social oppor-tunities offered by the lowland might no longer be interpreted as offensive and damaging to Akha society. In fact, some Akha are using those technologies to forward and preserve their culture. Resilience, adaptation, and hybridity seem to be programmed into the Akha social framework, and these traits will allow the culture to persist in some shape or form. During my video call with Ren San, he commented on the possibility that North Korean nuclearization could tip Asia into a state of conflict. I noted my worries, but he shared no common concerns. He said, "I'm not worried about war. That's something that big states do. We're Akha, and we survive. If things fall apart, then we'll just go back to swiddening. We still know how to do it."

5

THE GOLDEN TRIANGLE IN TRANSITION

My journey into the Lower Mekong began in 2004 during the last meeting of a graduate course on Southeast Asian Economics at the University of California, San Diego. In the final 5 minutes of class Professor Krislert Samphantharak listed some emerging trends in Southeast Asia and mentioned how trade was picking up between China and Thailand on the Mekong River. I immediately raised my hand and questioned his observation because I had been to Jinghong, Xishuangbanna a few years prior and remembered standing on a new bridge spanning the Mekong, seeing no activity related to river trade. The professor and I had a quick conversation after class, and 4 months later I was at China's major Mekong port at Guanlei, boarding a cargo ship headed for the Golden Triangle.

A small research grant from UCSD enabled me to shadow a group of agriculture exporters and government officials from Yunnan down the river. They wanted to know how their lettuce and broccoli were making their way to Talad Thai, Thailand's largest wholesale market located in north Bangkok. Prior to shoving off from Guanlei, porters loaded the ship with sacks of garlic and apples through the night. In order to reach Chiang Saen, Thailand 200 kilometers downstream, we had to leave port before dawn.

One of my companions described the trip as a journey through unruly territory. Between Guanlei and Chiang Saen, the river formed the border between Laos and Myanmar, and these frontiers were known to be the domain of warlords and drug-runners. Our course cut through the heart of the Golden Triangle, the region where Thailand, Laos, and Myanmar meet. In the 20th century opium produced in this region was worth its weight in gold, giving the region its namesake.

For the most part, the trip downriver was uneventful. With the exception of a few villages along the river, we hardly saw signs of life. My companions napped most of the way. The captain called me into his wheelhouse for the final 2 hours of the journey. We were entering Devil's Pass, a 20 kilometer stretch where the river speeds up through narrow canyons less than 100 meters wide. "In Devil's Pass, there are no signs to tell you where the rocks are," yelled the captain against loud whir of the boat's engine. "A few boats have capsized in this part of the river, and some sailors drowned here. I know the route because I trained alongside an experienced captain for 3 years before doing it on my own ship. In a few years, we'll blow these rocks out of the water, so the journey will be less risky."

The captain expertly guided the ship but not without coming close to several exposed shoals midstream. Eventually the canyon opened to a wide valley, and the river became wide and calm. "That's what they call the Golden Triangle," said the captain as he pointed to a giant statue of a golden Buddha facing the river. "There's actually a triangle of land formed by a smaller river emptying into the Mekong. It is where all three countries meet." Soon after, our ship moored along the levee at Chiang Saen's new downtown port, and a mixed line of Thai and Chinese deckhands formed to move sacks of cargo from the boat to trucks waiting streetside.

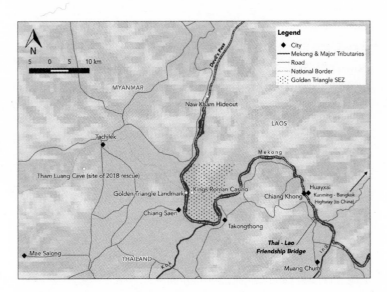

Map of the Golden Triangle

In the early aughts, the uptick in trade was the result of a bilateral trade negotiation that dropped import tariffs on a handful of agricultural products traded between Thailand and China. These increased economic ties fit well into the foreign policy goals of both countries. After more than six decades of unrest in its northern regions, Thailand sought to convert "battlefields into marketplaces"[1] by bringing state-sponsored economic development programs to its frontier. China, then a newly rising power, pushed a policy of "good neighborliness" to provide assurance to its neighbors that its regional ambitions promoted mutual benefits and economic development. China wanted to signal to Southeast Asia that its rise would not upset regional stability. This trust building was important because less than two decades prior, Beijing had provided military materiel and technical support to Communist insurgencies in Southeast Asia. To enjoin these efforts, the Asian Development Bank (ADB) launched its Greater Mekong Subregion

(GMS) program in the mid-1990s to build a series of economic corridors to promote commercial activity between mainland Southeast Asia and China. The program provided concessional loans for infrastructure development projects to better integrate the region. If things went according to plan, highways and railways would shoot out from Kunming to Myanmar on the west, Thailand and Laos to the south, and Vietnam on the east. These routes would cut through some the world's most unforgiving terrain. Some of the new transportation routes looked westward to access ports in Myanmar and Thailand on the Indian Ocean. This was part of China's strategy to keep the trade of goods flowing in the event the US or other naval power blockaded the South China Sea or the Straits of Malacca.

The Kunming-Bangkok highway served as the centerpiece of this strategy and would enable goods from Kunming to reach Thai markets in less than one day. Completed in 2007, the stretch from Kunming to Jinghong reduced transit time between these two points from 24 hours to 8. The 180 kilometer R3 highway bisecting northern Laos and linking Xishuangbanna to Chiang Rai province in Thailand was also completed in 2007. Before the R3 went through, the only viable transit pathways between China and the Golden Triangle were river transport and muddy tracks that looped through the upland villages in northern Laos and eastern Myanmar. Most of the overland passages were impassable during the monsoon season. China, Thailand, and the ADB each contributed one-third of the financing for this road. The government of Laos, which often does not have enough state funds to pay its officials, had no funds to pitch into the highway project. Clearly, the project's main beneficiaries were China and Thailand.

Over the years since 2004, I frequently returned to Chiang Saen to watch the lines of porters loading the Chinese fleet for return trips to Xishuangbanna. Going both ways, fruit and vegetables make up most of the cargo. Apples and garlic grown in Yunnan's more temperate climes dominate China's contribution to trade while Thailand ships mostly tropical fruits like bananas, mangoes, and longan – a lychee-like fruit known for its traditional medicinal qualities. Thailand also sends frozen chicken and pig parts up the river to China. A Chinese porter once told me how a small herd of live cattle was lost in the river when the ship transporting them ran into trouble in Devil's Pass. The Chiang Saen port is known to ship goods upriver that originate from such far-flung areas as Turkey or Iran. One time I watched deckhands skillfully maneuver 20 late model sports cars onto one ship. I later learned the cars made the journey from England and were *en route* to the personal collection of a Yunnanese government official.

On one visit to the port in 2015, a deckhand showed me something unexpected. "I can take you to one of the ships where the Chinese sailors were killed. After four years, the *Hua Ping* is still there. No one uses it because we are afraid of their ghosts," said Mr. Song as he led me down the concrete stairs to a large cargo vessel with its windows shot out and glass still on the floor. With exception of the windows and occasional spattering of dry blood, the cargo ship looked like its crew still inhabited it. But the toothbrushes in tin cups and worn shirts hanging in the closets would never be used again by their owners. On October 5, 2011, unknown assailants boarded the *Hua Ping* and *Yu Xing 2*, 7 kilometers upstream from the Chiang Saen port and murdered all 13 of the ships' crew. When local authorities boarded the *Hua Ping*, only the ship's captain was found. His dead body slumped over an AK-47 beside 900,000 methamphetamine pills later determined to be worth more than 6 million dollars. Over the next two days, the bodies of 12 other crew members were washed ashore. All were blindfolded. Some had wounds which suggested the sailors were tortured before they were killed.

This was the deadliest and most violent attack on Chinese people abroad in recent memory, and circumstances surrounding the gruesome crime were murky from the start. Eyewitnesses claimed that smaller speedboats accompanied the cargo ships out of Devil's Pass, and when the cargo ships docked south of the Golden Triangle tourist site, a gun battle ensued, and the speedboats raced back upstream. Yet others produced a conflicting account claiming uniformed agents from an élite Thai drug enforcement unit forced the boat to dock. They claim the gunfire came after the agents boarded the ship. A witness standing next to a drug enforcement officer alongshore heard him give the order to dump the bodies into the river because, "the fewer bodies the better."[2] The following day, 9 Thai drug enforcement officers were arrested without specific charges, but a motive for the killing was still unclear. Were the Chinese sailors smuggling drugs? Or did the drug enforcement agents plant the methamphetamines to make the Chinese sailors, whose presence was becoming increasingly unwelcomed in the Golden Triangle, look culpable? And who was driving the speedboats that accompanied the cargo ships downriver?

China's reaction to the incident was swift and concerted. All river trade temporarily stopped, and China convened a quadrilateral meeting with national security agencies in Thailand, Laos, and Myanmar to gather known facts and pen out a cooperative approach to bring the killers to justice. Through the process, Thailand named a suspect: Naw Kham, a local drug lord who had held sway over territory in eastern Myanmar and western Laos for more than a decade. Under China's guidance, the four countries rushed to sign an unprecedented joint security agreement permitting Chinese security forces to operate at will in Laos, Myanmar, and Thailand in the hunt for Naw Kham.

Throughout much of the latter half of the 20th century, the opium trade in the Golden Triangle was dominated by Khun Sa, an ethnic Shan warlord whose network and security forces controlled much of eastern Myanmar's Shan state. To maintain power, Khun Sa was rumored to have close ties with Myanmar's military government. Southeast Asian scholar Alfred McCoy wrote in his influential work, *The Politics of Heroin in Southeast Asia* that "Khun Sa was the world's most powerful drug lord with a market share never equaled before."[3] To lure Khun Sa into official retirement, in 1996 the Burmese military negotiated a cease-fire in exchange for amnesty. This paved the way for the rise of Naw Kham, one of Khun Sa's most loyal lieutenants. Naw Kham took command of one of Khun Sa's splintered army units and emerged as a major player controlling the heroin and meth routes connecting the Golden Triangle to China and the rest of the world. To insulate himself with protection, he taxed all drug runners, and to build local loyalty, he was known to give the proceeds to surrounding communities and security agencies. To add a further layer of protection, he was rumored to give 30 percent of his proceeds to Myanmar's military. This enabled Naw Kham to operate in the Golden Triangle with relative impunity. His main hideout was on an island only a few kilometers upstream from the Golden Triangle tourist site.

Into the early months of 2012, the Chinese net began to close on Naw Kham. Gradually, China's investigative team apprehended Naw Kham's associates and turned a few to aid in the investigation. However, every time China's security forces had Naw Kham surrounded, he successfully slipped through their fingers. China's state-led new agencies provided daily updates on the hunt for this villain, and Chinese television viewers were glued to the investigation's daily progress. In April 2012, Naw Kham was finally captured alive on a boat close to his island hideout without a shot fired. The Chinese government laid accolades on the team that apprehended Naw Kham. His extradition and trial in Kunming were aired on Chinese state television to convincingly demonstrate to the Chinese people that the Mekong murderer was brought to justice. Typically, Chinese authorities bar media coverage from judicial processes. This made Naw Kham's show trial a conspicuous rarity. Naw Kham was given a death sentence. He was executed via lethal injection on live television in 2013. In a country with the highest number of yearly executions, this live coverage was a first and drew disdain from human rights activists worldwide. All but Naw Kham's final moments were shown to Chinese viewers. The 9 Thai drug enforcement officers were tried in absentia and also convicted of murder. But no direct connection was made between these agents and Naw Kham. They have since disappeared into Thailand's judicial system.

The case was closed, but many questions remained unanswered. The trial never established a motive for Naw Kham to ruthlessly murder the 13 Chinese sailors. Naw Kham was not known to menace local merchants running boats through the Golden Triangle. Typically Myanmar and Lao security forces were his only targets of harassment. Certainly, someone with decades of experience taking advantage of and evading the law would know that such a brash move would bring the wrath of China down upon him. This would have been especially salient to Naw Kham since China was becoming more and more assertive in his own backyard. The naming of Naw Kham as a prime suspect by the Thai authorities seemed to conveniently shift blame away from Thai drug enforcement officers and by extension, away from the Thai government. Much of the evidence against Naw Kham was extracted from confessions of his apprehended associates. In all likelihood, these confessions came under duress since Chinese security forces have a long history of extracting forced confessions. Moreover, since Naw Kham did not speak Chinese, his court depositions were often subject to mistranslation. Those fluent in Naw Kham's Shan language said the translated "confession" of the murders, broadcast on television before the trial began, was mistranslated. They claim the video accurately documents Naw Kham saying he had nothing to do with the murders.

Journalist Jeff Howe, who detailed the events outlined above in a long-form article for the *Atavist Magazine,* has another theory as to who might have been responsible for the killings, and it has to do with the Kings Roman Casino. This sprawling entertainment complex sits across the river from the scene of the killings, just north of Chiang Saen.[4] Howe suggests that Kings Roman's owner, a businessman from northern China named Zhao Wei, was engaged in a turf war with Naw Kham and either orchestrated the perfect crime to oust his rival once and for all or used his influence to finger Naw Kham as a prime suspect. The struggle for control over Golden Triangle drug trade made headlines 6 months before the Mekong murders. In April 2011, Naw Kham's associates kidnapped more than 20 tourists headed from China to Kings Roman via boat and demanded $830,000 for their safe return. To avoid bad publicity, Zhao Wei paid the ransom. The tourists were returned without harm. In September of 2011, just weeks before the murders, the Myanmar military attacked Naw Kham's hideout, killing more than a dozen of his men. Then, in what appeared to be immediate retaliation, the Lao security forces, who were believed to be part of Naw Kham's protection racket, raided Kings Roman Casino and uncovered 20 sacks of methamphetamines worth $1.6 million. Two weeks later, the bodies of the 13 Chinese sailors washed ashore.

By the time of the murders, Zhao Wei and a group of unknown investors had invested more than $800 million in the 100 square kilometer Golden Triangle Economic Zone. The investment group gained control of the zone's 99 year lease in 2007. To date, it holds the record for the largest land concession in Laos. Flashy brochures advertise the economic zone as an "integrated trade and tourism zone, replete with luxury resorts, spas, golf courses, yacht clubs, and helicopter tours." Additionally, promotional materials suggest the zone will be home to a film institute, hospitals, and an international airport. To date, its only real attraction is the casino, a large concrete building topped with a neon crown and surrounded with overbearing Corinthian columns. A few blocks of hotels and restaurants surround the casino to cater to guests, most of whom are Chinese.

The last time I visited the Kings Roman Casino was in 2014, after a long day's travel overland on the R3 highway from Xishuangbanna. Chinese security guards dressed in uniforms common to China's urban areas zipped around the zone's grid layout in golf carts. Clocks in the hotels were set to China time, 1 hour later than official time in Laos. After paying for my hotel room in Chinese yuan, the young clerk behind the check-in desk said, "It's just like home here, only with better weather." He was from China's Hunan province. The street behind the casino was lined with restaurants and massage parlors where scantily clad women offered their services to the casino's mostly male clientele. One of the sex workers shouted to our group in a thick Yunnanese accent, "Come back for a massage later, foreigners. We have Lao girls and Myanmar girls. Lots of girls from different countries." Apparently, she forgot that she too was in a different country. Our Thai handlers from across the river in Chiang Saen ushered us into the casino.

Gambling and prostitution are illegal in both China and Laos, but the Golden Triangle Economic Zone's lease allows its owners to govern the grounds on their own terms. In addition to being a haven for drug and sex trafficking, the zone is an open market for consuming and purchasing illegal wildlife. Most restaurants sell liquor out of vats filled with tiger bones, illegally smuggled into the zone or harvested from tigers raised and slaughtered on the zone's grounds. The drink is a favorite of Chinese tourists and gamblers who through using the pseudoscience of Chinese medicine claim tiger products increase blood circulation and stamina. Cages placed in front of some restaurants are filled with live pythons, bear cubs, and pangolins all ready to slaughter and serve up for the restaurant's patrons. Pangolins are a small, scaly anteater and one of the most trafficked species in Asia. Chinese and Southeast Asians believe the pangolin's scales have medicinal qualities.

A 2015 report by the Environmental Investigation Agency (EIA) exposed the extent of wildlife trafficking going through the Golden Triangle Economic Zone. The undercover investigation found products made from illegal ivory, endangered hornbill, and tiger skins readily for sale throughout the grounds. A zoo behind the casino housed 26 live tigers and 38 Asiatic bears. The zoo's manager, a Chinese national, claimed to be an experienced butcher and gave investigators the impression there were no restrictions on keeping, breeding, or trading captive wildlife in Laos.[5] A few weeks after the report's release, Lao security forces raided the zone and confiscated stockpiles of tiger pelts, frozen bear paws, and elephant ivory. The zone's restaurants were only temporarily closed.

The report also details how illegal wildlife is moved in and out of China by linking Zhao Wei to the notorious warlord Lin Mingxian, who is also of Chinese descent and controls the Eastern Shan State Army just across the border from Xishuangbanna in a small city of Mongla, Myanmar. In 2003 the Chinese government shuttered Mongla's casinos, citing a border security threat. Apparently too many government officials were losing their cash to Lin Mingxian's casino tables. Zhao Wei operated Mongla's most popular casino, and after the forced shutdown he decamped to the Golden Triangle to find new business. The report also claims Chinese cargo ships have long served as mules for Zhao Wei and Lin Mingxian's operations by regularly shipping contraband up and down the river. After Naw Kham's capture, China, Laos, Thailand, and Myanmar set up joint river patrols to improve law enforcement and crack down on illegal activity. If the EIA investigation claims are true and China's cargo ships are aligned with King's Roman's illegal operations, then these official patrols also protect and help facilitate the illicit trade of drugs, wildlife, and possibly humans.

The day after I visited Kings Roman casino, I crossed the Mekong from Laos into Thailand to meet with Varin Sutavong, one of Chiang Saen's vice-mayors responsible for the town's tourism and economic development. Varin is in his sixties, has a deep tan, slicked-back hair, and on the handful of times that I have met him has always worn an untucked button-down shirt common of government officials in northern Thailand. Beneath the ruins of an 11th century Buddhist temple made of carved limestone and purple laterite, he told me of a business opportunity. "Zhao Wei wants to build a bridge from Chiang Saen to Kings Roman," said Varin. "He'll pay for all of it. The Thai government won't need to lift a finger. But I don't know if a Mekong bridge will be good for Chiang Saen."

Northern Thailand's Lanna Kingdom got its start in Chiang Saen in the 9th century before its capital moved to Chiang Mai 400 years later when Mongol invasions destabilized the region. Lanna culture is defined by its reverence for Buddhism, unique architectural styles, and spicy cuisine, among other factors. These arguably are what put Chiang Mai on the map as one of Southeast Asia's top tourist destinations and go-to choice of expatriation for Asian and European retirees. Chiang Saen, with a population of 5000, is surrounded by a low-lying brick wall constructed more than 1000 years ago. It contains the ruins of more than 60 temples which show layers of influence from surrounding Burmese, Lao, Indian, and Chinese cultures. Chiang Saen's ancient city too could be a top tourist destination, if it were not for so many other Thai cities filled with temple ruins and complex, layered histories.

"Kings Roman casino, that's 'Sin City'. Chiang Saen is 'Merit City'," Vice Mayor Varin told me while pointing across the river. "Chiang Saen is the place where gamblers can come and make good with the Buddha after they've lost all their money. Or they can first come to our temples and pray for good luck before crossing the river to Laos. The bridge could act as a kind of bridge between heaven here and hell over there. But who knows, maybe the tourists won't stay in Chiang Saen." In the past decade, over 30 guesthouses have opened in the town, but most tourists visiting the Golden Triangle are day trippers. The guesthouses are only busy for major Thai holidays. Lin Sumpatnua, the owner of the Golden Nakara guesthouse told me that more Chinese tourists are booking rooms in Chiang Saen. "They drive down the highway from Kunming and stop for a few days. We're happy to host more Chinese tourists because it's good for business. Now a third of my customers are Chinese," she remarked. Vice Mayor Warin who helped translate my interview with Lin interjected, "The Chinese like spas! Maybe Chiang Saen can be Merit City and Spa City! But the Thai government won't approve the bridge to Kings Roman because it's just another way for China to conquer Thailand." At the time of this book's publishing, Zhao Wei's bridge to Chiang

Saen was still a pipe dream, but China's naval vessels continued to patrol the Golden Triangle.

The other large Golden Triangle town on the Thai side of the river is Chiang Khong, roughly twice the size of Chiang Saen, located 60 kilometers downstream. For centuries, Chiang Khong thrived as a frontier trading outpost with neighboring Laos. Because of its remoteness, the town has historically been much less transient, making community ties much tighter than in Chiang Saen. In 2008, the completion of the R3 highway which terminates across the river from Chiang Khong in the Lao town of Huayxai, introduced a lot more traffic to Chiang Khong. Then in December 2013, a Chinese-built bridge across the Mekong opened, connecting the R3 to Thailand's road network. The bridge opened just months after Xi Jinping announced the Belt and Road Initiative, an ambitious series of infrastructure development projects built abroad and robustly supported by China's development banks. The initiative, which is often described by Western critics as China's Marshall Plan, will link China's markets to Southeast Asia, Central Asia, Africa, and Europe and instigate a sea of change in China's foreign economic policy which was previously much less ambitious.

Unlike the Marshall Plan, however, the Belt and Road Initiative supports projects abroad by issuing loans on a range of infrastructure development projects, many of which are rated as risky by other lending agencies. When countries cannot repay their loans, China gains access to free or low cost assets abroad. Such was the case in Sri Lanka in late 2017 when the government could not service the loan on its Hambantota Port, a Belt and Road project, China signed a 99 year lease on port ownership. Southeast Asian analysts worry how China's loan projects will affect weaker states like Laos and Cambodia where Chinese debt issuance is growing at a rapid pace.

To see how the bridge was affecting Chiang Khong, I caught up with my old friend Jib who owns and manages the Bamboo Mexican House Restaurant located on the town's main drag. Jib is one of Chiang Khong's more animated personalities. In his late sixties, Jib dresses like he is a 1970s Grateful Dead groupie. He is always wearing a knitted Rasta cap, and a blown glass medallion hangs around his neck fastened to an old knotted hemp rope. In Thailand, it is customary for most people to hang one or more photos of the late Thai King Bhumibol Adulyadej in their home or business, but the only photo of Thai royalty in Jib's restaurant is an old black and white photo from when the Thai king and queen met the King of Rock and Roll, Elvis Presley in 1960.

Jib feels the new bridge has severely impacted Chiang Khong's tourism economy. "Chiang Khong's guesthouses and restaurants used to be full during the high seasons from October to February. Now they are only busy for a few weeks." When Laos opened for foreign tourism in the 1980s, backpackers on a tour of Indochina (many of them French) would come to Chiang Khong to catch the ferry to Luang Prabang, 200 kilometers downstream. Many of these tourists expected a quick transit from Thailand to Laos, but they soon discovered that visa processing could take up to 1 week. With little to do, the foreign backpackers would hang out in a riverside bungalow, chat with the locals, and make a party of it. "They'd just walk or motorcycle into town and stay for a week. It was great business with the best people. One foreigner taught me how to make Mexican food. I found my niche. This is the only place you can get a burrito in the Golden Triangle," says Jib. But now, with the bridge open and Laos's visa-on-arrival service available to all, tourists skip the overnight stay in Chiang Khong and go straight across the river to Huayxai. Jib remarked how Huayxai is beginning to take off economically, "Their hotels are getting better. People over there are starting to dress like Thai people. They play golf and drive Toyotas. Their music is changing too. They used to blast real trippy tunes from that side of the river, but now all we hear is schmaltzy pop."

Jib, who transplanted himself from Bangkok in the 1980s, was always a fan of rock and roll. Over the years, wayward travelers also introduced Jib to blues, rock, and reggae. I was first attracted to the Bamboo Mexican House when I found Jib crooning away at Bob Marley's "Redemption Song" with his guitar in hand. And on this particular visit in 2014, after discussing the bridge at some length, Jib tossed me his guitar and said, "Let's do some Wilson Pickett!" Through a few verses of "Mustang Sally", we then ran through a handful of the Allman Brothers Band's songs, attracting a few tourists in from the roadside to listen. "Man, it was the relationship with the foreign tourists that showed me the power of music. They showed me the blues and now with business so low, this town is giving me the blues." He tells me this as he strums the chords to Crosby, Stills, Nash and Young's "Our House."

Locals in Golden Triangle communities on the Thai side of the river began to feel the effects of China's rise from upstream dams long before China's highways, cargo ships, and bridges encroached on the region. Like most riverside communities in the Mekong Basin, village markets are filled with fresh fish catches. In the Golden Triangle town of Chiang Khong, this is still true, but catches are magnitudes smaller than what they used to be. Niwat Roikaew, known by his followers as Khru Tee and profiled in the book's introduction, runs the local NGO *Rak Chiang Khong*. This name translates to "Love Chiang Khong." He attributes the drops in fish catches to China's upstream dams. "When China's first dam at Manwan began to fill in 1993, the water level immediately lowered here in Chiang Khong, 600 kilometers away," he said. Over the last 15 years, he has observed how the river's level can change on a daily basis. "In 2011, Xiaowan, the giant dam, began to store water. I had never seen the river so low. You could walk across it in the dry season. This day to day fluctuation gives the fish anxiety. They don't breed here anymore or maybe they just stay away."

Power generated from China's Upper Mekong dams is in greatest demand during the summer months when demand for air conditioning in China's coastal provinces is high. As a result, dam operators have a tendency to not produce electricity during the winter and spring. Water that would normally be flowing through the dam's turbines or spillways is stored in the dams' reservoirs. But in the Mekong Basin, the winter and spring months are the driest. With water stored for future use in China's dams, the Mekong River falls to unnaturally low levels downstream during the 6 month dry season. This often leaves China's cargo fleet stranded at the docks in Chiang Saen. If a major shipment comes in, the heads of the cargo fleet can call for a temporary water release from the Jinghong Dam. If a sudden dry-season weather event like an unexpected snowstorm or late season monsoon happens in Yunnan, dam operators are forced to release water to compensate for incoming flows impacting dam reservoirs. These factors make the last 5 years' hydrographs, the charts which track the day to day changes to flow volume and river level, look like an erratic stock trading chart.

Communities living along the Mekong and its tributaries have always planted dry season crops along riverbanks, taking advantage of nutrients naturally deposited during the monsoon season. This practice is often called flood-retreat agriculture. In December

2013, after a rare snowstorm hit Yunnan province, the river level in Chiang Saen rose 3 meters over a 24 hour period. The sudden floods affected 8 of Thailand's Mekong provinces.[6] Most riverside fields were destroyed by the river's sudden rise. Livestock and farm equipment left along the riverside were also washed away. Damage was roughly calculated in the tens of millions of dollars in Thailand alone. Chinese dam operators now have begun to share information on water releases from its upstream dams to Thailand's government in Bangkok, but no mechanism exists to get that information to the riverside communities who need it in a timely manner.

"In the past before all this dam construction, we ate well, lived well, and slept well. We only had to fish for one or two hours a day before there was enough to eat and sell at the market," said Polorng Taungsook, the leader of Huaileuk village at a meeting of local village heads at Khru Tee's Mekong School. In the past, most of his village's households fished the river for their livelihood, and now they are migrating to the city because the village has no jobs. With such fluctuations of the river's level, a river grass locally called *klainam* is no longer found in abundance. *Klainam* is a critical food source for fish. Its exposed root system provides shelter and encourages fish spawning. In the dry season, locals also harvest the grass to dry into sheets and eat as a deep-fried snack served with a spicy dip, but this practice too has waned in recent years.

"The river is no longer a river but a series of reservoirs," says Khru Tee at the Mekong School meeting. "We need to create strong community networks to stop the construction of dams on the Mekong. The Mekong is not for sale." In 2014, Thailand's highest court agreed to hear a petition filed on behalf of Khru Tee's *Rak Chiang Khong* group and a handful of other riverside communities. The petition detailed the impacts of Laos's Xayaburi Dam which is being built 300 kilometers downstream from Chiang Khong. It attested that the dam's builder, a Thai construction company called CH. Karnchang, did not consult with local communities prior to starting construction. The company neither provided adequate information on the dam's impacts nor assessed how the dam would impact communities outside of Laos in Thailand, Cambodia, and Vietnam. The hearing was a breakthrough for civil society action in Thailand, but it was scheduled before military general Prayuth Chan-Ocha ousted Thai Prime Minister Yingluck Shinawatra in a May 2014 *coup d'état*. A positive ruling could have stalled or halted CH. Karnchang's construction of the dam, but on December 15, 2015, the Thai court ruled that Xayaburi's builder was in full compliance with the law. Thailand's new military government was not willing to rock the boat on a multi-billion dollar Thai invest-ment in Laos, especially one that had already reached 50 percent completion at the time the petition was accepted.

This part of the Mekong was once famous for its seasonal catches of the Mekong Giant Catfish. In 2005, a group of Thai fishermen netted a female Mekong Giant Catfish that weighed 293 kilograms and was 2.7 meters long.[7] To date, this catch stands as the largest single freshwater fish caught since fishing records began to be written down. The Mekong Giant Catfish is the world's largest freshwater species and has been found in most reaches of the Mekong from the delta in Vietnam to Yunnan province. Little is known about the habitual patterns of the Mekong Giant Catfish, but the species is believed spend most of its time in deep pools in the middle sections of the Mekong and spawn yearly around exposed shoals just upstream from Chiang Khong. Since 2000 the popu-lation of Mekong Giant Catfish is believed to have fallen by 80 percent, and it is now designated as a critically endangered species. In 2008 a moratorium on Mekong Giant Catfish harvests went into effect, and since then only a few have been pulled from the river.

Fish conservation scientists claim only few hundred of these river giants are left in the wild.

To protect community fishing stocks, locals in Chiang Khong are beginning to take conservation into their own hands. Their action is a part of a long legacy of self-reliance in the Golden Triangle and reflective of the fact that communities have survived and thrived here for hundreds of years well outside the reach of the Thai state. To be sure, overfishing in addition to upstream dams' impacts also pose a threat to fish stocks. The populations of Chiang Khong and its surrounding communities have grown significantly in the last two decades. Also, better roads connecting Chiang Khong to the provincial capital of Chiang Rai mean that Mekong fish can now be sold at inland markets. These pressures contribute to overfishing. Khru Tee and his community network have introduced local solutions to fisheries protection by creating fish conservation zones in areas where fish are thought to breed. They also build fish ponds to raise native species of fish for release into the river and to sell on the market.

Villages in the community network have agreed on limiting the size of fish catches, identifying which fish are prohibited from harvesting, and when the fishing seasons begin and end. They also enforce regulations against illegal forms of fishing such as electric shock or using explosives to kill fish, forms of fishing unfortunately prevalent throughout the entirety of the Mekong Basin. Violators face a range of sanctions from fines to being reported to local authorities. Also, village leaders regularly meet to share best practices for fish conservation and discuss results. This is all done with zero guidance from the local government. To achieve success, Khru Tee also has to send his message practice across the river to neighboring communities in Laos. "If the Lao come and catch our fish, there's no point in doing conservation," said Khru

Tee. He claims that villagers are finally seeing how fish conservation, when carried out correctly, produces an abundance of fish. "It's taken a long time because at first, they thought we were protecting the fish and reducing their access. Now fish catches are getting better and so are the villager's livelihoods."

Khru Tee and his colleagues believe that incorporating traditional practices that help local communities adapt to or even push back on the forces of modernity and globalization is critical to both keeping communities intact and protecting the ecology of the Mekong River. But such an approach is seen as antiquarian and not widely respected in Thailand. Traditional practices are often deprioritized and undercut by modern agricultural methods imported from the West. However, Professor Apisom Intralawan, a US-trained ecological ecologist who teaches at Mae Fah Luang University in Chiang Rai would like to change this prejudice through promoting local communities as bases for research. "Villagers need to do the research, not the academics coming in from afar. The goal is to incorporate traditional knowledge so villagers can govern themselves," he said. "In the past, intellectuals and government officials claim that villagers don't have the knowledge to govern themselves. They claim villagers possess no knowledge since knowledge is science, and science comes from the West, not the upland areas of Thailand. But sometimes this scientific application doesn't fit the context of the people, and there's a backlash."

To better understand the marriage of traditional knowledge and conservation practices, Khru Tee took me to Muang Chum village located on the Ying River, one of the Mekong's Golden Triangle tributaries. We hopped in the back of a Toyota pickup truck driven by Panya Prombao, Muang Chum's university-educated village head. Panya is in his mid-fifties, and his black, thick-rimmed glasses and the curious eyes behind them give him the looks of a meticulous college professor. However, his worn, calloused hands reveal his life of farm work. Over the last decade he has successfully inspired the 515 villagers of Muang Chum to participate in community organized forest and wetlands preservations projects, all with very little support of the local government. When we arrived in a wetland forest populated with trees wrapped in orange ribbons adjacent to the village's rice fields, I asked him to describe the recipe that has made conservation in Muang Chum so successful. "You're looking at it. The trees in this forest are blessed by local Buddhist monks and the elders of Muang Chum respect these trees. It is taboo to cut these trees down."

Panya's daughter, who attends college in Bangkok, rolled out a picnic cloth, and we sat down for mid-morning pork-rind, sausage, and some home-made rice whiskey. An aging villager who accompanied us used his knife to convert a hacked piece of bamboo into a few bowls and five sets of chopsticks. Panya poured me a tall glass, and since it was January 2, 2015, offered a New Year's toast of whiskey to our collective good health. "Many professors from Thailand and around the world come to this forest to learn about community conservation," he said. He and Khru Tee began to teach me about the intermarriage of community space, ritual, and village elders. They pointed out the various man-made additions to the wetland forest: a Buddhist shrine, two pavilions with tables for village gatherings, and in the far corner of the forest, a raised concrete platform used to cremate bodies of recently deceased villagers.

"This space is for the community. After working in the fields, people come here for rest and eating – they like to joke around and talk about the latest gossip," said Khru Tee. "And they don't have to bring too much with them because the wetland forest is like a supermarket filled with wild herbs, tasty bamboo shoots, and lots of other things to eat," he proudly exclaimed. As he finished this sentence, the older man once again emerged from the forest with a large, red banana flower. He quickly cut it up into a tasty salad dressed with fish sauce and sugar kept in the truck. Khru Tee launched into a brief diatribe against Chiang Khong's recently opened, Tesco Lotus Supercenter. "The fish at the Tesco Lotus is cut up into fillets and brought in frozen from other parts of Thailand. Some local consumers get excited about goods from all over the world. But we've always had everything we need in Chiang Khong. If Tesco Lotus is a supermarket, then our forests, rivers, and wetlands are our super-supermarkets!"

We jumped back into the pickup truck and Panya drove us to other community spaces around the village. We visited a large, open-air pavilion used for community fish and chicken grills that Panya said also doubles as the community meeting and training center. In this pavilion, on another previous visit to Muang Chum with American college students, I participated in a *baci* ceremony where the local elders lay blessings upon white strings and tied them around the wrists of each newcomer to welcome them to the village. This ritual expression demonstrates the connection between newcomers, villagers, spirituality, and nature. It is found throughout northern Thailand and Laos and is similar to the black thread tying ceremony of the Akha people.

Panya also took us above the village to shaded groves of trees that lined the village's man-made reservoir which provides guided irrigation to Muang Chum's rice fields and drains through the village into the forested wetland below. "We have to maintain these trees because our village's couples like to come here to talk romance. Without these trees, our population would dwindle," Panya said with a smile. We ended the day on large flat rocks below a waterfall above the reservoir. "These spaces are the private property of no one person. We draw resources from them, but since the spaces belong to the community, those resources are maintained in abundance. We regularly hold rituals here, and it's important for the village elders to talk about the importance of ritual. This keeps the people coming back and our ecology intact."

After visiting Muang Chum, I followed up with Professor Apisom for insight on why maintaining community space served as the key to cultural and ecological preservation. Most importantly I inquired about why the "tragedy of the commons," the widely-held belief that shared space and a poor definition of private property leads to the overexploitation of resources and social dis-harmony, was not happening in Muang Chum. He answered, "Because the community space is not open access." Noting the taboo of cutting down trees, he said, "There are customary boundaries and social sanctions enforced by locals and their leaders. These laws and codes are not necessarily written down. In these Golden Triangle communities, the connections between the individual and nature, and the producer and the consumer, are clear. Individuals understand that their actions can impact a greater ecology." To provide contrast, Professor Apisom told me of the time he asked his niece, who lives in Bangkok, where rice comes from. "She quickly replied, 'Of course I do. Tesco Lotus Supermarket!'" he said. He told her that she was correct but only half-correct.

Other Golden Triangle communities have explored different approaches to adapting to ever-changing conditions. In Takongthong village, 50 kilometers upstream from Chiang Khong, Promma Setthasak has set up a community-based tourism project that involves most of the village's 300 residents. In addition to managing the tourist project, the entrepreneurial Promma wears many hats. He is the village sheriff, and starting at 6 o'clock am each day, he broadcasts all the news from the Golden Triangle and around the world from an FM radio station that he owns and operates. Promma is in his mid-fifties and like Panya Prombao, he responded to a need to protect the community economy and local ecology when he observed the negative effects of cash crop management and the flood of young people leaving Takongthong village. Also similar to Panya Prombao, Promma's action plan created and maintained shared social spaces to keep individuals in the community gelled together. The difference in the approach is that Promma's activities are profit-bearing.

One of these shared social spaces is in the rice field. In July 2014, I took the opportunity to get knee-deep in rice paddy mud to plant rice seedlings with a group of American college students. After a crash course in "How not to wreck our rice paddy" taught by a gregarious local woman in her sixties, we donned knee length waterproof socks and wide-brimmed straw hats and began to carefully construct neat rows of rice seedlings. A portable loud-speaker system began to blare traditional music, which for lack of a better comparison, is defined by bluegrass-esque guitar licks backed by a loud reggae off-beat. Standing on dry land, our rice planting instructor began to break into song and twisted her arms and hands to the beat of the music. When she finished a verse, we noticed that the male villagers who were planting rice alongside the group called to her in response with their own verse. At times, the song sounded like a competition between the men and the woman. Professor Apisom, who introduced our group to Takongthong village, said that the calls and responses were laden with dirty jokes where men and women often poke fun at the size of each other's sexual anatomy. "This makes otherwise tedious work enjoyable and helps to bring the villagers closer together," said Professor Apisom.

The call and response songs, those lewd and those safe-for-work, are part of a century old northern Thai and Lao rice planting traditions. I first learned of this tradition at a Thai studies conference at the University of Wisconsin-Madison where a young graduate student claimed the singing tradition had been erased when landowners began to contract rice planting to migrant labor pools. Villagers simply were no longer meeting in the rice paddies. She said the only living instance of this tradition had been preserved by a playwright in Chiang Mai, Thailand and that the songs were now performed for tourists seated in theaters. In other words, the only way to access this practice was like going to see a museum exhibit since it could no longer be found in contemporary practice. Discovering this tradition alive and well in the Golden Triangle served as a reminder of how community-based tourism provided opportunities to protect such traditions. Even though our activity was still a kind of paid-for performance, it reinforced community ties and continued an age-old tradition.

Central to Takongthong village's tourism experience is a homestay program in which more than half of the village's households participate. The first overnight tourists came to the village in 2012, and by 2016 the number of visitors increased to over 5000. Most of the tourists are urban Thai who are looking for ways to get away from the air pollution and traffic of their surroundings and return to nature. Less than 10 percent of Takongthong's homestay guests are foreign, and unlike Chiang Saen's guesthouses only 10 kilometers away, fewer than 10 Chinese tourists have stayed in the village. Promma oversees the operations, but community-based tourism efforts in Takongthong are very much led by the village's women.

Takongthong village absorbed refugees from the northeast Thai region of Isaan 40 years ago. Some of the refugees likely fled to Isaan from the civil war in Laos before ending up in the Golden Triangle. All of Isaan is located within the Mekong Basin, and the majority of people there share close cultural ties with the people of Laos which made the sparsely populated Golden Triangle a feasible zone of refuge. In Isaan, these villagers were skilled weavers, and many of Takongthong's older women still possess these skills taught to them by their mothers. In Takongthong, they set up a weaver's guild with some start-up funds Promma accessed from the local government. Tourists often enroll in week-long to month-long classes in Takongthong to learn how to weave, and the guild's products can be found in shops as far away as Bangkok. Additionally, the women have set up a local spa that offers steam baths and Thai massages to tourists. They also take tourists to their riverside gardens to help with picking fruit and vegetables. These activities are packaged into a circuit of activities aimed at promoting local values and practices to outsiders. But the most frequent beneficiaries of these spaces are the villagers themselves who spend the day weaving and quilting and happily taking steam baths and receiving massages. Once while I was receiving a massage, one of the village women told me, "Happiness doesn't just come from money. We get happiness, pride, and confidence from working together. When we see tourists enjoying our activities, then the happiness spreads."

Promma hopes these efforts will increase villager's incomes and entice them to stay in Takongthong rather than moving to urban Chiang Rai or other cities. He even has envisioned ways that college graduates can find work in the village by converting much of the community's agriculture to organic farming now that Thai consumers are more conscious about the quality of food they eat. "Some of our children are receiving agronomy degrees, and their return to the community will open up other service opportunities for young people with college educations," says Promma. To entice more youth to return, in 2015 he accessed 8 million baht ($250,000) from the provincial military to start a 150 kilowatt community-scale solar farm just outside the village boundary. "Operating the solar plant will require engineers and managers, so this could bring some of our children home." Before I left Promma, he parted me with words that reminded me I was still in Zomia. "This part of the world is changing faster than we can see, and we must adapt. The most important thing is to create the tools to solve these problems ourselves and not wait for the government to intervene," he said.

6

LAOS AS A
CONTESTED SPACE

The ancient capital of Luang Prabang is located in the center of northern Laos on a small peninsula formed by the Mekong and a tributary called the Nam Khan. It is officially promoted as "Asia's Best Preserved City," but with a population of around 50,000 living on the peninsula and in the surrounding area, Luang Prabang is more a sleepy Mekong town than a city. Underneath the old town's coconut palms lies a collection of ancient Buddhist temples, traditional Lao teak homes, and refurbished French villas, all of which suggest the town has been forgotten by time and modern technological advancements. Before sunrise each morning, young monks in saffron robes collect food and alms from the town's residents. Tourists who observe this timeless ritual are encouraged not to pollute the scene by taking photographs. Many of these tourists arrive by boat traveling downstream from the Golden Triangle, and others fly into the town's single runway airport.

Luang Prabang is also a dreamscape for local and expat gourmands in search of the perfect croissant at Le Banneton, a café which is consistently rated as one of Asia's best bakeries. Other seek out Southeast Asia's most savory papaya salad and sticky rice combination sold by a local family at a stand outside their home. Tourists gather daily at the top of Mount Phousy in the center of old town to watch the sunset over the Mekong and the foggy hills that line its western shores. Even after 20 years of designation as a UNESCO World Heritage Site and a major stop on the Southeast Asian tourism trail, Luang Prabang maintains its charm as a remote jewel amidst the tropical jungles and mountainous landscape of northern Laos

On New Year's Day 2014, local vendors set up canopied stalls in the middle of the town's main street ready to sell traditional Lao handicrafts at the town's famous night bazaar. As they did every night, they placed miniature elephants, prints of Buddhist art made on homemade paper, and a collection of other colorful souvenirs on canvas tarps. On this night however, they were rudely interrupted by the piercing blare of car horns. A caravan of 10 SUVs, all with license plates from China's Yunnan province, was attempting to force its way through the bazaar, despite it being closed to auto- mobile traffic. Local police soon showed up. The Chinese tourists, who had driven from Kunming 600 kilometers to the north for a New Year vacation in Laos, brazenly claimed their right to drive through the bazaar to reach their hotel. After a 15 minute voice battle, the police convinced the caravan to take a more circuitous route to its lodging. The situation de-escalated, but the story spread quickly throughout Laos's tight-knit communities.

In Laos, this story fits into an increasingly dominant narrative of a "Chinese takeover" of Luang Prabang and northern Laos that worries many locals. In a town that already struggles with a saturated tourism market (a large majority of Luang Prabang's 600,000 annual tourists are from outside of Asia), hotel owners and tourism operators are learning to cope with the needs and behavior of Chinese tourists. Relatively new to the international tourism scene but now leaving China in droves, Chinese tourists typically travel in large groups with mega-phone equipped tour guides, and they often eschew local food in search of Chinese cuisine. Among locals in Laos, Chinese tourists have a reputation of being loud and unruly. The stereotype

is cliché – certainly not all Chinese tourists to Laos or other countries are loud and unruly – but in 2013 China's government began
to issue new regulations to curb the behavior of its citizens abroad.
Some of these suggestions include cautioning against lying down in
public, going outside with disheveled hair and a dirty face, removing
one's shoes and socks in public. Other useful points of etiquette
read not to spit phlegm or gum, throw litter, urinate or defecate
wherever one likes. Continuing, one shouldn't cough or pick one's
nose in public. In 2015, the Chinese government created a blacklist
of citizens behaving badly abroad that prohibits those listed from
flying and affects various credit ratings. Some inside and outside
decry the blacklisting of Chinese tourists as an infringement on individual liberties and the application of Chinese law outside of China's
territory. The new regulations have achieved mixed results, and
for better or for worse over the last decade, the volume of Chinese
tourists abroad has increased by 20 percent year on year.

To be sure, the new tourism dollars brought into Luang
Prabang are much welcomed, but it is difficult to predict just how
big the future wave of tourists to Luang Prabang will be, given the
proximity of Yunnan's tourist towns, which attract tens of millions
of Chinese tourists per year. More direct flights are connecting
jumping off points in China to Luang Prabang's new international
airport, which was built and financed by a Chinese contractor. And
if things go according to plan, by 2021 a high-speed rail network
will link Kunming to Vientiane with Luang Prabang serving as a
major stop on the new line.

Laos only has about 10 kilometers of railway running through
it, and these rail lines historically served the needs of outsiders
more than they served Laos itself. A short railway bridge carries
passengers from northeast Thailand into a station near Laos's
capital at Vientiane. Laos's other railway, which is less than

6 kilometers long, lies in a deteriorated, unusable state near the country's border with Cambodia. It originates from the late 19th century, French colonials built a small portage railway there to pull military and cargo ships up over the waterfalls at Siphandone near Laos's southern border. The French long sought to transform the Mekong into a navigable pathway to connect its southern colonies and protectorates in Vietnam and Cambodia with those in what comprise modern-day Laos.

In comparison to its Western European counterparts, France's entry into the Asian colonial fray in the middle of the 19th century came late, and dominating the Mekong was a way to push back on both British and the Siamese imperial ambitions in Southeast Asia. French expeditionary forces in the 19th century also knew the Mekong led to China and imagined that a Mekong navigable from mouth to headwaters could serve as a spear for the French to penetrate and colonize China's south. Their eventual charting of the river in the mid-1800s revealed otherwise. They learned of the river's difficult passages in the Golden Triangle and concluded Yunnan's isolation would never give France a strong foothold in the rest of China. The railway at Siphandone operated at limited capacity into the 20th century and was taken over by the Japanese during the Second World War. When the French returned to Laos as re-colonizers in 1946, they abandoned the railway. Eight years later in 1954, France's colonial operations in Indochina ended in 1954 with its stunning military defeat by Vietnamese revolutionary forces at Dien Bien Phu, and the portage rail was entirely forgotten. Today, two of the train engines once used to shuttle boats from the low end of Don Khone island to a port on Don Det island are corroding away under open-air pavilions as a reminder of Laos's colonial past and French hubris. Nearly all of the narrow-gauge track was scavenged over and sold off to the local scrap metal market.

China's current railway plans for Laos are much more ambitious than those of the French. In January 2017, the newly installed Lao Prime Minister Thongloun Sisoulith broke ground for the construction of a 417 kilometer segment that upon completion will connect Kunming to Vientiane. This was not the first groundbreaking ceremony for the controversial project. The railway was first proposed in 2006 by the Chinese government which eyes the railway as its missing link to gain access to ports along the Gulf of Thailand and send its goods overland to markets in Malaysia and Singapore. Delays in negotiations centered around the ability of Laos to pay for the rail's exorbitant price tag of $6.2 billion – a little under half of Laos's GDP in 2016. The construction plan for the project is a technical nightmare: 154 bridges and 76 tunnels will cut through some of the world's most mountainous and unforgiving terrain. The combined length of the route's tunnels is 196 kilometers, just under half of the entire length of the rail itself. Construction workers and engineers will undoubtedly encounter patches of unexploded ordnance dropped by US bombers in the 1960s and 1970s. And to make matters even more complicated, the area of northern Laos that the rail bisects is also seismically active. On average, northern Laos experiences 6 earthquakes a year. These latter factors introduce much risk to the project's viability and, combined with the need for so many tunnels, translates into a cost of close to $15 million per kilometer.

Initially, China expected the Communist government of Laos to take on a massive loan to pay for the project outright and then back the loan with mineral resources as collateral. If issued, the loan would have totaled nearly all of Laos's annual GDP with interest payments sucking up 20 percent of total yearly government expenditure. The debt level would have immediately placed Laos as one of the world's top 5 indebted countries. Between 2012

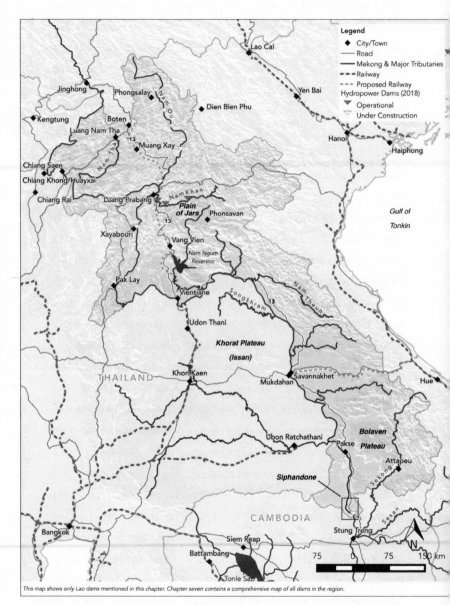

Lao Cai

Yen Bai

Jinghong

Phongsalay

Dien Bien Phu

Kengtung

Boten

Luang Nam Tha

13

Muang Xay

Hanoi

Haiphong

Chiang Saen

Chiang Khong/Huayxai

Chiang Rai

Luang Prabang

Nam Khan

Plain
of Jars

Phonsavan

Gulf of

Tonkin

Xayabouri

13

Vang Vien

Nam Ngum
Reservoir

Pak Lay

Vientiane

Songkhram

13

Nam Theun

Udon Thani

Khorat Plateau

(Issan)

Khon Kaen

Mukdahan

Savannakhet

Hue

THAILAND

Ubon Ratchathani

Pakse

Bolaven

Plateau

Attapeu

Siphandone

Sekong

Bangkok

CAMBODIA

Stung Treng

Sesan

N

75   0   75   150 km

Siem Reap

Battambang

Tonle Sab

This map shows only Lao dams mentioned in this chapter. Chapter seven contains a comprehensive map of all dams in the region.

Map of Laos

and 2015, Laos's ministries and National Assembly debated over the benefits of such an undertaking. Detractors argued how Laos would inevitably have to surrender a majority of its mineral rights to China and raised security concerns over China's ability to bring troops across borders should it ever choose to annex or colonize Laos. Proponents claimed that Laos had to shake off its landlocked mentality and become "landlinked" by reaping the advantages of sitting at the crossroads of Southeast Asia's major thoroughfares.

In late December 2015, Lao Deputy Prime Minister Somsavath Lengsavad, who is ethnically Chinese and associated with the majority of China's business interests in Laos, brought negotiations for the rail project across the finish line. Construction would begin immediately. The Chinese government agreed to pay for most of the project and issued Laos a $480 million loan backed by 5 of Laos's potash mines. The rationale for China's taking most of the project's risk was that it would benefit Chinese passengers and cargo much more than Laos. Two weeks later, Somsavath Lengsavad, Prime Minister Choummaly Sayasone, and a handful of their pro-China cronies were forced to retire and a new Hanoi-leaning government took power headed by Thongloun Sisoulith. After more than a decade of signing off on shady deals that saw Lao government officials selling off the country's land rights, mineral resources, and dam sites to outsiders, with Chinese investors taking the lion's share, Somsavath's railway deal was the straw that broke the Chinese camel's back in Laos. Immediately after his ouster, Somsavath Lengsavad sought hermitage as a monk in a monastery in his hometown of Luang Prabang. In July 2016, an anonymous source close to Somsavath told Radio Free Asia that "he wants to maintain mental tranquility for the rest of his life following his retirement from politics."[1] Many Lao people I talked to about Somsavath's religious turn suggest he is seeking atonement for a guilty conscience while others noted that he was merely biding his time in wait for a change in political winds. Today, he is often seen in the halls of government in Vientiane.

In March 2016, a Lao colleague who works in the finance industry told me, "Northern Laos is now like a Chinese colony. You know the saying 'Made in China'? Well, everything in northern Laos is 'Made by China, Made for China.' We hear these words every day on the streets of Vientiane, but since we're a small country, there's little we can do to stop it." Indeed, to construct the railway through Laos, 50,000 Chinese workers have already moved into the country. This number is highly significant for a country of less than 7 million. The population of its northern cities averages in the tens of thousands. In many of these cities, new Chinese arrivals already account for between 10 to 20 percent of the population.[2] The majority of the migrants are laborers who work on land concessions that were sold off to Chinese investors by the government of Laos or small holders of land rented to them by locals. They are responsible for cutting down unknown amounts of hillsides of old growth forest for conversion into rubber plantations. In low-lying areas, entrepreneurial Chinese migrants have established large plantations for growing cash crops like banana, watermelon, and cassava root. When harvest time comes, these goods are then sent northward for sale on the Chinese market. The success of this agro-economy is often determined by the demand for these goods in China. For instance, until recently, most of the land on Zhao Wei's Golden Triangle Economic Zone was used for planting bananas. When China's relationship with the Philippines warmed under the recent elected Duterte government in 2016, banana imports from the Philippines immediately outcompeted Laos's. Zhao Wei and most plantation owners switched to more profitable cash crops.

Chinese laborers are building and improving road networks that stretch out from Yunnan province, mining Laos's rich mineral deposits in the north, and supporting the construction of more than 40 Chinese invested dams north of Vientiane on the mainstream and tributaries of the Mekong. In 2017, I asked the chief engineer overseeing the construction of 7 Chinese built, owned, and operated dams on the Nam Ou River, an important tributary of the Mekong in northern Laos, why more local Lao people were not employed to construct the dams. He simply replied, "Chinese laborers are willing to work harder, and they are much more reliable than the Lao people. What's more, the Lao ask for higher wages."

Inevitably, service jobs ranging from machinery repair to boarding houses to restaurants offering the gamut of Chinese cuisines will follow the migrant clusters into Laos. The addition of Chinese storefront signs now makes northern Lao towns nearly indiscernible from those across the border in Yunnan. The gravity of Chinese migration is so strong that new immigrants need not learn to speak Lao. Upon arrival in northern Laos, Chinese immigrants can interact in a closed-loop system with their compatriots. On trips to Laos, I often walk through marketplaces in towns like Luang Namtha, Huayxai, and Luang Prabang and inquire with Chinese vendors how long they anticipate staying in Laos. Most new arrivals say they have trouble adjusting to the local culture, so they will likely return to China permanently in a few years after they stockpile enough savings in Laos. A small percentage, mostly men, prefer the Lao cultural milieu and choose to stay in Laos long-term. A Chinese man from Hunan province who had immigrated to Laos in the late 1990s to start a cattle business once told me how he adored Lao culture. As a convert, he picked up the Lao language, married a Lao woman, and has a preference for Lao food. He said, "Life in Laos is *sabai sabai*." In the Lao language as well as its sibling Thai language, the word *sabai* means happy and comfortable. He continued, "In China we don't have a word that combines these meanings in the Lao sense. We Chinese lack the patience of the Lao people. We've come to only care about making money and competing for this and that."

While stories of a rising China's encroachment into northern Laos often dominate the headlines of regional media outlets and draw criticism inside and outside of Laos, a trip through other parts of Laos will suggest that Vietnam and Thailand, Laos's other rising neighbors, also encroach on cultural space and economic development in Laos. Laos's central provinces are dotted with Thai invested special economic zones, purposed for export processing. The Bolaven Plateau, in the south of Laos, is over-run with Vietnamese-owned coffee plantations. Driving through Attapeu city, the capital of the southern province of the same name, an observer will find as many storefront signs in Vietnamese as in the Lao language.

With so many neighbors extracting Laos's abundant natural resources and carving up pieces of the country for their own economic dominion, it comes as no surprise that voices within the Lao National Assembly and other élite are calling for the Lao people to take back their country and curb the fleecing of its resources through strengthening rule of law. These voices cite the rhetoric of the Pathet Lao, the revolutionary forces that won victory over the US-backed Lao constitutional monarchy in 1975 and – somewhat ironically – laud Lao kings of centuries past who successfully fended off invaders and never bent their knee. But the real irony lies in two historical contradictions to this current rhetoric. First, Lao independence would not have been gained without the assistance of outsiders from the People's Army of Vietnam. And second, throughout history, without exception, all Lao kings bent their knee to one or more neighboring overlords.

In today's Laos, history books trace the beginnings of the country's history to the founding of the Lan Xang Kingdom in the 14th century. The story begins with a great king Fa Ngum who unified Laos's north and established a capital at Luang Prabang. During his prosperous reign, he brought Theravada Buddhism to the country and established the basis for Lao cultural identity. His descendants successfully converted Luang Prabang into an important regional hub for trade and commerce, but in the 16th century the Lan Xang Kingdom was forced to move its capital south to Vientiane to avoid invasion from the Burmese. This official historical narrative continues through periods of prosperity and decline, where successes and failures of the kingdom depended on the talents of individual monarchs. It eventually arrives at the 17th century when due to outside pressures, the kingdom split into three: Luang Prabang in the north, Vientiane in the center, and Champasak in the south.

Both Vientiane and Champasak would eventually be absorbed into the Siamese Empire, but Luang Prabang in the north never succumbed to outside invasion. Thus, according to the official narrative, Lao independence continued unwavering, but to a lesser degree. Under French colonialism, which lasted from 1860 to 1953, Vientiane and Champasak were re-incorporated into Lao space, but the official accounts accuse the Lao people of "sinking into a period of ignorance, venerating the French, forgetting their own lineage, and consenting to being slaves of the foreigner."[3] Finally, after decades of revolutionary struggle and violence against colonialist forces, the Pathet Lao restored the Lao nation to independence in 1975. These history books trace an unbroken, linear pathway of Lao national development from antiquity to the present, but lack a disclaimer reminding the reader that this official history was composed less than 40 years ago.

The word *Laos* first shows up in European languages in the mid-16th century when the Portuguese used it to describe all the people living north of the Siamese Kingdom. The "Lao" people were those who were not Siamese and included people in the kingdoms around Chiang Mai and Chiang Rai in modern-day northern Thailand as well as those in Lan Xang. The various Lao peoples, who were linguistically and culturally related to the Siamese but too far afield to control directly, collectively occupied the great periphery of Thailand called Laos. Thus, Laos is a plural word not dissimilar to Maldives or the Philippines.[4] The French who coined the term "Laos" never intentioned for the word to be pronounced with a final "s" sound. The Lao people pronounce the name of their country without the "s," and as a respectful practice, so should we all.

The reaches of kingdoms like Siam and Lan Xang had known limits but were unbounded by strict border delineations. Their strength was strongest around their capitals which housed their armies and administrative units but weakened in relation to distance from the capital city. In historical and political discourse, this kind of kingdom is known as a "mandala state," envisioned as a set of concentric circles of influence emanating from the core with influence waning in the peripheral zones. To maintain the economic and political viability of the mandala state, monarchs required smaller kingdoms or potentates on their periphery to pledge allegiance and give tribute in the form of food, gifts, and soldiers to the center in return for protection against invaders. This was by no means a system of an overlord imposing sovereign control over a strict and demarcated space, but the dictates of the overlords often influenced political outcomes and cultural and religious traditions in peripheral areas. If the monarch of a lesser kingdom refused to kneel or pay tribute or rebelled against its overlord, his capital was susceptible to invasion. However, one mandala state often overlapped with another or even multiple mandala states, so it was not uncommon in Southeast Asia for peripheral kings to craftily pay tribute to multiple overlords. The Lao Kingdoms were no exception. At the same time, lesser kingdoms like the ones found in Laos maintained control over their surrounding areas by replicating smaller mandala states.

To illustrate, at the beginning of the 19th century, Luang Prabang, Vientiane, and Champasak all paid tribute to both the Siamese king at Bangkok and the Vietnamese emperor at Hue. In 1828, armies from Vientiane led by Lan Xang King Chao Anouvong attacked Siamese military garrisons across the Mekong deep into Isaan, a region defined by the Khorat Plateau and heavily populated by culturally Lao peoples. In the previous decade, Lao cities in Isaan began to show deeper loyalty to Siam, and Chao Anouvong refused to let this most heavily populated part of his kingdom into Siam's grip. In response to Chao Anouvong's invasion, Siam dispatched troops to the Khorat Plateau, defeating the invading Lao forces. Chao Anouvong escaped to northern Laos to compel the Vietnamese to join his cause. But he was soon captured by the Siamese and sent to Bangkok where he was executed. The Siamese then sacked the city of Vientiane leaving it in such a manner that "only grass, water, and savage beasts remained."[5] To provide insurance against future uprisings, much of Vientiane and Champasak Kingdoms were depopulated and its dwellers were resettled to the Khorat Plateau. The resultant low population levels in the Lao Kingdoms would provide a challenge for the French who decades later established administrative centers in Vientiane and other parts of the country.

When the French began to colonize Indochina in the 1860s, their efforts mostly focused on direct rule over the Vietnamese colonies of Tonkin, Annam, and Cochinchina. The French grew anxious over prospects of the British Empire moving toward Vietnam from Burma, but were more squarely concerned with the expanding Siamese Empire just next door. To protect its interests, the French envisioned Laos as a buffer zone between French Indochina and

Siam with the Mekong River serving as a dividing line. To establish a logic of French control over the buffer zone, the French argued their own historical claims to the Lao Kingdoms since the Lao continued to pay annual tribute to the Vietnamese emperor at Hue who after French occupation was a subject of the French empire. By extension, the Lao kings were too subjects of France.

To establish Laos as a buffer zone, in his important study *Creating Laos*, scholar Soren Ivarsson makes a convincing argument that the French fabricated not only the boundaries of modern Laos but also the narrative of Lao national history and identity. The French used modern tools of national building to paint a disconnected and culturally disparate space into one defined by unity and a common cultural heritage. Ivarsson discusses how in the late 1880s the French employed the technology of cartography to mainland Southeast Asia for the first time. After consultation with Annamite bureaucrats and Lao kings, French cartographers produced a map of French Indochina that included all of the vassals paying tribute to the Hue emperor. This map included all Lao land east of the Mekong and also included the entirety of Isaan and the Khorat Plateau which was populated by ethnic Lao peoples. Ivarsson claims, "When the French took over Laos there was no sense of a Lao nation among the population that fell within the boundaries they mapped. Even for the French, Laos was at that time a mere cartographic reality than a social or historical one."[6] In response to the French mapping, the Siamese then hired British cartographers to map out the entirety of the Siamese empire which extended across the Mekong all the way across Lao space to the Annamite mountain range.

At the end of the 19th century, both France and Siam laid equal claim to Laos. Since no historical boundaries previously existed, the prevailing Western logic of historical claim could not settle the dispute. There was no consensus even among European colonizers for solving overlapping sovereignty claims. So, to force an outcome, in 1893 the French navy blockaded the Chao Phraya River at Bangkok, cutting off global trade to the Siamese Empire. The Siamese acquiesced with reluctance and signed a treaty which recognized France's rights to all lands east of the Mekong River.

Over the next five decades, to shed notions that the Lao were inferior subjects of the Siamese Empire, French administrators slowly invented the roots of Lao-ness and the Lao cultural identity. The Siamese long considered the Lao people a lower cousin and the Lao language a lesser dialect of their own language.[7] To elevate the Lao to a status of nationhood equal to the Siamese, the French sponsored the writing of a Lao national history that exalted King Fa Ngum as a unifier ruling over a strong and independent Laos, the territory of which conveniently covered the territory France's drawn boundaries. To underscore how things fell apart in Laos, historians noted the decadence of the later Lan Xang Kingdom citing how it subject to inner rivalry and anarchy.[8] Thus the French claimed that the merits of unity and good governance were not new values imposed by outside colonizers but rather historical lessons historical lessons to be learned by the Lao people they sought to civilize. Of course, the official history of the time also exalted the French as the providers of security to Laos. The French also codified a written Lao language that was distinct from Siamese language and put the new script into print through the publication of books and newspapers that told stories and news from around Laos. Discussions and illustrations praised the merits of the French colonials and also the Vietnamese administrators who were assigned to work in Laos. In this propaganda, the neighboring Thai were consistently depicted in a racist, pejorative manner. Ivarrson believes these efforts successfully de-linked Lao space from Siam which subsequently changed its name to Thailand in 1938 after the abolition of its absolute monarchy. While the cultural and historical thought-work that promoted Lao identity was designed to keep Lao space comfortably under France's thumb, it ultimately backfired against France by inspiring nationalist movements within Laos that eventually would eject the French overlords in 1953 and later the Americans in 1975.

Today the campaign for a common Lao identity is only about a century old. The French, Americans, and even the current Lao PDR government lacked the resources to convincingly deliver this campaign to settlements on the Lao periphery and up the mountainsides. The independent Lao state is weak in its ability to project a national identity and to defend law and order to the limits of its borders. This weak national fabric hampers national builders in the Lao government from pushing back against those countries and entities that erode its peripheral areas. Thus, even though Laos qualifies in every aspect as a modern nation-state, its interior and periphery remain as contested spaces highly vulnerable to the machinations of both neighboring countries and global powers.

Another outcome of France's nation building project in Laos was a close political and historical affinity to Vietnam. The French lacked the manpower to administer control over Laos and employed thousands of Vietnamese in its civil service. At any one time, only a few thousand French could be found in Laos. Since Lao space was depopulated by Siamese incursions in the previous centuries, the French encouraged the resettlement of thousands of Vietnamese throughout Laos to work on agricultural plantations and stimulate the economy. To illustrate, in 1937, census records from the Lao administrative capital of Vientiane show the city was populated by 12,400 Vietnamese and only 9,570 Lao.[9] After the French left Laos in the early 1950s, the Vietnamese influx was a cause for concern among the Lao élite. However, the Vietnamese population already in Laos served as the leading ally in to the victorious Pathet Lao, and linkages between both Communist governments remain strong today.

Into the 20th century, the Thai never gave up on reclaiming "lost" Laos. In the 1920s the Thai extended railroad networks north toward Chiang Mai and west to the Khorat Plateau. From these railways shot out new road systems extending to the Mekong that would facilitate Thai economic commercial and potential military influence over Lao space. The French colonizers were particularly worried about losing economic sway over Luang Prabang, which was 3 to 4 months' travel upriver from Saigon but now only a few weeks' travel from Bangkok. Because of its proximity to Burma, Siam, and China, a French consul once called Luang Prabang "the most important strategic point in eastern Indochina."[10] With so many new routes putting Laos within easy access of the Thai, the French responded by building the famous Route 13 which runs the length of the Mekong River and connects the historical Lao capitals of Pakse, Vientiane, and Luang Prabang. Route 13 was hailed as bringing Laos firmly into France's Indochinese family and breaking away from Siam.[11] The French also constructed a series of east-west reaching road networks which linked major coastal cities in Vietnam to Laos. These road networks, which are still virtually impassable during the monsoon season, were completed just prior to the breakout of the Second World War. Decades later these road networks would also prove very useful to Lao revolutionaries receiving materiel and support from Vietnam during its revolution. They also formed the trunk of the Ho Chi Minh trail used by the People's Army of Vietnam to channel munitions and personnel to Vietnamese revolutionary forces in what was then Southern Vietnam. The French built these roads to curb Thai ambitions, in the later decades of the 20th century, these roads determined strategic outcomes of greater significance by helping Vietnam's northern deliver defeat to the Americans in the south.

I believe China's railway strategy through Laos will also take on a strategic significance into the 21st century and possibly beyond. The goal of connecting China to Thailand by rail is an ostensible one. If this were the really the case, the rail could take a shorter and much more inexpensive route cutting directly toward Chiang Rai and the Golden Triangle once it enters Laos. This would reduce the length of the railroad by more than 300 kilometers and reduce risks considerably. However, the railroad connects Kunming to Luang Prabang and then further on to Vientiane. By imagining modern Laos not as a strong nation-state, but rather as a collection of weak mandala states, the railway forces Luang Prabang to bend its knee to China. This implies Chinese commercial control over Luang Prabang and the surrounding cities and provinces in northern Laos. Its construction presents an opportunity to more deeply impose Chinese culture and values on northern Laos. Considering Luang Prabang's historical importance as a crossroads of Southeast Asia, then logistical control over Luang Prabang implies access to a much broader swath of political and economic space in mainland Southeast Asia. It comes as no surprise that in response to China's railway ambitions for Laos, Vietnam's government is now signing agreements to build railways linking Vientiane to its coastal cities. Vietnam's moves reflect a geostrategic objective of preventing a Chinese dominated rail network to penetrate deeper into Vietnam's zone of influence in Laos's south. As it has been throughout history, Laos continues to be a zone of strategic competition among outside powers.

In my current occupation, while on business trips to the Mekong region it is common for my colleagues and me to drive for hours on winding mountainous roads to catch a glimpse of a newly built dam. I have jokingly called this behavior "dam tourism" especially after I personally began to seek out dams and reservoirs when traveling around the United States and the rest of the world with family members. When visiting dam sites on the Mekong and its tributaries, my team is most interested in observing how dams impact local communities and their surrounding environments. All too often, dam developers will overemphasize how resettled communities are made better off through the resettlement process, but in Laos this outcome is rarely the case.

A few years ago, a friend in Kunming returned from a trip to northern Laos with photos of colorfully dressed ethnic people standing alongside large dams being built on the Nam Ou River, a 350 kilometer tributary of the Mekong that flows into the mainstream just upstream from Luang Prabang. The Nam Ou, one of the Mekong's longest tributaries, is lined with aspiring peaks of jungled karst mountains and cuts through the length of Phongsaly and Luang Prabang provinces. The river's headwaters are on the border with China. I was curious to see these dams, but little about them could be found online. So when my team had a free weekend on a business trip to Laos in February 2016, we hired a few local translators and piled into a van to find out what we could. About an hour after setting off from Luang Prabang, we came upon a large resettlement village a few kilometers downstream from a newly operational dam.

Judging a book by its cover, from our perch inside the van, the resettlement village appeared to be organized in neat grids lined with about 100 relatively large houses roofed with red tiles. Its inhabitants were busy fixing up their homes or heading out for a day of work in the surrounding area. After we had parked, a few villagers approached us. Without any solicitation, a middle-aged woman opened conversation with a complaint. "We are suffering! We were forced to move here 18 months ago, and the dam company promised 2 years of funding for transitional assistance. So far, we've only received enough to cover 6 months! We don't have enough to eat." I quickly inquired whether she and the other villagers were given land on which to plant agricultural crops. "No. No. The company only offered land for the house and provided no fields for planting rice. We have no money so we must walk back to our old fields and forests by the flooded village. We're old, and it takes us a few hours to walk there."

Other villagers gathered around. From how they treated her with deference, I could tell the woman was an important community leader. Another man beside her added, "By the time we get to our old fields, it's already noon. So we spend only an hour or so working the field, and then we have to come back." Our local translator added that these villagers practiced swiddening agriculture, and since the Lao government does not recognize swiddening as productive activity, awarding the villagers with productive land was not part of the official compensation process.

The woman continued, "If we want to plant rice or other crops around the resettlement village we must rent land from the village next to us. Since we have no income, some villagers who rent land have gone into debt. They are forced to leave the village if they can't repay. In our old village, very few people had the need to borrow money. Now more than half of these villagers are in deep debt!" My colleague inquired with her about health issues, "As soon as we moved here, many of the village elders died. This was not normal. They were aging but healthy. And since moving here, five infants have died. This also rarely happened in our village. We're not able to take care of each other like we used to."

On a closer look at the homes and people of the village, I realized I had never seen such impoverishment in Laos, and this served in stark contrast to the bespoke French villas and gilded Buddhist temples of affluent Luang Prabang just a few hours away. Two flooded villages, one majority ethnic Khmu and the other made up of various upland Lao ethnicities, were merged to create this resettlement village of more than 300 residents. Newly built homes on stilts with a floor space of about 60 square meters were situated on 200 square meter plots. Two raised huts facing each other at the edge of each property formed the borders of a small dirt courtyard. One hut was designed for storage use and the other as a kitchen. I approached one woman preparing food on an open fire in the middle of the courtyard and asked what she thought of her new house. "This house is bigger than what we had in our old village, but there we had more land. Look around this village, no one is using these little huts. We had nothing like this in our old village," she said as she turned a few bananas roasting over the fire. "Our old homes were built with hardwood teak and never rotted." She pointed to the side of her home, "See how termites are eating the side of this building? The Chinese used the cheapest wood they could find to build these homes, and we will likely need to rebuild in a few years." When I suggested that the dam company could re-use the teak from the dismantled homes in the flooded village to build new homes, she replied, "The Chinese took the teak boards from our old homes and sold them on the market."

In rural Laos and Thailand, families plant heirloom gardens around the periphery of their home to raise chili peppers, tomatoes, papaya, and eggplants, and other staple ingredients which give food from this part of the world its unique flavor. However, in this village, I noticed that the homes were built entirely on barren patches of packed and cracked earth. There were no heirloom gardens, and no trees covered the village with shade to cool down its surroundings. I asked the woman why this was. "We planted gardens alongside the house, but now they are dead. The dam company used hard soil to make the resettlement village. It's not fertile." Her home was located alongside the river, so we walked down a steep path to the river's edge. She said, "In our old village accessing the river was easy. We could bathe, swim, and go for picnics on the sandy beach. Now we cannot even fish because this part of the river belongs to the village next to us."

The team spent a few hours talking to villagers and learning of their destitute situation. Considering Laos's tight security apparatus, we were surprised that they so candidly shared their experience with us. We learned that in the 18 months since moving to the village, no one from the local government paid a visit to the village to check on progress. Previously, the only other outside visitors were from a prominent international human rights NGO. Eventually we all sat down inside the village headman's home, which was no different from any of the others, to learn of his plans to improve the situation in the resettlement village.

"There's little we can do," he said. "When we were resettled, I saw a contract that promised 2 years of financial assistance. Then the dam company only gave us 6 months up front. I went to meet with the company, and the people there said they already paid the provincial government. They suggested for us to take up our concerns with the provincial government. The government is supposed to ensure benefits are distributed to us, but I fear corruption has taken away the money that is rightfully ours. We have no idea what's happening between the dam company and the provincial government. I'm planning a trip to Vientiane. Maybe someone there will listen to me."

The middle-aged woman who greeted us when we first arrive added, "It's all very confusing because even though it seems the government and company are trying to help us, it's not working. People are beginning to sell their houses and land. They are building smaller huts near the old village." Despite her obvious despair, her personality remained sunny throughout our visit. As our conversation came to its conclusion, we shook hands with many of the villagers and only hoped that their situation would improve. Since that visit I have discussed our observations with both the chief engineer for the Chinese dam developer who said that all resettlement needs should have been met and any remaining issues should be taken up with the provincial government. I have not returned to the village to follow-up on improvement and have no way to contact the villagers remotely. Upon leaving the village that day, the middle-aged woman left us with these parting words, "Come again. You're always welcome to tour our poverty!"

Not all resettlement villages in Laos face the same set of challenges to recovering a sustainable livelihood for their inhabitants. The newly established livelihoods of the 2000 villagers relocated for the construction of the giant Xayaburi Dam on the mainstream of the Mekong south are often heralded in the national and regional media as a positive example of relocation. But the Xayaburi Dam has been long under the microscope of international scrutiny, whereas the Nam Ou dams and their impacts are virtually unknown. The extra attention on Xayaburi guarantees better results – results about which government officials in Laos are quick to boast. In Laos and throughout the Mekong region, one can find plenty of resettlement programs where those affected are much worse off in comparison to their previous livelihood. In the early 2000s, the Lao government launched a round of UN sponsored resettlement policies to eradicate opium production in upland areas. The process involved moving mostly ethnic Hmong peoples from the tops of mountains to the mid-slopes. Without access to income from their key cash crop and after being transferred to a totally unfamiliar agricultural setting, the resettled Hmong were fish out of water. Death rates in these villages were four times as high as prior to resettlement.

Observers are quick to criticize the Lao government for a lack of regulation or standards in the resettlement process often equating this lawlessness to a "wild west" atmosphere. However, Laos specialist Mike Dwyer argues that it is wrong to expect regulation because this assumes the Lao government has the ability to serve as an adequate regulator and that standards in Laos can be applied relatively evenly across a homogeneous space.[12] In Laos, effective regulatory patterns are most observable near the centers of power and weaken toward the periphery and up the mountainsides. Thinking about Laos as a mandala state helps to add clarity when interpreting these patterns. Resettlement outcomes vary differently from community to community and tend to be better when the settlements are close to centers of power. To extend to other examples of what might be labeled as injustice, for instance, the Prime Minister's office issued a ban on logging exports in early 2016, but the ban goes mostly ignored in localities. It was widely reported in Southeast Asian media that Attapeu's provincial governor continued to oversee the logging of mountainsides in southern Laos and selling valuable timber to Vietnam. It took several months for national level officials in Vientiane to arrest the errant governor.[13] Laos too has strict laws against wildlife trafficking, but Kings Roman Casino on the northern periphery continues to thrive in the illicit trade of wildlife. The pattern continues.

About one in every three people in Laos qualifies as a Zomian. In fact, the Lao government used to officially define ethnicity not first by linguistic or cultural differences, but rather on which part of mountains and valleys ethnic groups generally settle. The *Lao*

Loum, literally lowland Lao, make up 68 percent of the country's population and occupy the country's valleys and plains. The upland Lao, or *Lao Theung* (22 percent of the population) live on the middle slopes of mountainsides while the highland Lao, or *Lao Soung* live near the tops of mountains. Unsurprisingly, the Akha, who are also found in Laos, are classified as *Lao Soung*. Along with other major groups such as the Hmong, Iu Mien, and the Khmu, they make up the patchwork of more than 150 ethnic groups living at an elevation higher than 300 meters. Like other Zomians described in this book, these groups practiced swiddening agriculture (many still cultivate opium) and foraged and traded valuable non-timber forest products like mushrooms, fur pelts, and medicinal herbs with the lowland Lao. Today, the government of Lao seeks to call ethnic groups by their ethnic names rather than lumping them together by their position on mountainsides. This is because the linguistic and cultural differences among the agglomerated groups are quite vast. However, the Lao government has few resources at its disposal to change the discourse on ethnicity within Laos, so the three common ethic categorizations remain popular in the Lao vernacular.

For Laos's Zomians, resettlement has become a fact of life during the past five decades. The purposes of resettlement have taken on many forms since Siam began depopulating Lao space centuries ago. In the 1970s, guerrilla warfare fought between the Pathet Lao and the Royal Lao government, a constitutional monarchy which the CIA would later support, often required both sides to forge alliances with ethnic upland groups. During the conflict and then into the 1980s after the after the Communist takeover in 1975, it was common for upland communities not allied with the Pathet Lao during the war years to be forcibly resettled along roadside villages in the lowland as to better monitor them and prevent linkages with enemy groups.[14] In the 1990s, economic development began to take off in Laos to a degree, and the government set the development of smallholder, private agriculture as a top priority. Since the upland areas lacked arable land (at least in the eyes of the lowland government) and the lowland had a low population density, the government of Lao began to resettle uplanders down to lowland valleys to engage in intensified agricultural production.

This approach had three goals. First was a goal to drop the country's poverty rate. This required putting an end to economic practices which did not participate in a cash economy. Even though many of the upland groups were surrounded by food and forest resources which gave them a life of relative affluence, they were labeled "poor" because they generated little cash income. Ending subsistence-based livelihoods also fed into a second goal of folding upland cultures into the broader narrative of the Lao identity – transforming Zomians into members of a Lao nation. A final goal, the eradication of swiddening agriculture was set to allay Lao government fears that swiddening eroded nation-building and the productive development of a Lao national population.[15] But by 2005, 50 percent of Laos's population still were planting swidden rice. The resettlement efforts did give some uplanders access to more modern amenities such as schools and health clinics, but it largely failed. Laos simply lacked enough flat, fertile land on which to grow robust yields of cash crops given the technology of the time. This led to a paradoxical situation described by Southeast Asia geographer Jonathan Rigg where a shortage of land occurred in the country with the lowest population density in Asia.[16]

Over the last decade, foreign investment, particularly that from China, and connectivity improvements served as game-changing factors to quicken the depopulating of Laos's hills. Mountaintops and remote valleys were no longer the marginal, untouchable homelands of ethnic peoples, but rather a newly mapped out treasure trove of natural resources such as hardwood trees, rare minerals, and sites for hydropower dams and rubber plantations that could make foreign investors rich while providing a new tax base for the Lao government. Given Laos's legacy as a zone of contestation among outside forces, opening the gates wide made to foreign encroachment sense to the Lao élite who would benefit from granting licenses and providing access for foreign investors. Further, the risky responsibility of resettling upland peoples could now be shifted onto the foreign investor. Resettled peoples could be put to work on rubber plantations high in the hills. Or through the use of imported pesticides and fertilizers, the labor pools of large lowland agricultural plantations could be efficiently employed. The new landscape has created a resettlement racket that completely marginalizes and overlooks the cultural needs and practices of Laos's Zomians. And as in China, the process has erased the value of swiddening agricultural and community managed forests. It has also replaced the value of culturally important non-timber forest products that came from those forests with the value of commodities like rubber, minerals, and electricity generated by hydropower dams.

A high-level Lao official once told me, "The resettlement issue involves minorities, so it's really a minority problem." In resettled villages, access to schools, television, or the internet could open the door to a more globalized way of thinking and lead an individual formerly tied to an upland community to a modern lifestyle. But at the individual level, resettlement only pays off as long as those resettled accumulate tangible benefits to their livelihoods or that of their children. Otherwise, they are likely to act in a typical Zomian fashion and head back to the resource-rich hills. But returning could place them at risk of conflict with the outside developers who now see the hills as regulated zones of commercial activity.

Indeed, this is what my team had observed during the visit to the Nam Ou resettlement site and also on a subsequent visit to a much larger resettlement town along the Nam Khan River just east of Luang Prabang. There, the construction of two Chinese-built and operated dams glommed together more than 1000 villagers from more than 10 upland ethnic groups. Patterns observed in the Nam Ou resettlement village repeated themselves here. Households did not have access to arable land, financial assistance was in arrears, and villagers were increasingly in debt. In this village however, most working-age individuals were recruited to work on a nearby Chinese-run watermelon plantation. Their wages were magnitudes lower than the Chinese migrants they worked alongside, and many complained of skin rashes that resulted from exposure to pesticides. The villagers said they received no training in the handling of these chemicals and noted how Chinese workers took prophylactic medicine and other preventative measures before going to work each day.

Some in the resettlement town had recently moved in because their former village, located 40 kilometers away, was flooded just a few weeks prior. My team subsequently drove to that flooded area to discover a thriving community of thirty households clinging to the mountainside just above the former village location. These holdouts had assembled tiny huts made from grass and bamboo established a well for collective water usage and set up a small roadside market. Children were playing on newly beat dirt paths, and the surrounding hills were busy with villagers planting rice, grazing sheep, and harvesting papaya and other fruits. I asked a man why he would rather live in these conditions when there was a large house waiting for him near Luang Prabang. He replied, "I tried it out last week, but I have everything I need here at my home. Being here is more important to me than living in a shabby home surrounded by strangers. And no one is going to come around this way and force me to stop what I'm doing. The Chinese and the government already made their money from resettling us."

The government of Laos would like to build more than 140 dams inside its portion of the Mekong Basin. A current dam building spree means displacement from hydropower projects has become a major driver of resettlement and internal migration in Laos. At of the time of this book's publication, more than 50 of those dams have begun construction. With only 2 dams currently being built on the mainstream (Xayaburi and Don Sahong) and another at Pak Beng on the way, a super majority of these dams will flood upland areas. In the eyes of the Lao state, the gravity of hydropower development conveniently brings upland peoples down out of the hills to ready them for involvement in the national labor market. Resettlement also orients uplanders to become upright citizens of Laos, as opposed to being rogue populations roaming the hills. But even more, to the Lao élite, building lots of dams is the only way to push back against encroaching appetites of foreign neighbors while still maintaining good relations with them.

Laos's rich mineral resources and precious timber stocks are all limited and exhaustible, and these commodities along with agricultural cash crops are subject to the fluctuation of regional and global market prices. Laos is a traveler's paradise, and like Costa Rica and many small island nations, it is endowed with an abundance of scenic wonders and unique cultural experiences that could make tourism a major driver of economic growth. However, tourism success, like income from commodities, is also subject to global market fluctuation. More importantly, tourism is a relatively decentralized industry that rewards a wide range of stakeholders, many of whom are poor.. Laos as a modern Communist country requires concentration of wealth into the hands of the state élite to maintain power. Tourism, arguably, works in the opposite direction.

But electricity, especially when it comes from dams the Lao élite believe will last for a century, is increasingly in demand around Laos's immediate neighborhood. As long as there is water in the river, a dam can produce electricity. Each of Laos's neighbors is rapidly urbanizing, and less developed countries like Cambodia and Myanmar have set ambitious goals to electrify their rural margins within the next decade. The Laos government has sought since the mid-1990s to position itself as the "Battery of Southeast Asia," a strategy which many have longed to be the silver bullet that will provide Laos with the hard currency it needs to finally graduate to the ranks of a strong, unified nation and strategically keep its neighbors at bay. However, more than 10 years into the process, Laos is at a crossroads in becoming the region's "hydro-powerhouse," and downstream ecological impacts of Laos's damming frenzy are beginning to manifest in Thailand, Cambodia, and Vietnam.

7

DAMMING THE
LOWER MEKONG

"I've been fishing my whole life. This is my life," says Nong, a middle-aged man whose livelihood has made his skin darkened and rough. A cigarette dangles from his mouth as he picks algae from his fishing nets. "My father was a fisherman, and so is my son. If there are fish in the river, I could fish all day. When I was young, my father took me out on his boat, and I still fish in those same spots," he says. Nong walks barefoot along a small sandy beach just below the roaring chutes of the Li Phi Falls at Siphandone in southern Laos. He and I have just returned from a trip to the base of the falls to check on his nets and fishing traps.

Over the last 2 hours, he has shown me at least 10 different kinds of ways to catch fish. His narrow boat, built for carrying up to 4 people, is equipped with a few nets with varying weights tied to their ends for use in different parts of the river, depending on the current strength and water depth. We inspect a few box traps in shallow, grassier areas of the riverside. At a cataract less than 1 meter high, Nong gets out of the boat and walks more than 10 meters along a single length of bamboo tied to a man-made weir that runs the width of the channel. His elongated toes grip the bamboo like fingers. A wrong step would send him into the fast running current below, but after decades of practice, this balancing act is performed with ease. "Want to give it a try?" he suggests in jest. At a few points, he checks reed baskets that catch fish as they pass through the weir but comes up empty. After returning to the boat he tells me, "I build that weir in December at the end of every monsoon season. To catch fish, we use bamboo from the village, cord imported from Thailand, and nets and line from the Nakasang market over on the mainland. Everyone in my generation knows how to use fishing line to weave the nets and make these traps, but not all of my son's generation can. Some of them leave the village for jobs outside, or they go to college."

Our morning fishing trip produced little results, and we returned to the beach with only a few small fish that barely covered the bottom of a black bucket. "Typically there are more fish at this time of year, but now they are harder to find. People are changing too," he says. "They are less honest, and I don't know why. It's all changed in the last 3 to 4 years. More fishermen are using illegal equipment and stealing fish. They are greedy and want more. Parents tell their children not to act this way, but the kids still do it. Monks in the temple tell everyone to be more considerate. Those who listen give the monks a bow to acknowledge the message, but then they go off and act selfishly." Nong continues to clean his nets alongside a posse of 4 other friends who he meets here every day. During the daylight hours, when he and his crew are not fishing, they join in on card games and snack on grilled fish and balls of sticky rice under the shade of giant palms.

Siphandone, which translates from the Lao language as "Four Thousand Islands" is one of the mighty Mekong's geological and scenic wonders. A major fault line that uplifts the bed of the Mekong cuts across the stream and forces the river to spread out into a maze of channels and rapids 14 kilometers wide. Countless islands, some large enough to support towns and others so small that only a few shrubs and itinerant birds find habitat, populate the channels.

Some of the smaller islands are entirely submerged for 6 months of the year during the rainy season. Siphandone's lush vegetation and numerous islands uninhabited by humans make it the ideal home to hundreds of migratory and local bird species. Some trees at Siphandone are the grandest and most impressive I've seen in the entirety of the Mekong Basin. On the tallest trees, 3 meters of root systems are exposed during the dry season creating a knotty, labyrinthine beard of roots that flows with the direction of the current. Other tall trees appear to be bent at the waist, their trunks and stems standing vertical but branches and leaves bowing horizontally parallel to the river's surface. This is a natural testimony to the power of Mekong's flood pulse which forces the treetops to submit to the high and strong current. The trees' persistence is also a testimony to their natural resilience. During the flooded monsoon season, water spreads out into the adjacent wetlands wiping out a portion of the wetland's vegetation which then rots and provides nutrient-rich feeding grounds for fish and other aquatic species.[1] As the river's channels approach Laos's border with Cambodia, the fault line causes a drastic, 20 meter drop which produces Asia's most impressive collection of waterfalls.

Island hopping in Siphandone, for the most part, can only be done by boat, and once on the inhabited islands, getting around is the work of motorcycles, bicycles, and flip-flops since most islands do not have roads wide enough for car travel. Boats filled with locals, robed monks, and the occasional tourists, taxi to the islands from the mainland port at Nakasang. The first time I visited Siphandone's Don Khone island, I almost put my rented motorcycle into the river as I nearly failed to drive it up a wooden plank into a narrow ferry less than a meter wide. For time unknown, the islands have been home to fishing communities that take advantage of Siphandone's unusual collection of shallow areas, deep pools, and waterfalls that promote the passage of a majority of the river system's migratory fish stock. Locals remember a time when there were so many fish that those not bought by the market were littered through rice paddy as fertilizer. That ended in the 1990s, not likely because fish catches were depleting, but because better roads opened up opportunities for middlemen to sell off Siphandone's fish to markets as far away as Vientiane and across the border in Thailand.

A Google search of Siphandone will inevitably come up with photos showing local fishers hauling in tons of fish in long traps called *lee* that force fish coming downstream onto an upward reaching ramp-like structure. Once high on the ramp, the fish are stuck, unable to return to the river. The *lee* are built downstream of falls to catch those migratory fish which get denied by the falls while on the search for an open channel to the upstream. The only major channel without a waterfall is the Hou Sahong channel which forms a border between Don Sahong and Don Sadam islands. Since the fault line appeared Hou Sahong is the only major channel that gives hundreds of different migratory species of fish unimpeded access to the river's upstream and downstream. At most, this 5 kilometer long chokepoint is less than 200 meters wide and a few meters deep. And Laos is building a dam on it.

Technically the Don Sahong Power Project, a 260 megawatt dam scheduled for completion around 2020, is being built, owned, and operated by a Malaysian company called Mega First, a light-bulb manufacturing firm that has never before built a dam. But after gaining the concession agreement, Mega First sub-contracted China's Sinohydro to build the dam. Because the dam closes off the chokepoint for fish migration through the Hou Sahong channel and its location is less than 2 kilometers from the Cambodian border, the Don Sahong project has by far become the region's most controversial. Among governments downstream, both Cambodia's and Vietnam's National Mekong Committees initially voiced opposition to the dam when it was first mooted in 2009.[2] Since then, a chorus of international and local civil society groups in Cambodia, Vietnam, and Thailand have organized campaigns and protests against the dam's construction.

In 2014, The World Wide Fund for Nature (WWF) launched a "Say No to Don Sahong Dam" campaign citing the dam's potential impact to the food security of millions in the Mekong region. "More than a quarter of a million people around the world are sending a strong and clear message to Mega First. Stop Don Sahong Dam or risk the dubious honor of precipitating the extinction of a species," said WWF former country director Chhith Samath in a 2014 online statement. He was referring to the possible extinction of a pod of freshwater dolphins that live in a deep pool a few hundred meters from the dam's wall. He continued, "Don Sahong Dam is a dangerous experiment and Mega First is gambling with the livelihoods of millions."[3]

Veteran journalist Tom Fawthrop, who has ceaselessly campaigned to stop dams on the Mekong by making documentaries such as *Great Gamble on the Mekong* and *Where Have All The Fish Gone?* told me, "The Don Sahong Dam and soon one more dam at Pak Beng is driving a process of cultural and ecological destruction. One of the world's great rivers, brimming with biodiversity and life is being dammed into the direction of a dead waterway. Its free-flowing currents will be crippled, starved of nutrients and sediment. Fisheries are already suffering a disturbing decline."

In October 2013, the government of Laos submitted a notification for the construction of the Don Sahong Dam to the Secretariat of the Mekong River Commission (MRC), an organization whose merits and failings are discussed later in this chapter.

The notification was a required legal procedure from the 1995 Mekong Agreement, a treaty signed by the four major Lower Mekong countries (Cambodia, Laos, Thailand, and Vietnam) to promote the sustainable use of the Mekong's shared resources and reduce transboundary tensions. January 2015 marked the end of a 6 month regional consultation process facilitated by the MRC where stakeholders could voice concerns over the dam's impacts and submit technical suggestions to mitigate those impacts. One of the outcomes of this process was Mega First's recognition of risk that the dam poses to fish biodiversity in the Mekong. The consultation process produced a new plan to deepen and expand seven other channels around Hou Sahong to promote the natural passage of fish instead of the originally targeted two channels. National governments collectively failed to endorse a consensus on the dam, and by the fall of 2015, construction commenced to close off Hou Sahong's mouth and headwaters with cofferdams that would drain the channel bed to make way for the dam's construction.

In January 2015, I visited Don Khone, Don Sahong, and the adjacent Don Sadam island and talked with more than 50 inhabitants from multiple villages to get their view on the project. Despite Mega First's and the Lao government's promise to deliver improvement in local standards of living, not a single interviewee voiced support for the dam. Sai, who operates boats that take tourists out to see the freshwater dolphins told me, "This dam will make life difficult. The government has banned fishing with *lees* and fence filter traps to ensure enough fish can pass through their newly dug out channels. So now our livelihoods are affected. No one on this island can survive just by doing one thing." He continued, "Our families all have to fish, plant rice, and provide tourism services in order to get by. The fish are both our food and major source of income." Sai earns a gross income of roughly

$30 per day as part of a 10-man rotation that takes tourists out to see the dolphins. As long as the dolphin pod remains at Siphandone, they provide a guaranteed source of income for these villagers, since as they are mammals needing to come up for air, the dolphins are sure to be seen. Tourism dollars are harder to earn in the monsoon season since the rains keep the tourists away, and the fast currents make it harder to see the dolphins. "So we fish in the rainy season, but again the dam will make fishing difficult," he said. He related a story of how a few years prior some foreign representatives from Mega First invited the headmen and other important community leaders from the surrounding villages to a meeting. Everyone who showed up was given 42,000 kip ($5). "They told us that the dam wouldn't cause any problems, but we walked away with many concerns."

I also talked to Luong Siri, a village elder from Ban Hang Sadam, a village that runs adjacent to one of the natural channels being widened to promote the passage of fish. He too was skeptical about the dam. "Those new channels are much narrower than the Hou Sahong channel. Some of them are only a few meters wide. Even if the fish do find those channels, I'm worried that locals will build fence traps across them and take all the fish. The price of fish is rising at local markets, and even though Mega First says it will put security guards along the channels, there will still be holes in the process. Fishermen will go at night and take fish or they will pay off the guards." Luong Siri is well versed in fish protection and conservation. He was trained by the WWF to manage a few fish conservation zones around Don Sadam island. "Before this dam business started, the biggest threat to our fisheries was the Cambodians who come across the border and illegally fish in our traditional fishing areas. They use methods like poison and electric shock to kill the fish." To be sure, my interviews also uncovered instances of local Lao using similar methods to kill fish. "We now have villagers who patrol our fishing grounds daily and nightly, but there's a high cost of doing this, and sometimes patrolmen shirk on their duties."

Luong Siri noted how recently catches were down for Siphandone's most prominent fish, the *pa soi*. "In October we usually catch ten to twenty thousand *pa soi* with one net!" he boasted. *Pa soi* refers to a few species in the cyprinid family, a small, light-colored fish typically found in great abundance in the Mekong's lower reaches. Fishermen sell off the majority of their *pa soi* catch to companies who dry and ferment the fish for processing into Laos's most common fish paste called *padek*. *Padek* is a major source of protein used nearly ubiquitously throughout Laos as a dip for sticky rice and condiment for cooking. A few years prior, Luong Siri also oversaw the expansion of fish conservation zones to include the freshwater dolphin pool. "Dolphins aren't like other fish," he said. "They only give birth every three to four years. If we don't improve our conservation efforts, they will disappear! Their numbers are already extremely low and occasionally one will come up dead in fisherman's nets." Indeed, at the time of this book's publication, the population of the dolphins at Siphandone had dropped to five, a level well below the natural ability for the pod to thrive in the wild. "We worry the noise from the dam's construction will injure the dolphins or scare them away," he concluded.

In response to concerns raised both locally and internationally, Laos's Ministry of Energy and Mines produced a fact sheet called "Don Sahong Made Simple: Questions and Answers about the Don Sahong Power Project" and distributed on its official website. The

Ministry of Energy and Mines is the line agency responsible for energy and hydropower development in Laos.[4] It is unknown from which source the questions addressed oriented, but the answers are myopic and unreferenced. Three questions and their official answers are listed below.

Q. What are the biggest threats facing the dolphin population?

A. The real risks to dolphin survival in the Mekong, have been well documented. They are: disturbance from tourism activities; gill nets and other fishing gear; and an unexplained high mortality rates of calves and juveniles.[5]

Q. Will DSHPP [Don Sahong Power Project] cut off one – some say the only – fish migration route across the Khone falls, harming the food security of millions of people in the region?

A. The fact is there are several other channels that support fish migration in the dry season, and the project research indicates that other channels can and will be modified to accommodate more fish migrations in both directions in both seasons. The statement that the food security of "millions of people" will suffer is pure speculation and exaggeration designed to scare the public and win support for anti-dam groups. Extensive studies and investigations confirm that the proposed project will cause no significant impact to the full mainstream flow of the Mekong; nor will it affect fish migration or sediment passage to any degree that would harm downstream communities. Furthermore, the Lao people also rely on the Mekong for their livelihood and we intend to enhance and improve their lives and the lives of their children as well as the fisheries sustainability of the area.[6]

Q. Fishermen say the amount of fish they catch above and below Khone Falls has been declining for years. Won't a dam on Hou Sahong make things worse for them?

A. There are several factors behind the decline in dry season catches in the region. First, because of climate change, the dry season is longer and there is less water in the dry season. Second, there is more water usage in the dry season due to irrigation, agriculture, domestic and industrial use by more and more people. Due to population growth, changes in fishing gear, enlarged fish traps, and market demand overfishing takes place all the way from Cambodia's Tonle Sap to Khone Falls. With so many fish traps and without environmentally sound regulations and conservation enforcement, fewer fish are reaching feeding grounds and spawning grounds. When these impacts are remedied, fish will return to the channels.

The fact sheet also implies that the dam's management team can actually improve fish conservation efforts, given the claim that the major threat to Siphandone fisheries is overfishing and not the dam's blocking of the channel. To cover all bases, the document does state "However, if all else fails (re fish passage promotion) the government of Laos will ask the Developer to decommission the dam." Lastly, the document states:

Local authorities and project staff are in regular contact with families regarding their income and livelihood. By and large, the people of Siphandone want this project to move ahead. They don't want to have to leave the islands to find work. They want training in new vocations: driving trucks and heavy equipment, auto repair, carpentry and the like. They want more tourists to visit the area by car and bus to see the future of Laos, not the past.

Ian Baird, an associate professor in the University of Wisconsin-Madison's Department of Geography who has spent much of his life in Laos and kicked off the efforts for fish conservation in Siphandone in 1993 told me that vilifying local fishing practices has turned local fishers into scapegoats. "Their most important fishing gears, wing traps, and fence-filter traps have been declared illegal in the name of the new fisheries law. But the Lao government only began enforcing this once the dam company gave money to the local government to do so," he said to make the point that the Don Sahong Dam company , not the government, was behind the interpretation and enforcement of the law. "In fact, originally the dam company wanted to compensate the fishers for not being able to continue fishing so that the channels in the Khone Falls area could be opened to mitigate the negative impacts of damming the Hou Sahong channel, the most important channel for fish migrations in the Khone Falls area. But the Lao government said what locals were doing is illegal, and that there was therefore no need to compensate the people for illegal fishing, even though the government was collecting taxes for the same type of fishing, which was not considered illegal, just a few years earlier. As a result, the local people have not received any compensation. Their livelihoods have been made illegal by law, and they have received nothing for essentially mitigating the impacts of the dam." Now that fishing is banned, Baird suggests that it is likely more fish will be able to pass through the channels, but this increase will only happen at the expense of local livelihoods. "Those most reliant on the banned fisheries have not been given other options, they don't have a lot of farmland. They have small land holdings and have been fishing for a very long time. To ban their main livelihood like this without giving the people compensation is a vast injustice."

In October 2016, I returned to visit the Don Sahong Dam, this time on an official visit facilitated by the government of Laos for a few colleagues and me. I met with the dam's fish conservation team whose members had been actively working onsite for 10 years to conduct research on fishing practices around the Siphandone area and prepare other natural channels for fish passage. The team had a budget of $14 million dollars to monitor the fish catches of 60 households over a 10 year period starting in 2009. Interestingly, the funding for fish research was scheduled to run out in 2019, the year the Don Sahong Dam will open for business. One of the team's leaders told me he was uncertain whether new funding would be found to continue research after the dam opened, the most critical period to research migratory fish passage.

The fisheries team had strong faith in the ability of newly widened and deepened channels to promote the passage of fish in the dry season. We were taken to inspect those new channels and shown data that indeed demonstrated key species were recorded moving through the altered natural channels especially during the peak migration periods in January and February. When I inquired what percentage of fish will be guaranteed to pass through the new channels, a team leader replied, "We're not sure, but we are trying to stick to the MRC standard of promoting the passage of 95 percent of fish species to protect the river's biodiversity." Fish might be passing through these channels now, but when the dam opens, more water will be diverted into its reservoir, reducing the amount of water to the altered channels. This runs the risk of water levels in the new passages being too low to promote fish passage, so the future abundance of the river's migratory fish still depends on a roll of the dice.

The fisheries management team also showcased a few innovations that could be used to prevent fish from being harmed or killed by the dam. We were shown a model of a screen that prevents fish from entering the penstock, a tube that channels water directly to the dam's turbines. The screen effectively prevented fish larger than 20 centimeters from going through the dam – these fish would be turned around and forced to find passage downstream through another of the river's channels. Even though such options are being explored, there is no guarantee of their usage. Because of expensive operation and maintenance costs, Mega First will likely not build the screen since it requires a costly "windshield wiper" mechanism to clean away flotsam that could get caught in the screen and stop water from flowing through the dam's turbines. Much attention has been given to the dam's "fish-friendly" turbines, the blades of which are rounded and spaced apart so that fish are not injured or killed as they pass by the turbine's spinning rotors. This seems to be bunk science since fish entering the narrow penstock will not be able to adjust to the sudden change in water pressure. Fish are kept buoyant by air sacs in their abdomen and the change of pressure will likely cause the fish to explode from within by destroying their air sacs. The same could be said for fish eggs and larvae passing through the turbines.

But these last two points only apply to fish going downstream through the dam's turbines, and fish do move downstream through a myriad of channels at Siphandone. So all things considered, if fish continued to pass upstream through the newly altered channels during the dry season, the mitigation scheme just might work. This conclusion has been acknowledged in conversations with more than a few critics of Mekong hydropower development; however, these critics are quick to point out that successful fish passage around Don Sahong sets a dangerous precedent for other dams in the

Mekong. Dam proponents could be galvanized by Don Sahong's results. But the difference between Don Sahong and the remaining 180 dam sites in the Mekong that none of the others have geological conditions that will permit natural alternative passages for fish. All of those dams will span the entirety of the Mekong River.

The Xayaburi Dam is often hailed as a global innovation in fish mitigation technology with a 7 kilometer long fish ladder and a navigation lock fitted for fish passage. The dam design also includes an untested "fish elevator" that reportedly will lift fish that somehow find their way into the elevator compartment 32 meters up and over the dam wall to the reservoir behind it. Most of the Xayaburi Dam's technology is based on models from the northwest United States where fish ladders aid the migration of a few species of salmon. How this technology will promote the passage of hundreds of species of fish of varying sizes traveling through the Mekong is unknown. Even if some fish make their way through the passage, what metrics demonstrate success? At peak migration, the Mekong around Xayaburi is known to have up to 30 tons of fish passing through it per hour. Flowing water is a natural hydrological signal that tells the fish to continue migrating upstream. Fish that make it behind the dam wall into the reservoir will encounter slow-moving or stagnant pools which will wipe out this signaling. As such, many fish will fail to complete the full migration upstream to their natural breeding, drastically dropping the success rate of reproduction.

Considering these uncertain results in the context of a cascade, such as the five mainstream dams planned above Vientiane in northern Laos, chances of fish mitigation preserving the river's biodiversity seem even slimmer. If 70 percent of fish migrating upstream can make it past the first dam (by most measures a high level of success,) and then 70 percent of those fish make it past the next, half of the river's fish are already wiped out. By the time fish make it past the fifth dam, only 16 percent remain. At a 50 percent success rate, only 3.1 percent survive by the time they pass the fifth dam. The cumulative impacts of the dam cascade make the billions of dollars spent on fish mitigation technology look like a gross waste of money. An alternative approach which leaves out fish mitigation infrastructure entirely seems contrarian, but given the low success rate, the resources spent on unsuccessful fish mitigation efforts could be spent on preserving other long stretches of the Mekong River and its tributaries, so migrating fish can access long, unblocked segments of the river system. This kind of basin-wide thinking could place focus on keeping dams off the main stem of important tributaries like the Sekong River, which runs through southern Laos and empties into the Mekong in northern Cambodia. To date, the Sekong is the longest undammed tributary remaining in the Mekong system, but developers are circling like vultures to dam it.

Damming the Lower Mekong was not an idea of local origin. In 1957 as American designs for economic and political dominance in mainland Southeast Asia were taking root, a United Nations committee was formed to explore the joint development of the Mekong among the 4 Lower Mekong countries.[7] To the Americans, a prosperous and unified Indochinese peninsula posting high economic growth numbers fueled by Mekong hydropower was an ideal strategy for pushing back against Communist forces expanding into the region from China. This was a classic defense against the now widely debunked domino theory that drew the US into a violent and prolonged conflict in the region. In April 1965, US President Lyndon Johnson remarked in a speech delivered at Johns Hopkins University, "The vast Mekong River can provide food and water and power on a scale to dwarf even our own TVA."[8] The Tennessee Valley Authority oversaw a grand-scale hydropower and water management project initiated by President Franklin Roosevelt in the deepest years of the Great Depression purposed to lift rural Appalachia out of poverty. Johnson's vision also included another strategic ambition. He believed that if the power of the American model of economic development could be demonstrated in Southeast Asia, then rebellious forces there would come to heel. He saw damming the Mekong as a way to entice Ho Chi Minh to the negotiation table and victoriously unify Vietnam.

President Johnson tapped David E. Lilienthal, an American public administrator who decades before directed the design and management of the Tennessee Valley Authority. By his own judgment, when Lilienthal arrived on the scene in 1967, he inherited a mess. Despite tens of millions of dollars spent on developing the UN plan over the previous decade, he noted, the Mekong master plan for 14 dams in the basin was a "typical 'project by project' approach" lacking a master plan of a nature "remotely resembling the comprehensive unified report the TVA published in 1936."[9] In other words, the dams were not envisioned in a coordinated manner to maximize power production and irrigation benefits. Nor were there guarantees that the Mekong plan adequately tamed the river to prevent natural disasters. His coordinated vision would utilize the storage capabilities of upstream dams to reduce flood risks downstream and release water during the dry season or in times of drought to irrigate the fertile Mekong Delta. As always, in the eyes of the American elite, South Vietnam – the US bridgehead against the growth of Communism in Indochina, would receive the lion's share of benefits from upstream planning.

In 1967, Lilienthal, like many American élite at the time, was optimistic about an eventual American victory in Southeast Asia. He contrasted the ephemerality of US-backed aid and welfare support in Southeast Asia to the robust economic development opportunities provided by his potential fleet of dams. But he misunderstood the nationalistic motivations and resolve of the revolutionary forces fighting to rid Indochina of colonial influences. His vision also gave little consideration to the natural abundance of the river's ecology and how the basin's communities would be impacted by environmental impacts introduced by the dams. Indeed, a UN report from the early 1970s entitled "Mekong and Ecology" fully demonstrates this lack of understanding. The report stated, "the Mekong has a built-in tolerance for change" because of its abundance of biodiversity. Applying the economic logic of diversification to ecology, the report continued, "diversity is inherent to stability, and because of this complexity, it is an irrefutable fact that environmental alterations [from dams] are far less likely to be disruptive in the Lower Mekong Basin."[10] The American defeat and retreat from Southeast Asia in 1975 temporarily halted the US vision for damming the Mekong Basin. Those plans would gather dust on the shelves of government offices throughout the Mekong until the early 1990s when the conflict in Cambodia finally settled. Mekong countries again could envision the development of the Mekong's resources, this time without an outside overlord managing the process.

Today there is no shortage of peer-reviewed analysis showing clearly how dams on the Mekong mainstream are a bad idea. In 2010, the International Center for Environmental Management (ICEM), an Australian-run environmental consultancy based in Hanoi, produced a strategic environmental assessment study (SEA) sponsored by the Mekong River Commission.[11] One of the study's most glaring conclusions claimed that not enough information was known about the volume and behaviors of migratory fish species in the river. Further, the study claimed that in 2010 the actual degree to which human communities in the basin relied on protein intake from freshwater fish catch also remained unknown. The SEA recommended a moratorium on damming the Mekong's mainstream for 10 years, so more studies could be conducted. The Mekong River Commission Secretariat endorsed this recommendation, but soon after in 2011, the government of Laos initiated the consultation process on the Xayaburi Dam. Construction began on the $2 billion project in March 2012, and since then the project has run into repeated delays and accumulated an extra $1.2 billion in cost overruns.

The 2010 SEA emphasized the high level of risk associated with moving too quickly on damming the Lower Mekong. In 2011, a group of international and local scholars produced what is popularly called the "Costanza Report" which assigned economic values to anticipated losses accrued through building dams. In addition to stating a business case for not building dams on the mainstream, the Costanza Report was interesting because it examined the net value of several possible future scenarios of dams on the mainstream. It explored a "definite future" which incorporated the impacts of 30 dams already completed or under construction at the time of the study, a second scenario including 6 dams on the Mekong mainstream in northern Laos plus 30 new tributary dams in Laos and Cambodia, and a third scenario that included 11 mainstream dams plus 30 new tributary dams. The Costanza Report put dollar values on losses of wild fish catches, forest and wetland loss, impacts to other biodiversity and other impacts. It also included economic estimates of some of the benefits provided by dams such as flood prevention, the opportunity to use dam's reservoirs to raise fish and other aquaculture, and most importantly electricity generation. Across all three scenarios, Costanza's analysis showed Laos and Thailand reaping net positive economic gains, but the collective losses for all four Mekong countries outweigh individual gains in Thailand and Laos. For instance, in the more conservative scenario with 6 new dams built on the Mekong mainstream, the net loss is $1 billion – essentially a zero-sum game that provided all of Laos's and Thailand's gains from losses in Cambodia and Vietnam downstream.[12] The net impact of building all 11 mainstream dams plus 30 on the Mekong's tributaries is negative $66 billion.

Maureen Harris, Director of International Rivers Southeast Asia Program, told me, "Despite the number and impact of previous studies, there is insufficient research to understand how drastically the proposed developments will disturb the state of the Mekong's rich ecological systems and the food security and millions of livelihoods that depend on them." International Rivers is a non-government organization that has been at the heart of the global struggle to protect rivers and the rights of communities that depend on them. The organization works with an international network of dam-affected people, grassroots organizations, environmentalists, human rights advocates and others who are committed to stopping destructive river projects and promoting better options. Maureen's team is very active in the Mekong region. In our conversation, Maureen indicated that a regional crisis is looming: fishing communities report major drops in the number and availability of fish and changes to seasonal flows and flooding regimes. She added, "The impacts of multiple dams are cumulative, increasing pressure on the region's fragile ecology and local populations. While it is not too late to change course, with each new project, the basin is descending deeper into uncharted territory."

Laos and Cambodia plan to build many more than 180 dams on the Mekong's tributaries. In Laos alone there were over 50 large dams completed or under construction at the time of this book's printing.[13] In the Mekong region, the benefits and impacts of mainstream dams are studied more closely than tributary dams. This is partially due to the mandate of the Mekong River Commission, which only covers planning and analysis of mainstream dams due to their obvious transboundary impacts. MRC mandated processes invite criticism of mainstream dams from downstream countries and outside observers. To some extent, the MRC mandate makes it more difficult to dam the mainstream. This to a degree shifts political will towards damming the Mekong's tributaries. But damming tributaries can deliver equally disastrous downstream impacts. In 2012, a group of scholars led by Guy Ziv, a water expert from the University of Leeds, concluded that building all planned tributary dams would have graver impacts on fish biodiversity and floodplain fish productivity in Cambodia and Vietnam than mainstream Mekong dams.[14] Their conclusions emphasize the importance of protecting fish spawning habitats which are mostly located in Mekong tributaries far away from the mainstream. An additional study was done in 2012 by scholars from Australian National University asking how local protein diets would be impacted by the loss of fish catches caused by dams. The authors found that with eleven mainstream dams, Cambodians would lose up to 60 percent of their protein intake and Laos up to 24 percent. Accounting for additional tributary dams, the total loss in Laos could reach 43 percent and in Cambodia up to 100 percent loss due to impacts on the Tonle Sap Lake.[15]

In the discourse of Mekong hydropower, these studies, among many others, are canonical and consistently held as standard bearers among serious Mekong watchers. Unfortunately, they hold little water with the policymakers in Lower Mekong countries who make decisions about where the next dams will go. Richard Cronin, the retired director of the Stimson Center's Mekong Policy Project which has engaged with policymakers in the region over

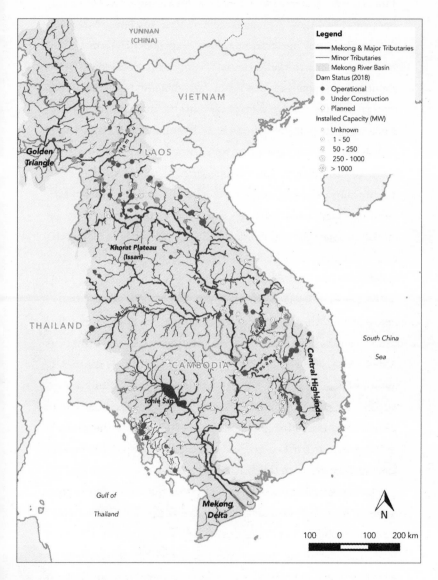

Map of Lower Mekong dams

the last decade over the risks dams pose to the river's ecology and downstream communities told me about his struggles connecting with policymakers. "Stimson's own efforts to 'close the science-policy gap' were ineffective against the combined impact of the desire of countries like Laos and Cambodia to base their development on exploiting their water for domestic development and export revenues, and powerful economic and financial interests." He continued, "The latter seek to exploit these resources for profit and in some cases energy security by obtaining concessions to develop dam projects under long-term, so-called public-private partnerships. Because of the authoritarian nature of most of the governments, the impact of these destructive projects on the Mekong's ecology and its citizens, especially ethnic minorities, receive little consideration."

Over the years, I have developed some sympathy for water and energy planners inside the halls of government in countries like Laos and Cambodia, for they are ultimately pawns in a larger game of élite interests that hold sway over economic progress. The careers of these officials depend on demonstrating progress, which typically means building more dams or coal plants to meet growing demand, but ultimately their actions are performed at the behest of others. In Laos, it is a dam developer that first approaches government agencies to begin the process of constructing a dam. The developer is almost guaranteed to be foreign since few Lao companies have the financial resources or expertise to build a dam. Indeed, to date more than 50 companies from 10 different countries are building dams in Laos.[16]

A developer will never gain a license for a dam without an off-taker market that will buy the dam's power, so ultimately the fate of the Lower Mekong Basin is determined by the electrification needs in major urban centers such as Bangkok and Ho Chi

Minh City. Much of Laos's hydropower is currently sent directly to Bangkok where giant shopping malls like Siam Paragon use air conditioning to cool down the *exterior* of their premises. These malls consume more power than smaller provinces on Thailand's periphery.[17] Thailand alone has a required electricity reserve of roughly 40 percent which means at any given time, the country needs access to nearly one and a half times its peak electricity demand. Ostensibly, Thailand attributes the high electricity reserve to buttressing grid instability on its periphery. In reality, élite politics in Thailand guarantees that its energy firms and regulators receive major subsidies for investing in energy assets outside Thai border. The Thai firms that build dams abroad receive a guaranteed rate of return on projects abroad. In total dams on the Mekong will meet only about 7 percent of total electricity demand in mainland Southeast Asia. Finding a way to lower Thailand's high reserve rate and introducing better energy efficiency measures throughout the Mekong region could easily erase the need to dam the river.

Energy planners in Laos and Cambodia also act on arbitrary decisions of élite officials above them who benefit politically and personally from dam construction. The Don Sahong Dam makes very little economic sense for Laos because of its remote location, its lack of a national grid connection, and minor export volume to Cambodia. But Don Sahong Dam has long been said to be a pet project of a former prime minister of Laos whose hometown is near Siphandone. He wanted a dam to feed cheap power into new businesses around Siphandone. Most infrastructure deals are black boxes in terms of how much individuals actually benefit from dam construction, but between the procurement of concrete, machinery, and labor there are many opportunities to channel funds into personal bank accounts. Much of the extra $300 million spent on improving the Xayaburi Dam's fish mitigation and sediment flushing mechanisms is believed to also have ended up in the hands of individual benefactors. In Laos, Chinese companies are said to pay off government officials in kind with new villas and sports cars.

The controversial Lower Sesan 2 Dam, which blocks two major tributaries of the river, the Sesan and the Srepok, was built to improve the political lot of Prime Minister Hun Sen prior to national elections in 2018. Because of a low level of electricity supply and a poorly built transmission structure, Cambodians pay more for electricity than any other consumer in mainland Southeast Asia. The Lower Sesan 2 was Hun Sen's chance to drop the price of electricity just prior to the 2018 elections, so he asked Hydrolancang, the developer of the upstream Mekong dams in China, to build the $800 million dam in a short time frame of 3 years. The aforementioned Ziv study suggests that this dam's blocking of major tributaries will reduce the Mekong's population of migratory fish by 9.3 percent. Because of the need to build 300 kilometers of transmission lines from Phnom Penh to the dam site, the price of electricity did not drop after the dam began to generate power in late 2017.

The basin and its planners are, by and large, held hostage to a process dictated by foreign market demand and the personal ambitions of political leaders. This produces an uncoordinated and somewhat anarchic "project by project" process. Extending David Lilienthal's criticism above, the 21st century approach to dam planning in the Mekong Basin is currently less coordinated than the way the US approached damming the Tennessee Valley nearly a century ago. Relying on foreign developers only exacerbates the problems created by the "project by project" approach because the foreign developers who operate the dam have no incentive to work with each other. Further, agreements signed with foreign firms often give ownership of the dam to its foreign operator for a period from 25 to 30 years. Typically, these operators will turn a profit 12 or 15 years after the dam's commissioning. Until the dam is turned over to the government of Laos several decades later, Laos itself only receives a very small portion of electricity sale proceeds. Since most dams have yet to be built, this means that the real monetary benefits of Laos's dam fleet will not hit the country's coffers until around 2050. In 2015 Apisom Intralawan and group of scholars updated the Costanza Report mentioned above to calculate how much income Laos will actually generate from building out its dam fleet. The study results showed in consideration of losses of fish catch, sediments, wetlands, and other social impacts, Laos will generate a net income of only $700 million over 50 years from its hydropower exports.[18] To prepare for the handover decades from now, Laos will need to groom an army of skilled laborers to manage the inherited super-fleet of dams, and to date, little has been done to prepare such a cohort. Lastly, the uncoordinated "project by project" approach is the main driver of criticism from downstream governments and communities because it creates a situation of unknown trigger points that will inevitably deliver disastrous consequences for those impacted downstream.

In October 2016, my team released a report focusing on hydro-power development in Laos which, among other things, discussed how in the months prior, the Mekong River Commission had cut its organizational capacity to one-third its traditional level and closed its Phnom Penh Secretariat office in 2016. The Mekong River Commission has always been funded by foreign government donors, mostly from Europe and Australia, and our report attributed MRC attrition to foreign governments decreasing their funding based on their perception that the MRC has been an ineffective platform for transboundary management.[19] Given that the next 5 years would likely determine whether damming the Mekong passes a point of no return, the report continued with a plea to donor governments to continue their support. A few days later, the Associated Press ran an article which was also published in the New York Times entitled "Mekong effort fails after years of lavish foreign funding." Citing our report, the article accused the MRC of wasting $320 million of foreign funding over the course of two decades "on ineffective studies, lavish trips to tour rivers in America and Europe, and a poor handling of the legal processes that should protect the river's resources and the millions of people who live in the basin."[20] In 2016, donor countries slashed their traditional funding of the MRC by more than $50 million dollars which required the organization to shed about 100 of its 160 employees, many of them water and hydropower experts from those foreign donor countries. "There is a risk that an MRC without donor support could further lose influence," said Kurt Morck Jensen, lead advisor to Denmark's development agency supporting the Mekong, in the AP article. "On the other hand, donors should not be babysitting the MRC forever." Denmark's government gave $85 million to the MRC over two decades before ending its funding in 2015.[21]

The Mekong River Commission was created in 1995 as part of the Mekong Agreement, a multilateral treaty signed by Cambodia, Laos, Thailand, and Vietnam which pledged to actively collaborate over the sustainable development of the Mekong's water-based resources. The MRC is overseen by a council formed by the top leaders of these 4 countries, but most of its work is done inside of its Secretariat, which prior to 2016 was split between two locations in Vientiane and Phnom Penh. The Phnom Penh office focused on fisheries research, and Vientiane handled all other issues related to transboundary water management. The Secretariat, led by a CEO, is responsible for producing research, analysis, and technical studies related to a range of complex issues like hydropower planning, fisheries management, and irrigation. It also works on analyzing impacts of climate change and disaster prevention related to droughts and floods. This work is delivered to member countries through the channel of a National Mekong Committee located in each member's capital and staffed with government employees who then disseminate results and policy advice to relevant ministries in those countries. National Mekong Committees also pass along data and analysis from those ministries back up to the MRC Secretariat. The Secretariat is also responsible for carrying out the protocols related to new hydropower and irrigation projects that affect the river's mainstream.

So what's not working at the MRC? One of the first major disappointments came soon after the MRC released the 2010 SEA which recommended a 10 year moratorium on mainstream dams until further studies could be completed. The government of Laos widely ignored this recommendation, despite the protests of Cambodia and Vietnam, and announced the construction of the Xayaburi Dam soon afterward. Another blow to the MRC's credibility came when the government of Laos permitted preparatory work on the dam sites at Xayaburi and Don Sahong without going through the regional consultation process clearly mandated by the Mekong Agreement. For the Don Sahong Dam, the government of Laos avoided the consultation process by originally stating the dam's location was not on the Mekong mainstream, since it did not span the entirety of the river. Eventually Laos acquiesced to mounting regional pressure and put the Don Sahong Dam through the consultation process. Laos had little to lose since member countries have no right to veto the actions of other member countries when it comes to damming the river. Laos continued to espouse its sovereign right to damming the river. The MRC took the brunt of the heat from critics who ridiculed the organization for lacking the teeth to prevent Xayaburi or Don Sahong from being built without gaining consensus from downstream member countries.

Some MRC member states have called for China's inclusion as a full member since the Mekong Agreement was signed in 1995. China has never joined, and its lack of participation dogs the organization's effectiveness. The four member states came together out of the legacy of the joint UN commission on Mekong development which started in the 1950s partially as a way to push back on China's Communist bamboo curtain. But by the early 1990s, China was emerging as a regional player and three of the Lower Mekong countries, Laos, Cambodia, and Vietnam were led by Communist parties. Political differences did not preclude China's joining the MRC. But historically China has eschewed participation in multilateral mechanisms which require it to cede sovereignty and open its closed doors to outsiders. This partially is a reaction to China's legacy of encroachment by Western foreign powers which carved the country up into spheres of influence and sent it into a century of decline. Downstream countries too were scarred by the colonial experience and weaker ones like Laos and Cambodia needed equal footing with Thailand and Vietnam. As a result, the Mekong Agreement granted no ability for one Mekong state or a group of members to veto the actions of another. Thus, joining the MRC requires no surrendering of sovereign rights. But China's real reasons for not joining the MRC were more practical. Given the geological advantages of building dams in Yunnan province, the Chinese government needed to maintain the right to build dams on the upstream without a single delay or interruption from downstream countries. Joining the MRC would inevitably introduce outside criticism into China's damming plans. When the Manwan Dam was completed in the early 1990s, downstream protests, particularly those from Vietnam, began to mount. At the same time, the government of Laos now had an impetus to dust off the old plans for damming the Mekong. Lao officials thought if China was damming the river, then so should downstream countries. These two factors together galvanized the process which resulted in the 1995 agreement.

Additionally, if China were a member of the MRC, its dam operators would be obligated to share data on a range of issues from water release to power generation to fisheries impacts with the MRC. Also MRC staffers would have free reign to conduct studies on dam impacts and how climate change affects the Himalayan snowpack feeding the river. This data is kept under close watch in China, much of it labeled as state secret. The data that is released publicly is often curated and censored to meet the needs of the Chinese government. In the early 2000s China agreed to send updates on water levels and dam releases to downstream countries during the monsoon season to as a method of flood warning, but to date shares little else.

As discussed previously in this chapter the MRC mandate only accounts for dam and irrigation projects that are built on the Mekong mainstream. This focuses 100 percent of the MRC Secretariat's efforts on the plans for 11 mainstream dams and widely avoids analysis and research of the impacts of more than 160 dams planned for the Mekong's tributaries. MRC efforts have proven to delay dam construction on the mainstream, and its technical reviews can help to alleviate some of the worries downstream countries voice about the dams. As a result, after more than 2 decades, only 2 dams have begun construction on the mainstream. Neither was finished by the time of this book's publishing. The

MRC technical review process has made the Xayaburi Dam one of the most technically innovative in the world in terms of fish and sediment mitigation. The same can be said for additional mitigation at the Don Sahong Dam. Whether that mitigation actually works remains to be seen. At the same time, the cascade of 7 dams on the Nam Ou less than 100 kilometers upstream does not have anything built into it that permits the passage of fish or sediments. I asked Sinohydro's top engineer overseeing the Nam Ou cascade, why this is. He replied, "The government of Laos didn't ask us to build fish ladders or sediment flushing gates. It didn't seem important to the government."

Despite the criticism, the funding poured into the MRC has indeed produced meaningful work. The MRC has established an effective flood warning system for the lower basin and is a clearinghouse for regional climate change analysis. The organization manages a sophisticated battery of hydrological research stations located throughout the region. Data derived from the 2010 SEA and other studies produced by the MRC Secretariat are used by technical planners at the national level. MRC studies have demonstrated the value of the river's wild caught fish catches and these too are used in building an economic case to promote a smarter strategy to damming the Mekong.

The deep slashes to MRC funding certainly came abruptly as donor countries withdrew their support in 2016, but a gradual transfer of the MRC's funding stream away from foreign donors and toward member countries themselves was always part of the vision for MRC progress. For too long, the MRC Secretariat was a revolving door of expat hydrologists, and dam and fish experts whose value to the organization ceased when their short-term contracts expired. This was no way to run a sustainable and impactful organization. Foreign hires also came at a much higher price tag than local hires. As part of the MRC restructuring and localization plan, in-country river monitoring and other aspects of river management will be delegated from the MRC Secretariat to national government agencies. Twenty years after the Mekong Agreement, member countries now can provide the resources and technical capacity to monitor the parts of the river inside their respective national boundaries. Whether they choose to invest in these resources is a different question.

MRC CEO Pham Tuan Phan was hired in January 2016 to oversee the localization and restructuring of the organization. As a Vietnamese national, he is the MRC's first chief executive from a member state. Phan told me that the MRC prefers the word "riparianization" when referring to localization because the word suggests MRC control is being returned to those who are from the Mekong Basin and know the landscape well. "For the first 21 years of the Mekong River Commission, CEOs were western. With Xayaburi hydropower project coming up in 2010, riparianization was coming necessary as Laos was determined to harness hydropower potential for their economic development, while the strategic environmental assessment in 2010 conducted under Jeremy Bird – a British CEO, recommending a delay of hydropower projects by 10 years," Phan told me. "A riparian CEO is a milestone of ownership by the riparian member countries when Mekong member countries really take the sustainable management and development of Mekong into their hands. But it took a long time for the MRC to decide that now is the right time to hire a riparian CEO."

Phan is widely lauded for his management of the regional consultation process related to the Pak Beng Dam, the third mainstream project announced by the government of Laos in late 2016 which has yet to begin construction. The Pak Beng consultations were appraised as more transparent and inclusive of stakeholders' opinions than previous rounds of consultation for Xayaburi and Don Sahong which most critics labeled as a sham. CEO Phan also ended the member country yes/no voting process on individual dams since no country has veto power over another. He introduced processes which give member countries a wider berth to suggest conditions and alterations that should be applied if an individual dam moves ahead and produced a set of recommendations to be delivered directly to the project's developer and host country. "International CEOs that came before me did not have the feeling of ownership and did not act decisively. There is no guarantee that future riparian CEOs will manage the organization as I have. I hope they will do better. But Riparian CEOs are important as we have deeper insights into how riparian governments work," concluded Phan.

In the spring of 2017, a group of researchers from George Washington University in Washington D.C. conducted a study of perceptions toward the MRC's impact and its future. They interviewed more than 50 stakeholders active in the broader discussion of Mekong hydropower development, many of whom were currently working for the MRC Secretariat or had worked there in the past. I found their analysis very useful when thinking about the future of the organization as it goes through a critical period of restructuring and localization. Broadly speaking, the George Washington University study found that its interviewees could be lumped into three categories: optimists, skeptics, and abolitionists.[22]

The optimists believe that the MRC has played a critical role in enabling cooperation and coordination around regional resource management. They also believe the MRC as has been unfairly blamed for the inability or unwillingness of the member countries to more effectively engage in sustainable development matters – especially given the organization's relatively narrow mandate. This group is generally composed of those working directly with the MRC, including those within the organization, and those acting on behalf of the MRC's closest development partners. Optimists generally believe that the restructuring process will address many key concerns and that the organization's future will be assured if it can successfully transform into a body that successfully helps to manage resources within member countries.

MRC skeptics view the institution as lacking the capability to truly fulfill its mandate to enable sustainable and cooperative water resources management due to its lack of political authority and weak institutional capacity. They are skeptical that a decentralization of the MRC will actually improve the management of the Mekong River's water resources or the living standards of riparian populations. On the whole, however, they believe that the river basin is better off with the MRC despite its inefficiencies, and they argue that enhancing the MRC's authority and capacity for political engagement would make the organization more effective. This group of stakeholders tends to include those with more experience with policy and diplomacy who view the MRC in the context of broader regional relations. They also frequently cite the critical nature of the technical work undertaken by the MRC, and in some cases, argue that the organization should refocus its efforts in those areas, collecting data and developing analyses that others can then use to push member countries to take action. They assume that without the MRC, countries will not communicate with each other and this will lead to a rapid degradation of the lower basin's resources and ultimately to the deterioration of regional relations and stability.

Abolitionists accuse the organization of "doing more harm than good" and view the functional purpose of the MRC as shielding member countries from criticism for their failure to appropriately address development issues in the Lower Mekong Basin. This group is composed of stakeholders with substantial work experience on development issues in the region, including some who have worked directly with the MRC. Arguing that the MRC is ineffective and inefficient as currently structured, these individuals believe that the MRC should be disbanded if the member countries are unwilling to more aggressively support its mandate. When questioned about the MRC's localization process, these individuals typically argue that the problem is systemic, not structural and that the MRC will continue to be ineffective unless the member countries commit to ceding actual decision making authority to the organization. Abolitionists believe other NGOs and research institutions can better serve to conduct technical reviews of dams and important analytical research regarding the river's future.[23] The only way to implement the abolitionists' suggestion to restructure the mandate and authority of the MRC is to revise the 1995 Mekong Agreement. Richard Cronin of the Stimson Center believes it is dangerous to try and renegotiate or rewrite the 1995 Mekong Agreement. He told me, "There will never be another 1995 moment. Despite its limitations, it's the only possible game in town. Of course, the member states could hand its functions over to a Chinese-run mechanism. China would welcome that but this would cede the future of river development over to China."

At this critical juncture of MRC restructuring and localization, it is uncertain which view above, the optimists, the skeptics, or the abolitionists, accurately depicts the future of the MRC. Other Mekong watchers wonder if China's rise as a regional overlord, and China's effective control of the upstream could draw the countries of the Lower Mekong so closely into its orbit that China will begin to dictate the future of the river's development. In March 2016, senior leaders from China, Myanmar, Thailand, Vietnam, Laos, and Cambodia met on China's Hainan island for the first meeting of the Lancang-Mekong Cooperation Mechanism (LMC). The LMC, said to be mooted by Thailand after a suggestion from China, could finally bring China to the negotiation table in an effective manner. However, despite an initial focus on water management, the Chinese government quickly expanded the LMC's scope to include a wide range of issues including educational exchange, poverty alleviation, and infrastructure development. China has offered an $11.5 billion line of credit to downstream countries for infrastructure projects. This all ties neatly into the ambitions of China's Belt and Road Initiative. The LMC promises to set up a secretariat to promote transboundary water management and research, but to date most almost all of its progress has given little consideration to water-related issues. Like the Belt and Road Initiative, the LMC is mostly focused on infrastructure investment opportunities and persuading countries to become a more important part of China's manufacturing supply chain.

Since the LMC's founding, China has been more forthcoming in sharing data with downstream countries through channels inside of the Mekong River Commission, a noted improvement from past practices. Additionally, for the first time, officials from downstream countries were invited to tour China's upstream dams. While early observances suggest China is finally coming around on pursuing cooperative channels with downstream countries, one cannot help to think that the economic heft behind the LMC could easily eclipse the MRC. In fact, many Mekong watchers fear that it is only a matter of time before the LMC creates an institution that puts the MRC out of business.

When surveying a basin for hydropower development, planners and engineers develop an inventory of possible sites on which to build dams. Laos has more than 140 dams in its inventory and has built just over a third, and Cambodia's inventory has more than 40 dams with only 7 currently operational. History tells us that the inventory of dams is rarely constructed to its fullest potential. The easiest and most profitable dams are usually built first, while the technically more difficult projects and those farther from power demand centers are often foregone. Technical challenges could arise from the dam's remote location, the need to resettle a large amount of affected peoples, or environmental risks posed by the dam often discourage developers from certain projects on the map. The Nature Conservancy estimates that globally about 40–70 percent of a basin's dam sites will be constructed.[24] To illustrate, the US has a fleet of more than 3000 dams. Most of these dams were built prior to the 1960s. Since the 1960s, the US has introduced environmental protection and water management laws that have essentially slowed the construction of hydropower within the US to a snail's crawl, despite a multitude of potential sites that still could be built. Hydropower, despite its claims as a clean and renewable energy, lost its popularity in the US more than 50 years ago. The same can be said for many other countries, especially those in Europe. And now Brazil and India are beginning to slow the process of damming their rivers.

In February 2016, I asked one of Laos's top energy planners exactly how many dams would need to be constructed to become the "Battery of Southeast Asia?" He could not give me a specific answer. Nor could he tell me how much income Laos needed to generate from the export of power across borders to meet its economic goals. For a country that has placed its top economic development priority as the sale of hydropower to its neighbors, I was banking on more confidence in his answer. Despite all of the hype and dreams to become the "Battery of Southeast Asia," the government of Laos has no concrete plan for how to reach that finish line. Its agencies do not know where the finish line is, they just know they are running towards it. This mindset is symptomatic of the "project by project" approach to damming the Mekong, but it could also be what prevents the river from reaching its ecological tipping point.

Evidence published by the Stimson Center suggests the rate of issuing new contracts for dams in Laos and Cambodia is actually slowing down. This emerging trend has been consistently confirmed through conversations with energy planners in Laos and Cambodia and the foreign dam developers interested in investing in the Lower Mekong. A top Sinohydro executive in Cambodia told me in February 2017 that he has left Laos because most feasible projects are already spoken for, and it is harder for him to find a good project in Cambodia. In November 2016, I spent a few days in Vientiane with a Chinese executive from the Yunnan Energy Investment Group who told me his team marched around Laos for 3 years looking for a dam site worth investing in and came up short. He told stories of how they were stranded on mountainsides and his cars were washed away in floods in his quest to find the perfect dam site, but in the end, his company settled on building a cement factory in northern Laos. Some developers, particularly Chinese, are moving out of the Mekong because it will take too long to turn a profit in Laos and Cambodia compared to building a dam in another part of the world. "A dam site might be perfectly feasible to get a good rate of return, but Laos makes us pay for transmission lines which is cost prohibitive," said one Chinese developer.

Other Chinese developers simply are not showing up due to a lack of financing available to bring the project forward. After decades of unfettered economic growth, China's total debt level is more than three times its GDP, and its commercial banks are now much warier when issuing loans to risky projects.[25] This is not to say that the seemingly endless government funding provided by China's Belt and Road Initiative or the LMC could not be used to support hydropower development in the Mekong, but since China no longer needs to import electricity from its neighbors, its dam developers are only interested in making a commercial profit. Further, the Asian Development Bank, which provides low interest loans for infrastructure development projects throughout Asia, does not finance new dams in the Mekong Basin because of the widely documented environmental and social risks. It is possible funds for future financing of dams are shifting into less risky forms of energy generation such as natural gas and non-hydropower renewables such as solar and wind.

With financing options on the decline, a few other important inputs that bring dams to fruition may also be drying up, the most important of which is water. Dams on the mainstream of the Mekong will only be viable if enough water is in the river to generate enough electricity to sell to the market. Water availability is never a problem in the monsoon season, but in mainland Southeast Asia, energy demand is highest in the dry season when high temperatures drive up the price of electricity due to a spike in air conditioning use. During the spring 2016 dry season, an El Niño induced drought sent a chilling signal to hydropower proponents throughout the basin: people were literally walking across the Mekong in Vientiane, Laos. Because Laos's mainstream dams are all purposed as run-of-the-river schemes, they cannot store water for use in times of high energy demand.[26] Climate change is predicted to lengthen the dry season and China's mega-dams upstream which store enormous quantities of water in their reservoirs historically have not provided the downstream with a regular flow of water in the dry season. There is nothing to suggest this pattern will change. In the dry season, Mekong flows are nearly entirely reliant on snowmelt from China's portion of the Himalaya, and much of this is predicted to melt within the next decades due to rising temperatures.

China's perennial water shortage gives it every impetus to use or store every drop of that water before it is gone. As suggested in this book's first chapter, this could be the real reason why China is building 19 mega-dams on the Upper Mekong upstream. If developers and investors realize that not enough water will be available in the dry season to spin the turbines of downstream dams at a time when power is at its highest demand, they might think twice about investing in dams on the Mekong.

Globally the price of other renewable energies such as solar, wind, and biomass is falling at a rate more rapidly than can be anticipated. Courtney Weatherby, a research analyst at the Stimson Center's Southeast Asia program told me "The global price of solar technology dropped more than 80 percent between 2009 and 2014, and further significant drops are projected to continue through the mid-2020s. This has resulted not only in record low prices for renewables but record low electricity prices period. Even without battery storage, the right policy environment and loan terms for investors allow solar and wind to outcompete fossil fuels and older hydropower projects in developing countries around the world. These welcoming policies and financial terms are not yet wide-spread in the Lower Mekong countries, but investor interest has spiked even without welcoming policies from Laos and Cambodia and with Vietnam and Thailand's policies in flux." Since 2017, the announcement rate for new scale solar and wind farms in the Lower Mekong Basin has exceeded that of dams. To be sure, most of these renewable projects will be built in Thailand and Vietnam which no longer build dams inside their borders. But it is only a matter of time before the price of solar and wind generation in Laos and Cambodia reaches parity with hydropower.

It is important to recognize that until battery storage technology improves, these forms of intermittent energy production will not be as reliable as hydropower. However, a large dam contract awarded today will likely take 7 years until its turbines begin to produce electricity. Looking at energy trends, it's a good bet that solar, wind, and biomass will be more profitable and energy storage more reliable than hydropower by 2025. Thus, hydropower is quickly becoming an obsolete technology that will, in the medium term, likely be globally priced out of the market and without exception in the Mekong region.[27]

Both Laos and Cambodia are well endowed with solar and wind potential, and added together these energy sources make up more than half of the hydropower potential of these countries. Cambodia in particular, with its wide swaths of flat and unproductive land could harness its solar potential and specialize as an exporter of solar power, becoming the region's sun belt. At a public forum on the Pak Beng Dam in Laos, Dr. Daovong Phonekeo, Permanent Secretary of Laos's Ministry of Energy and Mines acknowledged that after 2020, a portion of Laos's power exports to Vietnam will be in wind and solar. This points to both a recognition of Laos's non-hydropower renewable potential and the slowdown in hydropower availability. Considering his statement, perhaps Laos still will be a "Battery of Southeast Asia" but one that is more diversified and less reliant on hydropower as a driver of economic growth. Indeed in 2017, a study produced by the University of California at Berkeley revealed that if Laos were to plan its energy generation through 2030 by simply using market price trends across a spectrum of energy generation choices, it would develop an energy mix that with more than 50 percent non-hydropower renewables. This energy mix provides as much power as the current hydropower heavy plan and costs $2.6 billion less!

Thus, it is not too late for Laos to chart a new, alternative pathway for energy development, one that drastically reduces social and environmental impacts to its downstream neighbors.

Over the last four years, China's dams in Yunnan province wasted tens of millions of dollars per day in foregone power generation by sending water over its spillways rather than through its turbines. Similar trends are playing out on rivers in neighboring Sichuan province. Power grid operators and developers in China are keen to find new markets outside of China for this power, and the Mekong countries, excluding Laos, provide a ripe market. This gives Laos an opportunity to earn valuable income by charging transit fees for China's power as it is wheeled to markets in Southeast Asia.[28] But downstream countries, Laos included, are becoming increasingly leery about overreliance on China. Buying power from China could further slow the need to build dams and provide valuable time for the prices of solar and wind power to drop, but downstream countries are unlikely to reward China with cash for decades of ignoring their decades-long call to join the MRC. Perhaps one way to make this deal more palatable would be for China to finally join the MRC.

Clearly, a sustainable pathway forward can only be delivered through strategic coordination that involves multiple countries in the Mekong to explore an alternative pathway for energy development. Vietnam can lead that exploration. If Vietnam were to meet its rising energy demand by investing in a large portfolio of energy generation assets in Laos and Cambodia – a portfolio that maximizes solar, wind, and biomass and minimizes hydropower – it could effectively negotiate and guarantee a brighter economic and ecological future for the entire region. As the most downstream country, Vietnam is the most interested in promoting a positive outcome for the Mekong River. However, to date Vietnam's response has been to collectively lead a rally protesting mainstream dams rather than suggesting constructive pathways forward for Laos or Cambodia. Vietnam must triple its energy consumption capacity through 2030, and because it has maxed out its own rivers with dams and finds nuclear energy unpopular, to do this, planners must make a balanced choice between importing power from Vietnam's neighbors or importing coal from the rest of the world. Importing too much coal will increase air pollution levels beyond an acceptable limit and could threaten political stability in Hanoi in a similar manner as bad air quality threatens Beijing. Yet importing too much hydropower from its neighbors could spell the end of the Mekong Delta, a topic explored in this book's final chapter. But Vietnam could strike a balance in its energy mix planning by helping its neighbors develop their solar, wind, and biomass assets and importing power from those assets rather than dams. This is a win-win solution that could also protect the core ecology and natural provisions of the river because it would negotiate the most impactful dams off the project map. Vietnam is uniquely positioned to assist its neighbors, with which it enjoys favorable relations, to chart a new course for energy development in the Mekong.

8

PHNOM PENH AND
BOEUNG KAK LAKE

When the Mekong passes from Laos into Cambodia, it abandons the 3000 kilometers of mountainous valleys it has carved upstream and transforms itself into a wide river that bisects the whole of Cambodia. In northern Cambodia, the river's wandering path creates braids of flattened islands, some more than 40 kilometers long. The Mekong's margins form countless wetlands, many of which are protected by the international Ramsar Convention on wetland conservation. These islands and wetlands are the habitats of dwindling populations of migratory birds such as the critically endangered White-Shouldered Ibis, and the largest remaining pods of freshwater Irrawaddy Dolphin are found in deep pools nearby. Some of the islands were settled in the 1970s by refugees fleeing the brutal rule of the Khmer Rouge regime that was responsible for the deaths of 2 to 3 million people. In a kind of "wet Zomian" setting in the middle of the river, these refugees found new solace out of arms reach of the Pol Pot's oppressive government.

Moving downstream, at Stung Treng, the tributary waters of the Sekong, Sesan, and Srepok Rivers, often glommed together in name as the 3S Rivers, flow into the Mekong. During the monsoon season, the westward flowing 3S Rivers are swelled by the heavy rains in Vietnam and Laos's upland areas and contribute a significant portion – 20 percent – of all water in the Mekong system.

Below Stung Treng, with the added waters of the 3S Rivers, the powerful Mekong widens even more. Here, roads run parallel to both sides of the Mekong, and under the shade of palm trees, stilted houses, roofed with orange tiles or red, rusty tin, line the spaces along the river and the roadside. Together, these homes form a nearly seamless chain of villages that runs more than 400 kilometers all the way to the Vietnam border. Altogether, more than a quarter of Cambodia's 15.75 million inhabitants live within sight of the Mekong mainstream. Another quarter lives along the shores or in homes floating on top of the Tonle Sap Lake and its tributaries. The river's resources, cooler temperatures, and fertile floodplains are a magnet for human settlement.

Generally, when a river floods, it deposits sediment, sand, and silt in the low-lying areas surrounding its channel. This replenishes the land with nutrients and raises the level of land around it. As a river approaches its outlet at the ocean, its channel fills with more water and more sediment and has the full force of its system pushing its contents onward. Because of this, floods that occur closer to the ocean tend to be more intense and deposit more sediment. This, in turn, creates more land. Over time, this process forms new land that is pushed outward into the ocean, lengthening the channel of a river. As it approaches the sea, the gradient of a river bed flattens out, slowing down the river's speed, and more of the river's sediment naturally settles in the bottom of the riverbed. This process causes the riverbed to rise, and then it is only a matter of time, usually a few hundred to a thousand years, before the river jumps its main channel in search for a new steeper, faster path to the ocean. A new channel is created as the old one is abandoned. Sometimes, as in the case of the Mekong, the old channel is not entirely abandoned, and the river will split into multiple channels called distributaries (in contrast to tributaries) that send water into the sea. Cumulatively, millennia of flood cycles and channel jumping sends the river system to and fro across the landscape forming an ever-widening and lengthening swath of land called a river delta.

By many counts, the Mekong's Delta is said to lie entirely within Vietnam, but the aforementioned delta forming process actually begins in Cambodia just below Stung Treng, long before the river enters Vietnam. More than 5000 years ago, the river took a major leap that set up conditions for the rise of the Khmer empire and the Cambodian nation. Cambodia's largest urban settlement, its capital Phnom Penh, is located alongside the Mekong at the spot where two rivers, the Tonle Sap River and the Bassac, meet the Mekong. This point of convergence, called Chaktomuk or "four faces" in local Khmer language, produces four channels of the Mekong (the Tonle Sap, the Bassac, the Mekong main upstream, and the Mekong main downstream). The French, who colonized Cambodia in 1863, called the convergence Quatre Bras — the four arms — and these arms are easily seen on a map or better appreciated while on a stroll down the newly constructed riverside promenade in central Phnom Penh. The Tonle Sap and Bassac were once connected to form a river system entirely isolated from the Mekong Basin from its headwaters to its mouth at the sea. Then 5000 years ago, the Mekong jumped westward, splitting the Tonle Sap/Bassac in two. The Mekong not only captured the Bassac, turning it into the Mekong's first major distributary to the ocean, but it also turned Tonle Sap, which prior to the change only flowed in one direction, into a distributary in what is often described as one of nature's miracles. Each monsoon season, the Tonle Sap River reverses its flow and takes on water from the Mekong. By sending water up the Tonle Sap River, this event suddenly caused the Mekong's floodplain to increase by a third of

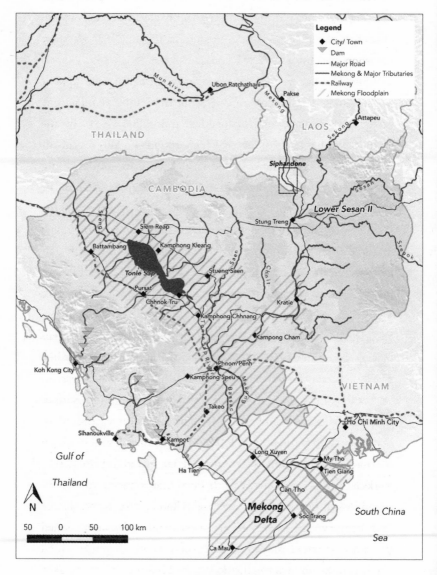

Map of Cambodia

its previous size and more importantly created the Tonle Sap Lake, Southeast Asia's largest body of freshwater. From this point in the Mekong's geological history onward, the Tonle Sap Lake began to expand to five times its dry season footprint like clockwork every monsoon season.

The first recorded histories of the Khmer people appear in the annals of Chinese empires more than 1500 years ago. A group of city-states, lumped together and called Funan by the Chinese, transitioned in the 7th century into a more centralized polity called Chenla which paid tribute to China's Tang emperor in modern Xi'an. Eventually, the early Khmer living along the Tonle Sap figured out how to store a portion of the lake's monsoon pulse during the dry season and take advantage of fertile plains in the receding flood zone for planting rice. Gradually, with advances in irrigation and rice cultivation techniques, combined with the lake's abundance of fish, the Chenla peoples produced a great surplus of food, allowing them to develop into a grand civilization which supported a large army, a robust government bureaucracy deriving its regalia from Hindu and Buddhist traditions, and classes of artisans and other skilled laborers. In 802 AD, out of this innovative mix sprung forth the Khmer Empire, the dominion of which, by the 12th century, covered all of modern-day Cambodia, Laos, most of Thailand, and southern Vietnam. The empire was sustained by grand infrastructure works like giant reservoirs, stone bridges that connected an extensive network of roads, and massive religious structures. In the 12th century, the Khmer King Suryavarman II commissioned the construction of Angkor Wat, a grand temple structure which embodied the physical replication of the Hindu universe. Angkor Wat, like many of the empire's bridges and reservoirs, still stands today and is the world's largest religious complex. At its zenith, the city of Angkor was about the size of modern-day Los Angeles, making it by far the largest city in the world in physical size and home to more than 1 million inhabitants.

Much of what we know about the Khmer Empire time was recorded by a Chinese explorer named Zhou Daguan who arrived in Angkor at the end of the 13th century. Bas-relief murals on the numerous stone temple complexes that remain intact or in ruin around Angkor Wat and around mainland Southeast Asia also tell much about the historical and cultural milieu of the time. The carvings show a complex religious society steeped in rituals and festivals, many of which are still observed today in Cambodia and inspire the modern Khmer nation. Ubiquitous carvings of fish now remind Khmer and foreign visitors alike of the importance of the Mekong's natural provisions to the Khmer diet. The representation of enemies like the Cham who occupied the central coast of what is now Vietnam and allies like the Chinese suggest an inter-linked system of regional relations based on conquest and tribute. Zhou Daguan's records confirm these relationships.

Imperial record-keeping ceased in the 13th century, so today historians and anthropologists are uncertain of the exact factors which sent the Khmer Empire into decline. Some have suggested that gradually the technical knowledge of maintaining the empire's complex irrigation system was lost. Others point to an extended period of low precipitation and drought, a period of acute climate change between the 13th and 14th centuries that naturally would have impacted agricultural production and water availability. Some historians suggest kings and élites competed to see who could build the largest and most elaborate temples, requiring more canals to float large stones to the construction site. Over time, too many canals and the intensified temple construction caused a competition over water which weakened the Khmer empire. At the same time, the world surrounding the Khmer Empire was rapidly changing. Droves of people who would eventually form the Siamese and Lao Kingdoms on the periphery of the Khmer Empire were hemorrhaging out of China. The Mongol invasion of southern China at that time forced out a last big push of Tai/Lao refugees. Burgeoning European maritime trade with Asia took advantage of coastal ports and likely restructured some of the Khmer Empire's tribute economy away from Angkor located far inland. The Tai Kingdom at Ayutthaya, situated just north of modern-day Bangkok eventually began to antagonize the Khmer and eventually sacked Angkor in 1431, incorporating what remained of the Khmer Empire as a vassal of Ayutthaya. To take advantage of global commerce, the remaining Khmer élite moved down the Tonle Sap and founded a new capital at Chaktomuk, naming it Phnom Penh.

The new location at Phnom Penh guaranteed that no sailor coming up or down the Mekong would miss out on commercial opportunities with the Angkorian Kingdom. Soon, Japanese, Malay, and eventually Portuguese and Spanish traders began to visit and conduct commerce with the city's inhabitants. The monsoon season created a traffic jam of water all converging on the "four faces" sending water throughout the floodplain. This provided a robust agricultural advantage to feed the city's burgeoning masses. But the unpredictable floods might have discouraged Khmer kings to stick with Phnom Penh as a permanent seat of government. The capital moved from Phnom Penh to surrounding cities a few times before the king returned to the city in 1863 as the installed figurehead of the newly established French protectorate of Cambodia.

When the French arrived in Phnom Penh in the mid-1800s, the interior of the capital, except for a few palaces, was dominated by lakes and wetlands managed by the Angkorian monarchy. Royal decree prevented commoners from owning land in the city, so most of Phnom Penh's residents lived riverside, along the Mekong, Bassac, and Tonle Sap, in stilted homes made of wood, bamboo, and thatch. These homes faced natural levees on their river banks, and they were supported by stilted beams dipping into the water.. The French broke down the monarchy's power and eventually permitted commoners to settle on land, but this required draining a portion of the city's lakes and wetlands and converting them for residential and agricultural use. To manage the city's ethnic population, the French built canals and drainage systems to zone off urban districts exclusively designated for Europeans, Chinese, Khmer, and Vietnamese. As the city's population became more diverse, city space became more exclusive. Toward the end of the century, the French laid out wide boulevards and a street grid system that emanated from Wat Phnom, the city's highest point and most important religious monument. Over time, the French built the new royal palace, hotels, schools, and public offices. Many of these buildings still stand today. Over the course of several decades, a space that previously could only be navigated by boat and was often known for serious cholera outbreaks was converted into a Western-inspired urban landscape that could support a population of several hundred thousand.

By 1920, Phnom Penh, like many French-built cities in France's Asian colonial sphere, was known popularly as the "Pearl of the Orient." Prior to the Second World War, the French doubled the size of Phnom Penh's urban plan, moving it southward. This meant even more lakes and wetlands were filled in. The city's largest remaining French-built structure, the Central Market, opened for business in 1937. At the time, this art deco structure was said to be the largest commercial space in Asia. Before 1935, the area on which the market now stands was a large lake. Urban planning stalled during the Japanese occupation of Southeast Asia between

1941 and 1945 and did not resume until 1953 when King Norodom Sihanouk negotiated independence from France which after the Allied victory in 1945 had returned to re-colonize Cambodia. To transform the Pearl of the Orient into a city of modern Khmer pride, Sihanouk, who downgraded himself to the status of a prince in order to lead the country as its prime minister and head of state, tapped a young Paris-trained Khmer architect named Vann Molyvann as Cambodia's State Architect in 1956.

Between 1956 and 1970, a period known as Phnom Penh's Golden Era, Vann Molyvann, with Sihanouk's full backing, designed and oversaw the construction of scores of innovative structures that combined modern architectural styles with Khmer cultural elements. Alongside the Mekong he built the zig-zag spired Chaktomuk Conference Hall and oversaw the construction of the iconic White Building, mainland Southeast Asia's first low-income housing project. Vann Molyvann's designs were a creative combination of function and form. For instance, the multi-storied buildings of the Royal University of Phnom Penh's Foreign Language College are raised off the ground, like traditional stilted Khmer homes, allowing air to pass underneath to cool off the building's interior and prevent the occasional flood from damaging the classrooms. Virak Ellis-Roeun, a young Khmer architect who gives informative tours of Vann Molyvann structures told me, "I think what I find inspiring about Vann Molyvann's architecture is his ability to transform Cambodian identity into the modernist utopian ideal. He was not shy to use traditional elements when it comes to his design. The way he incorporated water, air, and natural light in his rough concrete buildings shows how brilliant he was as an architect." Like many structures built in the West in the 1960s, Vann Molyvann used concrete as a decorative medium. Concrete-formed Naga, the serpent guardian of the Mekong, guard the doors to the library of the Foreign Language College, and scores more Naga align the lotus flower layers of Cambodia's Independence Monument, the city's most recognizable landmark. When Vann Molyvann designed the Independence Monument, he wanted to pay homage to the grand architectural style of the Khmer Empire.

During his tenure, Vann Molyvann doubled the city's French-era footprint, preparing for a city that in the future would be home to 1 million people. Like the French, Molyvann's vision for Phnom Penh's urban expansion pushed it farther southward along the Bassac River where a natural levee protected adjacent land from flooding. Molyvann knew how city's north often flooded when the monsoon pulse sent water back up the Tonle Sap River. He did not build northward and preserved the large lakes and marshes there to act as a buffer to keep water out of the city. In a 2014 interview with the *South China Morning Post*, Molyvann said, "The history of this city is working and fighting against water."[1] His proudest creation, the National Olympic Stadium built to host the 1963 Southeast Asian Peninsular Games, is a testimony to this struggle. The singular structure houses an outdoor stadium which can hold more 60,000 fans, an indoor arena, and an Olympic-size swimming and diving pool. The stadium grounds sit in a low-lying area of the city that is susceptible to flooding. Ellis-Rouen told me, "Unlike many European architects, Vann Molyvann respected the topography of his structure's locations and avoided filling in land to raise the level of the structure." Importantly, the stadium needed to function during the monsoon season. Drawing inspiration from Angkor Wat which is surrounded by a wide moat, Molyvann designed the stadium with a moat and drainage system that cleared the outdoor playing field, surrounding parks, and parking areas within minutes after a downpour.

The National Olympic Stadium is still used as the city's main athletic venue, most importantly for indoor events in its arena. Its exterior walls are designed with open-air slats that provide the arena with natural light and a constant breeze. This non-air-conditioned space is home to Cambodia's national basketball league and has hosted major cultural events such as the February 2017 Cambodian premiere of Angelina Jolie's feature film *First They Killed My Father*, an adaptation of the 2000 book by Khmer Rouge survivor Luong Ung. In recent years however, real estate firms from Taiwan and China have developed parcels of land around the complex's periphery. This required filling in much of Vann Molyvann's moat system and today 20-story residential high-rises surround much of the stadium. These buildings offer good views of sporting events but also cut off much of the air-flow that kept temperatures around the complex cool. To host the 2023 Southeast Asian games, a Chinese contractor will build a new stadium in the north of the city, placing the future of Vann Molyvann's prime creation in limbo. Many other Vann Molyvann structures face could face similar fates. Into the 2000s, the iconic White Building fell into disrepair after being occupied by squatters and the city's incoming migrant population. What was originally intentioned as government-provided housing for the city's poor and to a degree filled that purpose, was demolished in August of 2017 to make space for another new residential highrise.

Today Phnom Penh is one of Asia's fastest growing cities. Each time I visit the city I am greeted by what seems to be a different skyline formed by new office towers, hotels, residential complexes, and the occasional casino. In 2010, the city had not a single structure taller than 6 stories but within the space of 7 years, on my last count, more than 100 buildings with more than 10 stories now challenge the sky. Each of these bland new additions lacks the nationalist flare of Vann Molyvann's New Khmer architectural style. Most of these buildings are Chinese invested and built by teams of Chinese laborers. Many of these new buildings are related to the slowdown of China's real estate market which has sent Chinese developers farther afield to zones ripe for investment. Chinese president Xi Jinping's anti-corruption campaign has also flushed untold volumes of cash outside of Chinese borders into investment projects such as these which launder ill-gotten gains into ostensibly legitimate assets.

In January 2018, intrepid writer Chris Horton published an article in the *New York Times* on Phnom Penh's real estate boom. When talking with a Chinese real estate agent Chen Jinging, he discovered most of these newly built luxury apartments were sold to Chinese buyers. Chen said, "In terms of purchasing, it's basically all Chinese. Most people will buy for investment, but some will live in their flat because they have a company or business here."[2]

Horton also met with a political risk consultant George McLeod who said, "Businessmen with wealth in excess of a few million dollars are scrambling to squirrel cash outside of China and the reach of unpredictable authorities." McLeod noted how Cambodia's banks have lax internal controls and policies around anti-money laundering making them wide open to serve as vehicles to launder cash from criminals and corrupt government officials. "Given my experience doing investigations in Cambodia, I am convinced that laundered money from the PRC is a substantial portion of property investment in Phnom Penh," concluded McLeod.[3]

Half a century ago, Vann Molyvann designed a city blueprint to support 1 million, but now Phnom Penh's population is pushing the limits of 3 million, making it the largest urban space in the Mekong Basin. The city is a magnet for migrant workers employed by a globally competitive clothing manufacturing industry. It is also an attractive place to settle for educated Khmer youth schooled in the country's emerging academic institutions or returning from abroad. Many returning from abroad are the second and third generations of refugee families who fled to Europe and the USA in the 1970s.

Developing Cambodia is still reliant on overseas aid and has brought Westerners in droves over the last three decades to occupy key positions in government agencies and non-governmental organizations. The city's most recent wave of foreign residents comes from China. Likely numbering in the tens of thousands, this cohort is redefining the city's skylines, invests heavily in the infrastructure and commercial development, and interestingly has carved out space for, by my own measure, one of the widest selections of Chinese cuisine outside of mainland China, Hong Kong, and Taiwan. As a rapidly globalizing space, many businesses in Phnom Penh now choose to decorate their exteriors with signage displaying Khmer, English, and Chinese languages.

The city's municipal government lacks the resources and planning foresight to meet the infrastructure needs of the recent population boom. As a result, traffic jams and the need for extended commutes are now a fact of life in Phnom Penh. On these roads, tuk-tuks pulled by deeply tanned motorcyclists jockey for space alongside luxury Porsche SUVs and Maserati sports cars owned the capital's emerging *nouveau riche* class. Once, while sitting in a Lexus SUV taxi imported from the United States, I was stuck in traffic on Russian Federation Boulevard during a monsoon downpour. I watched a motorcyclist draped in a plastic poncho raincoat maneuver his way through rainwater half a meter deep only to disappear into the soup when his bike hit a hidden pothole. The shaken cyclist popped up a few seconds later completely drenched and defiantly continued on his way.

In Cambodia two-thirds of the population is under the age of 30. Those with disposable incomes choose to hang out at trendy, locally owned café chains such as Blue Pumpkin or Brown Café. Restaurants and bars around the Phnom Penh's famous Russian Market have reportedly been over-run by upbeat Khmer hipster entrepreneurs. Japanese and Chinese commercial real estate developers seem to be in constant competition to see who can build the country's biggest shopping mall and attract the hard-earned dollars of Cambodia's rising consumer class.

One of these shopping malls sits on the edge of a large open patch of land in the middle of the city's north section across from the seat of national government. Next to the mall, a large red sign marked with "Phnom Penh City Center" leads deep into an open, undeveloped area dominated by tall grasses and a half-developed grid of paved streets. At first glance, the City Center sign appears to be mislabeled. During the colonial era, this desert of sand and grasses could have fit most of the city. Its curved perimeter is now defined by urban buildup. Today, little remains to suggest that less than a decade ago, this barren space was once home to the city's largest lake.

The area formerly known as Boeung Kak Lake sits about 1 kilometer from the Tonle Sap in the north-central part of the city adjacent to the former French Quarter. Looking at French colonial era and Vann Molyvann blueprints for the city, Boeung Kak lake was set in the heart of the city. Those who remember it talk about how its shaded palm trees and cooler temperatures provided year-round respite from the heat of the concrete-laden city grid. The lakeside was dotted with hotels and guesthouses that serviced the city's burgeoning tourism industry. Cambodia's current, long-serving Prime Minister Hun Sen was known to occasionally drink brandy at his favorite lakeside restaurant. Most importantly, however, it was home to more than 4200 households who lived along its shoreline or on floating homes at the lake's edge.

Many who lived along the lake sought refuge there after living through the horrors of the Khmer Rouge regime. To provide context, in 1975 the Khmer Rouge government ousted the American supported Lon Nol government. The new regime completely evacuated the city and left it mostly uninhabited for more than three and a half years between 1975 and 1978. Phnom Penh's residents and most of Cambodia's population were forcefully sent to rural concentration camps for re-education. Those who were thought to have ties to the CIA or influenced by Western education or values were summarily executed in one of the country's many "killing fields" sites. More than 1 million people were executed in the killing fields. In 1979, the Vietnamese army invaded Cambodia and ousted the Khmer Rouge. The two groups would engage in a bloody civil war that lasted into the early 1990s. During the 1980s, Boeung Kak's lakeside started to attract more and more inhabitants. In the early aughts, the lake's most recent arrivals were those evicted by real estate developers in other parts of Phnom Penh.

By and large, Boeung Kak's residents always lived on the margins, literally and figuratively. They were some of the city's poorest inhabitants. The lake provided those who lived alongside it with a new community space that gave low-cost access to food resources like fish, crabs, and frogs and a place to raise water-borne greens like morning glory which could be sold on the local market. Being the city's last remaining large lake, Boeung Kak also played a critical role as the "lungs of the city" absorbing the monsoon rains instead of sending the waters to flood the city. The lake also naturally filtered wastewater that otherwise would infiltrate the surrounding water supply.

In February 2007, the Phnom Penh Municipal Government leased the entirety of Boeung Kak Lake's 133 hectares to Shukaku, Inc. to develop the lake into a residential district. The

233

deal's announcement took the surrounding community and most of the country by complete surprise. Just a few years earlier, the Phnom Penh municipal government hosted a competition to promote the lake as an important part of its urban plan, acknowledging the critical ecological services the lake provided to the city. Now the lake's future and that of its residents looked very uncertain. The deal's price tag was set at $79 million, a steal for such prime, downtown real estate. Despite the low price, few Cambodian companies in Phnom Penh could afford such a price, so locals correctly assumed Shukaku, which was nominally owned by a prominent Cambodian senator, was also backed by foreign investors. Lakeside residents launched an early protest outside of the South Korean Embassy based on the assumption that Shukaku sounded like a Korean word. However, they soon discovered that the deal was backed by a Chinese firm from Ordos, a city in Inner Mongolia. They also discovered that this was Shukaku's first ever venture into real estate development.

Many of the residents had ownership papers for their properties and others claimed right to their homes and land from a Sihanouk-era rule that granted access to land ownership if those who lived there possessed it peacefully, continuously, and unequivocally for 5 years. But since Sihanouk, the country had passed through four systems of government each with its own legal approach to land use and ownership.

After the 1978 Vietnamese invasion, residents returned to Phnom Penh after the fall of the Khmer Rouge regime, only to discover that the Khmer Rouge completely destroyed all former records of land ownership. The newly installed socialist government, which was fully backed by Vietnam, labeled all land as state collective property not to be sold or rented. Hun Sen, a former Khmer Rouge commander who defected to Vietnam in 1977, eventually rose through the ranks to lead this government as its Prime Minister in 1985 at the age of 33. In the 1980s, families were given plots of land on an ad-hoc basis, but old records were not recognized. The 1991 Paris Peace Accords ended the decade-long civil war between Hun Sen's Vietnam-backed government and the Khmer Rouge and paved a pathway for a democratically elected constitutional monarchy.

In the 1993 UN-administered elections, the Cambodian People's Party (CPP), which was actually Hun Sen's former party renamed to get rid of its communist affiliation, came in second to FUNCINPEC, a party founded by Sihanouk in the early 1980s. Neither party gained majority votes to form a government. As a result, a dual prime-minister system was formed with Hun Sen sharing power with Sihanouk's obedient son and selected appointee, Prince Norodom Ranariddh. Sihanouk, who had returned to Cambodia after years in self-imposed exile, and Hun Sen both saw themselves as the builders and saviors of modern Cambodia, albeit from differing eras since Sihanouk was three decades Hun Sen's senior. Neither would cede power to the other without a fight, and each political bloc commanded its own set of ministries. In reality, most government officials were still loyal to the CPP. Time after time, this arrangement resulted in deadlock. In 1997, after 3 years of political boxing matches in Cambodia's parliament, Hun Sen took advantage of the regional and domestic chaos caused by the Asian Financial Crisis to successfully launch a military-led *coup de force* against Ranariddh. The CPP executed more than 50 military commanders loyal to FUNCINPEC. This neutered Sihanouk's power over future political outcomes and fully consolidated Hun Sen's power. Once again, fighting between military factions returned to the streets of Phnom Penh and resulted in the deaths of hundreds of soldiers and citizens caught in the fray.

Into the 1990s, as Hun Sen jockeyed for power against Sihanouk, a poor land distribution process favored powerful individuals, and according to Kry Suyheang, executive director of Women Peacemakers Cambodia, this led to a "significant increase of social stratification, enriching those in a position of power, particularly those with power over privatization of land resources."[4] Hun Sen held sway over the land distribution process, granting land concessions and investment opportunities to powerful elite players, both foreign and domestic, in turn for political support. Sebastian Strangio, author of *Hun Sen's Cambodia*, a comprehensive account of Cambodia's recent political history published in 2014 told me, "July 1997 left Hun Sen in a position of unparalleled power. The coup crippled FUNCINPEC's military capability, sent its politicians scampering into exile, and cemented Hun Sen's primacy over factional rivals within his own party. Henceforth he ran the country like a family business, in which loyalty was repaid with access to business opportunities and lucrative state resources. Resources were used to secure political power, which was used to obtain further access to resources, in an endless cycle of patronage and enrichment."

Cambodia's powerful élite now had the means and political backing to evict rural peoples and the urban poor from long-standing land holdings, either by gaining possession of economic land concession licenses or by laying personal claim to parcels of occupied land. As people were evicted from their rural communities, the rural poor to begin crashing on Phnom Penh in search of homes and employment opportunities. Some of those new arrivals ended up around Boeung Kak Lake. In the run-up to the 2003 national elections, Hun Sen, well aware that high-profile eviction cases could tarnish his local and global reputation and impact his political future, issued a new land law which laid a better foundation for land ownership. The law prevented the expropriation of land except when "in the public interest and after fair and just compensation."[5] Possessors could apply for definitive ownership, but possession only counted for land possessed prior to 2001. Possession of state land and collective property was prohibited. Hun Sen's CPP won 47 percent of the vote and was challenged by Sam Rainsy, a former finance minister who criticized Hun Sen for being corrupt and ran a campaign promising to improve Cambodia's welfare system. In order to form a government, Hun Sen banded once again with the FUNCINPEC party. Sam Rainsy continued to politick and build his opposition platform.

Sebastian Strangio suggests land-grabs really took off once the CPP had fully consolidated its control over the system in mid-2006. This was when a constitutional amendment allowed the CPP to form a government alone, rather than in coalition with Funcinpec. Hun Sen kicked Ranariddh to the curb. From then on, the CPP went to town, leading land-grabs and the granting of economic land concessions to spike. For instance, the lease agreement for Boeung Kak Lake was signed in February 2007. When the Shukaku deal to develop Boeung Kak Lake was announced in 2007, some of the lake's residents who had settled there prior to 2001 were already applying for ownership of their properties. Around the same time, the World Bank set up a program called the Land Management and Registration Program (LMAP) to provide assistance to individuals in filing claim for land ownership. Upon learning of their possible eviction, many of the 4200 families rushed to file ownership claims in 2007 under the LMAP program. All of these claims were summarily rejected.

Unwilling to concede defeat, residents continued to question the legality of the Shukaku deal. Through engaging with domestic and foreign legal experts, locals pointed out a major flaw in the leasing of the lake. Boeung Kak Lake, like all rivers and lakes in Cambodia, is legally defined as state public land which cannot legally be leased. This made the lease illegal in nature. The law further defined that state land can only be converted if it loses the public interest. In early 2008, the municipal government settled this contradiction by issuing a *fiat* sub-decree that transferred the designation of the lake from "state-public" to "state-private" land. Citing the law, the municipal government also declared all lakeside residents of being illegal occupants settling on state property. Legal experts continued to inform locals of the discrepancies inside the Shukaku lease. For instance, Cambodia's land law reads that "state private" land can be legally leased for up to 15 years. The Shukaku lease had a term of 99 years. It also clearly defines that lessees are not permitted to change the function of the land in providing public services. Prior to 2007, the city master plan officially recognized the public service of the lake as a "storm reserve" and important "ecological zone." But because Cambodia has no independent judiciary, these valid legal issues fell on deaf ears.

In the July 2008 national elections, Hun Sen rode to electoral victory after deftly navigating a border dispute with Thailand over the Preah Vihar Temple. The Sam Rainsy party won 21 percent of the vote, fewer seats than in 2003. The Boeung Kak Lake conflict had little effect on the electoral result because the controversy over the future of the lake's residents did not reach full boil until later that year. In August 2008, Shukaku began to pump sand in from the Mekong River on average of 18 hours a day. Boeung Kak's residents erupted in protest with a major march on City Hall on September 1, 2008. Not only did they face eviction but resettlement terms offered by Shukaku forced lakeside households to move to small plots of land in a resettlement village 20 kilometers away from Phnom Penh's downtown area. If they moved to the resettlement village, no longer would Boeung Kak's residents enjoy convenient access to their jobs, schools, and medical services.

Further, for those residents who owned successful businesses like guesthouses and restaurants, a small plot of land would hardly provide equitable recompense.

Over time, 500 families agreed to move to the relocation site. Many were forced to acquiesce because their homes were inundated by lake water as the pumped-in sand pushed flooding into the residential areas. The protests continued despite constant intimidation from Shukaku security forces. One protester said, "I am not against the government's development plan, but any development in which the poor have to be evicted without proper compensation will only benefit powerful people."[6]

The World Bank LMAP program conducted an investigation into the legality of the Shukaku lease and claims of Boueng Kak's residents. The investigation's findings favored residents. It acknowledged that their claims were indeed eligible for titling and that many residents had pre-existing rights to the land. But this did little to stop Shukaku. In 2010, power was cut off to remaining holdouts which still numbered in the thousands. Rising waters in what remained of the lake increased the threat of water-borne diseases. Partially in response to the World Bank findings, Shukaku changed its terms for compensation. Residents who had not previously agreed to a benefits package could choose between resettlement 20 kilometers away, a one-time cash reparation of $8500 or could build their own home inside the development zone. Many took the cash and by early 2011, more than 3500 families were resettled or compensated. But to many business owners, $8500 was poor compensation for their ventures which could earn that much or more in a few years' time. The option to build a home inside the development zone had certain appeal, but Shukaku offered no guidance toward when these homes could be built and where residents would live while waiting for land to be prepared and designated for their new homes.

In response, the remaining residents, most of whom were women, petitioned for land sharing plan of 15 hectares to build their own homes. Despite their frequent protests, these demands were not heard. In July 2011, a ground-breaking ceremony officially marked construction of the Boueng Kak Lake Development project but more than 500 households still remained within the development zone. In an attempt to force a solution to the impasse, the World Bank announced the immediate ceasing of all its loans to Cambodia. Within days, Shukaku granted more than 12 hectares of land within the development zone for remaining residents to build homes upon. However, 10 percent of the remaining households were designated as falling outside of the land grant zone. Their homes were marked for immediate demolition. As a form of protest, one of these residents, a young female, committed suicide by jumping into the Mekong. On April 19, 2012, Boeung Kak Lake was completely filled in and ceased to exist as a body of water.

During the eviction process, residents were not allowed to collect possessions while their homes were being covered in sand and mud. Many were threatened at gunpoint by Shukaku armed guards. One man who refused to the resettlement terms, Pich Samol, was in the hospital unconscious when Shukaku staff came and dipped his finger in ink for use in signing an agreement to demolish his home.[7] He received no compensation for his home. Protests did not end when the lake's last drop of water dried up. On May 22, 2012, a group of women protesters, later to be dubbed as the Boeung Kak 13 were chased down and arrested by Cambodian security forces. They were quickly tried and convicted of being illegal occupants and obstructing the work of public officials. The youngest of the group was 25 and the oldest 72. All were sentenced to two and a half years in prison. Shortly after their sentencing, then US Secretary of State Hillary Clinton met with Cambodia's

Foreign Minister to discuss the obvious violation of the Boeung Kak 13's human rights, and 2 weeks later the women were set free, although their charges were upheld.

As the 2013 national elections approached, Sam Rainsy banded with Kem Sokha, the leader of Cambodia's Human Rights Party to form the Cambodia National Rescue Party (CNRP). The CNRP placed the Boeung Kak Lake controversy at the center of their opposition platform using it as the prime example of the CPP corruption and the injustices the Hun Sen regime imposes on Cambodia's people. The CNRP campaign also pledged to protect the country's resources from encroaching neighbors, but instead of focusing on China's deepening ties with Cambodia's élite, its campaign rhetoric placed most blame on the Vietnamese as the puppet masters pulling the strings of Hun Sen's regime. In the July elections, the CNRP won 44.46 percent of the national vote causing the CPP to lose 22 seats in the national parliament. The CPP declared victory with 48.83 percent of the vote, but international and domestic election monitoring agencies and the US and European Union pointed to irregularities in the voting process. The final vote count was announced by CPP-controlled Ministry of Information and little light was shed on the tallying process. Many critics, including the CNRP's Sam Rainsy and Kem Sokha accused the CPP of rigging the election. CNRP elected delegates, citing election fraud as their rationale refused to take their seats in parliament. The CNRP organized protests throughout the fall of 2013. These continued into 2014 when security forces killed 3 garment workers and injured several others at a demonstration where protesters demanded an increase to the textile sector's minimum wage. Protests were banned for 1 month. Later that year, several CNRP leaders were arrested and remained in prison until Sam Rainsy and Hun Sen struck a political deal in July 2014 that allowed CNRP elected officials to take their seats in parliament.

Roughly about the same time in 2014 after 7 years of peaceful protest, despite constant intimidation and the threat of violence, 631 households received land titles for their former lakeside properties. For those who held-out, theirs was a bittersweet victory that left many scars. Their success can be partially attributed to the rise of an effective opposition party folding their cause into its platform, but most importantly, this success demonstrated the power of civil society organizations in Cambodia to respond to the needs of individuals when the government failed to do so. Legal organizations provided knowledge and capacity for individuals to understand their rights while human rights organizations provided the skills to empower individuals and inspire effective collective action. These organizations also built linkages with key international allies to effectively apply pressure from outside countries. [8]

At the relocation village 20 kilometers from Boueng Kak, resettled community members claim they now earn much less income than in the city, and they have poor access to health care, education, and water. They also have yet to be granted titles for their new homes and land. Unemployment there has doubled since relocation. Symptoms of depression and anxiety are palpable. Many of these people were victims of the Khmer Rouge regime as well. Life, for them, has been a continuous series of tragedies.

In 2014 Shukaku's Chinese partner pulled out of the lease for undisclosed reasons. In June the HLH group, a firm from Singapore, purchased 1.3 hectares from Shukaku for $14.9 million, allowing Shukaku to recoup a significant portion of its investment for a minor lease of land. This plot is now being developed into a luxury real estate complex while the rest of the dry lake bed sits empty. Hun Sen's antagonism against Boeung Kak's residents continues. In early 2018, Cambodia's Supreme Court upheld the conviction of Tep Vanny, one of the leaders of the Boeung Kak 13, and sentenced her to 30 months in prison.

Against Vann Molyvann's advice to expand the city southward to avoid floods, Phnom Penh continues to expand toward the floodplain in the north and northwest of the city. In the wet season, plots of pumped sand stick out like a sore thumb against the flooded fields. Although the city lacks a clear urban plan for future development, it is known that the northwest floodplain will be designated for middle- and low- income housing investments. Without Boueng Kak Lake and other wetlands surrounding Phnom Penh, the impacts of a major flood event on the city are unknown, and the city is at risk. In a December 2013 interview, Vann Molyvann, then in his late eighties, said, "We would fill lakes too, but we would do it precisely. Those that remained were purposefully left to collect floodwater. Hun Sen rejects all of the plans that have been designed. Why? To sell land."[9] Vann Molyvann died at his home in Siem Reap in September 2017, less than a month after the iconic White Building was demolished.

At the time of this book's publication, Hun Sen at the age of 65 is the world's longest-ruling prime minister. He has publicly voiced his willingness to rule for 20 more years, but watchers of Cambodian politics suspect that he is grooming one of his Western-educated sons to soon take his place. Hun Sen will not concede a loss to a major opposition party. After all, he oversees a vast patronage network, created by his own design and this makes the country's economy run and guarantees a degree of security. Hun Sen is also concerned about his own personal safety, the safety of his family, and the ability to access his vast accumulation of wealth should he be ousted from power.

In July 2016, Global Witness, a corruption watchdog agency, issued a report which estimated Hun Sen's wealth and business holdings range between $500 million and $4 billion. Three days after the report was released, Kem Ley, a popular critic of the Hun Sen regime, was murdered in a coffee shop. Since Kem Ley's hitman-style assassination, Hun Sen has increasingly used the rhetoric of violence and political tactics to stifle all opposition to his rule. Prior to the local commune elections held in June 2017, Hun Sen said he would "eliminate 100 to 200 people if necessary to preserve national security."[10] This was a direct reference to his 1997 military coup which had as many casualties and a reminder to the populace of his willingness to use force to settle political disputes. Earlier that year Hun Sen deftly forced Sam Rainsy into exile using a battery of criminal charges. This made Sam Rainsy's partner Kem Sokha the head of the CNRP opposition party.

In the June 2017 local commune elections, the CNRP performed better than expected, winning 43 percent of the vote. This seeded much of the Cambodian countryside and urban areas with CNRP officials for the first time ever. In response, Kem Sokha was arrested in a pre-dawn raid in August 2017 and was accused of treason and conspiracy with the United States to overthrow the government. Shortly afterward, the Cambodian government forced the popular English language newspaper *The Cambodia Daily* to shut down after more than two decades in operation and shuttered all independent radio and television stations throughout the country. The government laid bogus claims that the newspaper owed years of back-taxes. Under the duress of uncertainty, the CNRP expressed reluctance to elect a new leader and into the fall of 2017, most of the CNRP leadership had fled the country. On November 16, 2017, Cambodia's Supreme Court dissolved the CNRP on the basis of conspiracy to overthrow the government sending the future of Cambodia's democracy and governance into uncertainty. Effectively stifling all opposition, Hun Sen easily won re-election in July 2018.

While most of the world has condemned Hun Sen's actions, his regime continues to rely on China, the country's biggest investor, for economic and political support. In light of these recent maneuvers, the role of opposition parties in determining the country's future political discourse remains uncertain. The CNRP, while never taking power, exposed flaws in Cambodia's governance structure. It also influenced Hun Sen to cancel dam projects, raise the minimum wage, and end the sale of economic land concessions to foreigners. Sophal Ear, a professor at Occidental College in Los Angeles is a prominent critic of Hun Sen's rule. He views the future of Cambodia's political structure and Khmer society itself with tense anxiety. "Hun Sen said in 2015 that he needs only 7 hours to arrest anyone who insults him on Facebook, but completely unchecked, the most recent arrest, in February 2018, involved a 29-year-old man who called the regime 'authoritarian'," he said. "Without an opposition as buffer, Hun Sen's powers are downright Orwellian, especially in an age of electronic surveillance which the ruling party Congress says it wants to intensify in the next 5 years. The economic and political outcome will be ever more rents – as gatekeepers – and control over the body politic."[11]

After the 2013 elections, Hun Sen also placed young, Western-educated leaders at the helm of the country's education and environment ministries. Many attributed this move as a way to appeal to the country's youth in coming elections. However, without an effective opposition party to challenge Hun Sen's rule, the current political instability will remain until Hun Sen dies or passes power on to one of his sons or deputies. Cambodia has slipped into full-authoritarian mode entirely backstopped by the country's close relationship with China. For the future of the Mekong River and the millions of people that depend on its resources, this timing could not be worse.

9

THE TONLE SAP

Sorn Pheakdey, the head of the Cambodia office for the International Union for Conservation of Nature (IUCN) and I stand in the middle of a muddy road in Chhnok Tru, about 120 kilometers upstream from Phnom Penh on the Tonle Sap. The road runs above a low-lying levee about 10 meters wide surrounded by the waters of the Tonle Sap Lake on both sides. Just ahead of us, the road disappears into the lake. If it were April, at the peak of the dry season, the road would extend a few more kilometers before it met the lake, but this is the end of November 2017 and the Tonle Sap had only begun to drain back into the Mekong a few weeks ago. Pheakdey, who is in his early thirties, brought me to Chhnok Tru, the point where the Tonle Sap Lake narrows into the Tonle Sap River, to show me the annual harvest of *trey riel*, which translates into English as "money fish." He did not disappoint.

We are surrounded by hundreds of local Khmer people either bringing in the morning's fish catch or engaged in one of the steps of making *prahok*, a fermented fish paste. Storable for many months after the year's peak fish harvest has ended, *prahok* is consumed as a protein-packed condiment and used as a dipping sauce with rice or other dishes or an ingredient in soups. The shoreline serves as a parking lot for long, narrow boats made of various colors of Plexiglas all fitted with outboard motors. Fishers, men and women alike, all wearing long-sleeved shirts and pants for protection against the sun's rays, unload an endless line of yellow, green, and red plastic tubs filled with fish onto the muddy shoreline. The tubs, which look like oversized plastic laundry baskets, have slits to drain water. They are filled with hundreds of white and silver *trey riel*, no longer alive but very fresh, each no more than 10 to 15 centimeters in length. I note to Pheakdey how some of the fish have differing colorations. He says, "Yes, these are different species, but all part of the cyprinid family, the most abundant species of fish in the lake." I immediately make the connection that the cyprinids here on the Tonle Sap used for making *prahok* are the same used in Laos for making *pa dek*.

A deeply tanned man in his late twenties lifts a tub onto a green portable scale. The woman who runs the scale records the tub's weight in a small notebook before the man places the tub at the end of a double line of 20 others, each brimming with freshly caught fish. Pheakdey says, "It will be this busy for about the next 2 months." All around us the reverberation of off-board motors makes conversation difficult. Almost all of the colorful building structures that align the road for more than 3 kilometers are temporary. Small huts pieced together with wood and aluminum are purposed for resting and sleep during this time of the year when locals are too busy to return to their homes. Vendors sell water and fresh food from make-shift stalls shaded by red and purple umbrellas.

Other open patches are covered by large tarpaulins hoisted high above to provide shade to those who are processing fish. Thirteen women and children squat around a high pile of a few thousand cyprinids. Each person, including the children, the youngest of whom is 7 years old, uses a knife to gut and clean the fish. Prepared fish are then collected by women and transferred back into clean tubs. As piles of innards and fish heads accumulate, these too are collected. Later, these by-products will be used to feed farms of snakehead fish or other animals raised by local villagers. Within eyeshot, 6 circles of people are doing the same thing. Pheakdey tells me how some people in Cambodia are critical of the use of child labor in the fishing and *prahok* making sectors, but he also highlights the importance of making *prahok* as a cross-cutting tie, the tradition of which helps to keep families and communities together around the lake. The annual cyprinid harvest also helps to bind together much of the country's population since farmers come from outlying provinces, some as far as 200 kilometers away, to trade rice or exchange cash for a year's worth of *prahok*.

We pass by an area where tubs of prepared fish are cleaned by soaking them for a few hours in the waters of the Tonle Sap. After this, they are extracted, packed with salt, and left to sit for up to 2 weeks before being pounded into paste and then packaged, ready for consumption or trade at local markets. All together in Cambodia more than 70,000 tons of *prahok* are made between the months of November and March each year, and most of this comes from the lake's cyprinid catch.[1] Counting fresh fish consumption and *prahok*, Cambodians consume around 75 kilograms of fish each year, much more than the per capita fish consumption of most developed countries. However, unlike other countries, fish consumption makes up 65–75% of animal protein intake of households in Cambodia.[2]

I wander over to an area where tubs of fish were fermenting. Walking closer, an overwhelmingly pungent odor gives pause to my approach. Pheakdey laughs, "We're all used to this smell here in Cambodia." Two men wearing football jerseys load tubs of finished *prahok* onto the back of a flatbed trailer, rusted over from use or exposure to the monsoon rains. Each tub, now filled with much more fish than those just coming in with the morning's catch, is much heavier and requires the strength of both men. They slip a pole through the tub's handles and move it onto the trailer. After

10 minutes, the flatbed is fully loaded with 8 tubs holding what I estimate as 15,000 fish. One of the men starts up his motorcycle rigged to pull the trailer. Moving forward a bit, the trailer becomes stuck in a muddy rut, but with a little push from Pheakdey and me, the motorcycle gains speed and drives up the road, eventually disappearing over the long, flat horizon.

All Cambodians know the proverb *"mean tuek, mean trey"* or "where there is water, there are fish." And nowhere does this adage ring truer than the Tonle Sap Lake. By all accounts, the Tonle Sap is the world's largest inland fishery. More than 500,000 tons of fish come out of the Tonle Sap each year.[3] To put this into perspective, *all* of North America's freshwater lakes and rivers combined produce about 450,000 tons of fish each year. During the dry season, the Tonle Sap river drains the great lake and sends its waters into the Mekong mainstream at the Chaktomuk confluence in Phnom Penh. But shortly into each year's monsoon season, typically sometime in June, the pulse of water flowing down the Mekong mainstream from Laos and the 3S rivers is so intense that it causes the direction of the Tonle Sap river to reverse. This reversal, which sends a massive amount of water into the Tonle Sap Lake, is the main ingredient in a recipe of nature's magic that produces an astonishing abundance of fish.

When the monsoons come, gradually the lake expands more than 5 times its dry season area, from a footprint of 2500 square kilometers to 15,000 square kilometers. Its height rises from an average of less than 1 meter to more than 9 meters deep, and the lake's volume of water grows more than 60 times that of the dry season. The rush of monsoon waters is filled with nutrient-rich sediment, rotting organic material, and most importantly, loads of fish eggs and fish larvae and adult fish that come from spawning grounds far in the upstream of the Mekong system. As the lake expands, the flow carries these fish and ingredients into freshly flooded areas. The combination of nutrients in the soils, sunlight, and the fresh influx of water teeming with microscopic life results in an ecosystem explosion from the bottom of the food chain up. Algae and plankton thrive, and as a result, the fish population does too.

When the monsoons wane in November and the dry season approaches, those flooded areas recede, and the force of gravity sends the contents of the lake back down into the Mekong mainstream. Juvenile fish migrate out of the Tonle Sap and look for refuge in deep pools throughout the Mekong system. Those which have reached adulthood return to traditional spawning grounds far upstream to lay eggs and wait for the cycle to begin again. At its peak, the fish migration out of the lake could reach more than 30 tons per hour.[4] The waterfalls at Siphandone on the Mekong mainstream near the Laos-Cambodia border mark a natural upstream barrier of this migration for many fish species. Some make it past the falls while others choose to migrate deep into the upstream reaches of the 3S rivers. This natural rhythmic process has played out annually without losing a beat ever since the Mekong joined with the Tonle Sap Lake 5 millennia ago.

Since I began coming to Cambodia, many years ago, I had visited the lake numerous times at several different spots. But I had never visited the lake at the right time to observe the annual cyprinid harvest which marks the beginning of the massive out-migration of fish from the lake to the mainstream. The day before our visit to Chhnok Tru, Pheakdey and I had hoped to see the cyprinid harvest just upstream from Phnom Penh where commercial fishers had licenses for 14 bag net fishing lots, locally know as *dai*, stretched over 30 kilometers of the Tonle Sap river. We stopped to see one of these lots from an open-air fish market alongside the river. In the middle of the river, fishers positioned a series of 10 anchored boats and platforms running parallel to the river. They were spaced about 10 meters apart and tied together with bamboo. The open ends of large nets were fastened to these platforms while the closed ends of the nets were tied to anchored houseboats about 100 meters downstream. In between, the nets' wide openings collect schools of fish which are then trapped by the force of the river's flow. One *dai* system could link as many as 10 nets across the width of the river, but this one was located the farthest downstream and had only 5 nets. When the nets are filled, fishers waiting in the boats downstream pull their bounty out of the water onto platforms rigged to the houseboats.

Before this, I had seen photos of *dai* nets being pulled out of the river teeming with several tons of fish and hoped to see it in person on that day. I inquired with a local fisherman standing on the shoreline whether the fishers on the river planned to pull up their nets today. "You came too early," he said. "We will bring the nets up in 10 days from now just before the full moon." Until then fishers watching the nets would remain on the houseboats midstream.

Over the last 3 decades, Mekong geographer and fisheries expert Ian Baird has researched the complexity of the Tonle Sap's ecosystem and discovered a relationship between cyprinid migratory behavior and lunar phases by observing fish catches north of Phnom Penh and around the waterfalls at Siphandone near the Lao-Cambodia border. He and most fishers in these locales will tell you that most cyprinids are harvested in Phnom Penh's *dai* fisheries just before the full moons of December, January, and February while the highest catches of cyprinids in Siphandone are about 2 weeks later, at the time of the new moon. This suggests that the timing of the Tonle Sap departure and the arrival at Siphandone is linked to lunar patterns, and this behavioral "knowledge" is programmed into the cyprinids' DNA. Baird has found that when *dai* fishery catches are low near Phnom Penh, Lao cyprinid harvests tend to be high at Siphandone. Conversely, when catches near Phnom Penh are high, they tend to be low in Siphandone.

Baird wrote in a seminal report called "Rhythms of the River" that fishers around the world have long believed that the most successful fishing times are associated with particular lunar periods.[5] Baird thinks the cyprinid exodus from the Tonle Sap is linked back to the time when the Tonle Sap river did not flow into the Mekong but rather emptied into the ocean. Rivers close to oceans are subject to the tidal effects of saltwater intrusion. A full moon brings the highest tides and thus sends the most saltwater deep into a fresh-water system. Prior to converging with the Mekong, the Tonle Sap River could have taken in saltwater, which is no friend to a fresh-water fish. The cyprinids that migrated into freshwater tributaries and wetland areas just before the biggest saltwater tides were more likely to survive. Over time, natural selection programmed this migratory trigger into the cyprinid's DNA. To prove this linkage of the Tonle Sap's original connection with the sea, Baird observed that cyprinid migratory patterns from other Mekong tributaries were not linked to lunar effects and did not occur simultaneously with the outward migration from the Tonle Sap.

When the Tonle Sap was captured by the Mekong 5000 years ago, these successful cyprinids had a new pathway to fresher water – a migratory route into the Mekong's upstream and into the 3S River system. But the waterfalls at Siphandone proved a problem and marked a natural barrier for the cyprinids' upstream journey. Locals have long observed how most cyprinids would attempt to pass upstream through the falls at night when fewer predators, those on land and in the water, could see them passing through the shallow waters. Night time, then became the preferred time for local fishers to ready the fishing traps at Siphandone. The darkest night, that of the new moon, always pulled in largest catches. Baird thinks that pulses of cyprinids arrive just before the new moon of each month and communicate with each other to stay in deep pools to remain unseen by predators. When the fish see no moon, they then somehow signal to each other that it is time to make a run for it.[6] That the fish have yet to adapt to the presence of fishermen in both the Tonle Sap and at Siphandon suggests that the massive harvest of fish in the early dry season by humans is a relatively new phenomenon compared to the thousands if not millions of years of fish migration. The cyprinids that make it to their spawning grounds look for mates, lay eggs, and wait for the monsoon waters to come and return them downstream, many ending up once again in the Tonle Sap Lake.

To gain a better understanding of the how the Tonle Sap's complex ecology works, the lake can be divided into 3 zones forming concentric circles. The innermost zone is the permanent lake, always filled with water. Next is a zone of flooded forest and grasslands, inundated for about 5 to 8 months of the year during the monsoon season and populated by trees and bushes. Finally an agricultural zone forms a peripheral area that is flooded for only a few days a year. The diagram below shows the relationship and size of these zones.

By far, the flooded forest, which measures more than 7,000 square kilometers, is the most important zone for producing the Tonle Sap's fisheries and the overall abundance of biodiversity in the lake's ecosystem – if not the entirety of the Mekong. Some trees in the flooded forest can grow to heights of 15 meters and are adapted to survive with their trunks submerged in 4 to 6 meters of water for 8 months at a time. When the forests flood, incoming water causes some trees and bushes to rot, tossing organic matter that is otherwise land-based into the water. Fish that arrive too

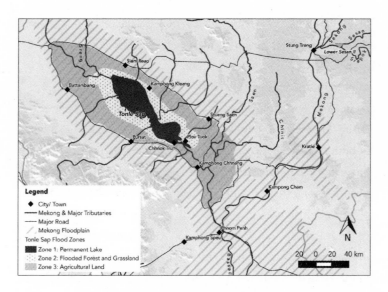

Map of the Tonle Sap Lake and Mekong floodplain

early find the water too toxic for habitation since the sudden burst of organic matter depletes the water of oxygen. This has indeed been recorded to cause massive fish die-offs, particularly if a storm drives fish into the shallows too early in the monsoon season. However, gradually after a period of several weeks, the oxygen mix balances and the flooded forest becomes fit for habitation. Juvenile and adult fish find the flooded forests to be a virtual smorgasbord of food. More eggs are washed into the flooded forest. Here these fish mature, feed, and form the schools of more than 150 species of fish that eventually leave the flooded forest. In the dry season, many exit the lake system while others return to the deep parts of the permanent lake.

The floodplains introduce material that typically would stay on land into the lake's system. This includes rotting plants, trees, and bushes, but also insects and smaller organisms. Floods cause an explosion of nutrients into a lake's system and the living organisms within that system, fish not excluded, take full advantage of the natural bounty. The more nutrients provided, the more fish thrive, and the more fish are then caught by fishers. So as long as the floods come each year, there is a direct relationship between the height of the flood and the fruitful bounty of the Tonle Sap.[7] Early and high floods also transport more sediment into the lake which not only promote the growth of plants on the bottom of the lake increasing immediate food availability for fish, but when the floods recede, more land is naturally fertilized with deposited sediment. This aids in the recovery of the flooded forests, a timeless cycle of decay and replenishment that is now coming under threat.

Today, the flooded forest around more than half of the lake is severely degraded. The fertile deposits of sediments induce communities to cut down the forests and plant cash crops in the dry season. At the same time, locals use the forest's timber for building homes. Along with commercial operations, locals also cut down trees for fuel use as firewood and charcoal and sell the largest trees for timber. To be sure, local community usage of the flooded forests' resources is not a new phenomenon. Just like the other forest areas of the Mekong, the Tonle Sap's flooded forests contain a variety of resources such as herbs, animals, and wood that have supported a unique livelihood. Village elders living in lakeside communities remember a time when local communities effectively managed the forests as a shared resource. But as markets develop in Cambodia and the price of fish and agricultural products rise, community populations around the lake have increased at a rate that puts the usage of flooded forests resources at great risk. This is particularly the case when the trees of the flooded forests, which served as custodians of the forest ecosystem, are cleared permanently for farming.

The Tonle Sap is home to more than 800 species of fish, birds, reptiles, mammals, and amphibians. Seventeen globally threatened or near-threatened species of birds live around or migrate annually to the lake, and most find habitats within the flooded forests. As the result of conservation efforts, the waterbird population is recovering, but other species continue to be threatened. Within recent memory, the lake was home to large populations of various monkey species, otters, and the flying fox, but these animals are often poached for use as medicine or food. Historical records dating back to the Angkor Wat period show elephants and Irrawaddy dolphins populated the lake and its shores. Today neither mammal is to be found. What is left of Cambodia's elephant population has retreated to mountains in the country's periphery. The lake's dolphin population was completely culled by the Khmer Rouge who harvested oils from freshwater dolphins for fuel use.

In the 20th century, the French colonials overexploited the lake's flooded forest by parceling out lakeside plots of land for agricultural concessions and did little to stop local communities from cutting down the forests for firewood. This colonial blueprint set the tone for future exploitation of the lake. In the 1970s, the Pol Pot regime cleared large tracts of flooded forest as it instituted slash-and-burn agricultural techniques related to its plans for agrarian reform, which subsequently met catastrophic failure and resulted in a massive famine that killed hundreds of thousands. After the Vietnamese National Army ousted the Khmer Rouge and put Hun Sen on the pathway to Cambodia's top leadership, half of the flooded forest was cleared between 1985 and 1993[8] to expose and reduce the hiding spots for Khmer Rouge holdouts.[9] Today, by and large, what remains of the flooded forests are secondary growth forests dominated by shrubs and bushes. As agricultural lands encroach into the flooded forest zones, irrigation canals for the delivery of water during the dry season and access roads now restrict the natural flood cycle and fragment the natural habitats of remaining flooded forests.

Even though the diets and livelihoods of most Cambodians rely on the Tonle Sap's fish catch, very little is done in-country to emphasize the importance between the maintenance of flooded forests and yearly fish catch. Local fishers frequently comment on recent declines in fish catches, but most attribute this to the effects of overfishing since more fishers are rushing to take part in the Tonle Sap's fishing industry. Others are quick to blame the upstream effects related to damming the river system.

According to Cambodia's Inland Fisheries Research and Development Institute (IFreDI), more than 4.5 million people, slightly less than one-third of Cambodia's population, are directly involved in the country's fishing sector.[10] But this number excludes those who fish for subsistence purposes. Cambodia's census form gives individuals an option to tick only one box as their main method of generating a livelihood. Fishing and farming among other occupations are listed as singular choices. But around the lake, individuals who tick the farming box also engage in fishing for up to half of their time. Excluding these individuals results in great underestimations of official records showing how many are involved in fishing and how many fish are caught per year. Importantly, this causes the government to grossly underestimate the percentage of protein intake derived from subsistence fishing.[11] IFreDI now reports that Cambodia's yearly fish catches range between 570,000 and 625,000 tons of fish, but this number is likely undervalued since subsistence fishers, which exceed more than 1 million, still are not accounted for. Cambodia's annual fish harvest is currently valued at up to $600 million per year when fish finally hit the end market.[12]

About 1.2 million people live in villages in or near the flooded forest zone around the Tonle Sap. Officially, another 100,000 live in communities of floating homes on the lake itself, although this number also excludes tens of thousands of ethnic Vietnamese whose roots can be traced back to refugee groups fleeing southern Vietnam centuries ago as Vietnam's northern dynasty began conquering the south. Not unlike mountain-based Zomians, these ethnic Vietnamese fishers escaped to the middle of this resource-rich waterscape and thrived as mobile exploiters of its resources. Today, these communities tend to possess more sophisticated fishing gears, and their floating homes allow them to access fish-rich areas more quickly.

Most of the households on and around the lake fish daily during the wet season, and half of these households continue fishing during the dry season.[13] On average, these households catch more than 100 kilograms of fish per year. The farther you go away from the lake in any direction, the more households are involved in wage labor and cash crop production. Communities around the lake continue to grow albeit at a slower rate than Cambodia's urban areas. Most people are not willing to migrate out due to the abundance of the lake's and flooded forest's resources. Between the 1990s and the early aughts, the population living alongside the Tonle Sap tripled. The influx of fishermen caused a doubling of the annual fish catch. This resulted in an overall decline of fish catch per person, and the trend of decreasing catches per person continues to play out today.[14]

These numbers can be somewhat deceiving, however, because they suggest a somewhat equitable, yet declining, division of the fish catch to those who have fished the lake over the past decades. In actuality, individual access to fishing resources began to decline in the 1990s when Hun Sen issued licenses to commercial fishing enterprises which subsequently controlled most of the Tonle Sap's fish harvest. Hun Sen's move divided the lake into 250 large scale lots that could trap nearly all the fish inside of them with bag nets. In the 1990s, almost 100 percent of the shoreline was covered by commercial fishing lots.[15] Locals fished the lake without a license and were not taxed for their catch, but they were excluded from the most productive areas of the lake. Many of the fishing lots were patrolled by armed security guards.

If the Tonle Sap's ecosystem and the resources it provided were valued as an important public good for Cambodia, regulation of commercial fishing lot system in the 1990s and early aughts could have been combined with conservation efforts to protect fish species and promote the abundance of fish in the lake's system. Quotas could have limited the amount of fish caught each year. Regulations on fishing equipment could have protected valued and threatened species, and earnings from the sale of commercial licenses which were valued in the millions of dollars could have been set aside to protect and prevent human encroachment on the flooded forests. But such regulations were not considered, and the earnings from fishing license sales disappeared into government coffers used for unknown purposes. Further, the important link between the flooded forests and fish abundance was never made clear to lot owners by governing authorities. Otherwise, lot owners would have been incentivized to protect the flooded forest and prevent local communities and commercial industries from cutting them down. Bribes paid by commercial lot owners who were making money hand over fist from their catches made pre-determined quotas entirely useless. Also, fishing lot owners could easily increase the size of their lots with under the table payments.

With such poor regulation, larger fishing lots crowded out local fishers even more. In late 2000, instead of issuing regulations to conserve the lake's fish and flooded forests, Hun Sen decided the problem was related to the ease of the ability of licensed fishing companies to bribe local officials in charge of monitoring the lake. That year Hun Sen recalled all fisheries officials to stay in Phnom Penh while he considered a set of new fisheries reforms. With the monitoring authorities sequestered away and out of sight, the commercial lot owners and locals, long kept away from the lake's key fishing grounds, engaged in a fishing frenzy. A report by Patrick T. Evans, a researcher for the UN Food and Agricultural Organization claims that as a result of this free-for-all behavior, the Tonle Sap has never been fished so thoroughly as between February and May 2001.[16]

Eventually, the fisheries authorities returned to the Tonle Sap, and little happened to change the practices of commercial fishing companies which over the next decade removed most of the fish from more than 20 percent of the lake.[17] In 2012, Hun Sen issued an unexpected and sudden decree to cancel all large-scale fishing on the Tonle Sap. Overnight, the commercial fishing lots were shut down. Ostensibly, Hun Sen justified his move as a response to locals complaining about declining catches and the need to reduce conflicts between locals and the powerful commercial firms. But his *fiat* announcement came one year prior to the 2013 national elections, and Hun Sen already had an established legacy of populist maneuvers in the run-up to national elections. Further, the CNRP had already begun to mount an impressive opposition campaign and was aligned with civil society organizations that were appealing to the concerns of local fishing communities.

Later that year, Cambodia's fisheries administration divided up about a quarter of the lake into fish conservation zones and made what was left open for access as communal fishing grounds. Local fishers could now engage in small-scale fishing practices and sell whatever was not consumed to the local market. To Hun Sen's credit, this was a much-needed action that by design sought to conserve the lake's fisheries, but it was issued with little guidance. The safeguarding practices of local authorities saw little increase as officials preferred to stay in their air-conditioned district offices rather than patrolling the lake. With the commercial lots removed from the lake, the 2012 monsoon season produced more fish than normal, causing thousands of new local fishermen to descend on the lake and fish deep into the dry season. Fishers were catching more than ever, and photos of catches of rare and endangered species were passed around social media sites. More fish hit the local markets, driving the price of fish to a recent low. While the Tonle Sap's fishing communities were experiencing a short-term boom in income, Hun Sen declared victory over Sam Rainsy's CNRP winning the June 2013 national election by less than 300,000 votes. But the situation on the lake descended into total anarchy, a repeat of early 2001. Fishers used illegal fishing techniques and plundered areas designated for conservation long before authorities could demarcate the zones.

Kampong Khleang is a fishing community located in the Tonle Sap's flooded forest zone about 50 kilometers southeast of Siem Reap. The town sits 3.5 kilometers up a small river from the Tonle Sap's permanent lake and is home to more than 30,000 residents, all whom, with no exception, live in houses raised several meters high off the ground by stilts. I first visited there in January 2014 when there was still plenty of water in the lake's system, not long after the transition point from the monsoon season to the dry season. Traveling down the river by speedboat from a small port 4 kilometers upstream, it was difficult to take bearing of Kampong Khleang's layout because the entire town was submerged in water, the only exception being a dry patch of land where a large Buddhist temple and a handful of stores sat. Most of the long, rectangular homes were made of clapboard, painted dark red, green, or white, and were about 2 meters above the water level. Roofs lined with terra-cotta tile or rusty aluminum zig-zagged horizontally to support the elongated structures. In Kamphong Kleang, most houses are organized with covered back porches facing the river and steep stairways made of thin wooden slats. Rows of potted herbs and flowers lined back porches. Below, small docks moored fishing boats, and pigs, chickens, and vegetables are raised on floating platforms. The river was abuzz with fishing boat traffic, and I noted that some boats were occupied by merchants ferrying around the town by paddle, selling wares such as blankets, foodstuffs, or offering other services. Others paddled their families and friends short distances from house to house for neighborly visits, choosing to save the fuel of their outboard motors. Large patches of water hyacinths clogged the town's canals, and the occasional tree provided shade along the town's periphery. My driver guided the speedboat through an opening between two houses and docked alongside the front of parked alongside a red clapboard home. Behind the riverside houses, I discovered another row of homes some made of clapboard and others of simple thatch.

I was there to visit the family home of Bunseun, a colleague who lived in Siem Reap running ecotours for foreign tourists. I was scouting the home as a potential homestay site and Tonle Sap base for American university students to learn about life on and around the Tonle Sap. After clambering up the stairs, Bunseun's mother greeted me on the front porch with a smile and invited me into her home. Hanging on the front porch wall was a traditional Chinese painting of running horses with the Chinese characters for "Strive for Success" written across the top. I asked if her family was ethnic

Chinese. She replied that she was not but noted her affinity for things related to Chinese culture. Inside, the house was composed of an open room 20 meters long and 6 meters wide with a few divisions in the back that served as bedrooms and storage spaces. Since Kamphong Kleang has no public utilities, a diesel generator supplied electricity to lights in the room and powered a few electronic appliances including a flat screen television and DVD player sitting off to one side. The open back door faced directly opposite the front door to allow cool air to fill the room. On the floor below, she and her husband ran a small convenience store, and she noted that they spent most of their time manning the store and on the front porch. She said the family had hosted groups as many as 30 overnight in the home before and welcomed our group to visit later in the year. Fulfilling my administrative duties, I asked about the home's safety features. She said, "See, none of the floorboards are nailed down, this way we can remove and store them quickly in the rafters above in the event of a major flood."

Four months later at the peak of the dry season, I returned with a group of students to find an entirely different Kampong Khleang. This time instead of jumping on a boat several kilometers upstream, our van drove us to the Buddhist temple in the middle of the town. Since January, the waters had almost entirely receded. The river which divided the town in two was now a muddy stream less than 30 meters across. We crossed a makeshift bridge and made our way in 5 minutes to Bunseun's home dragging our luggage along a dusty road. Previously I had no idea this road existed since it was entirely covered by water a few months prior. None of the stilts supporting the homes was now touching the water. In fact, the backs of the riverside homes were now more than 50 meters away from the narrow river's edge. The houses sat on the sloping riverbank, so I could now see the stilts used to prop up the front of the home were more than 2 meters shorter than those at the back. The boats and platforms previously tied to the back docks were now sitting far away in the river, tethered to the house by long ropes. From the back of each of the houses ran a PVC pipe that took sewage and wastewater into the river. The land underneath the homes was used to store boats, firewood, nets, and traps for fishing. One home caught my eye with thousands of small shoe-box size circular traps bunched together in a pile that took up the entire space under the house. The river, which 4 months previous had plenty of boat traffic, but little congestion since it spanned more than 100 meters in width, now was jammed with fishing boats slowly navigating the waters so that they would not bump into each other. The town's roads were crowded with piles of logs, upturned boats waiting for repair, motorcycles, the occasional automobile, and throngs of children playing jump rope or whatever games were popular in Kampong Khleang. In contrast to the flooded town just 4 months before, I found the differences totally astonishing.

Everyone who is able-bodied in Kampong Khleang fishes out in the lake or performs services that support local fishing. I would regularly take student groups by boat out onto the lake and observe entire families hard at work pulling up nets, sorting fish, or coming home from a long day on the lake. One small boat that particularly stuck out in my memory had two smiling children on it, each less than 4 years old, waving at the boatload of foreigners with their father at the front holding an infant and their mother running the boat's motor and rudder in the back. When the waters are high, boating out into the permanent lake from the center of town takes less than 20 minutes. But in the dry season, the 3 kilometer commute could drag on for more than an hour especially if your boat gets stuck in the shallow waters. This happened to my group and surrounding fishers more than a few times as we ventured into the lake during the dry season. To cut down on the commute time, some of Kampong Khleang's residents move to smaller, temporary homes along the lake to have better access to the fishing grounds. With low water levels, these fishers would otherwise have to commute between 3 to 5 hours each day to reach their fishing grounds and check their nets.

Each time we visited Kampong Khleang over the next 2 years at various time of the year, we would wake at 3:00 in the morning to go check nets in the middle of the lake, arriving just before sunrise. Of the 6 times the groups went fishing at Kampong Khleang, we pulled in an average of about 60 fish across 15 different species. On the last visit in April 2015, we caught the fewest fish but logged 25 species ranging from small silver cyprinids to a snakehead fish 30 centimeters long. Visits in the middle of the dry season yielded fewer fish but offered glimpses of other economic activity going on around the village. Returning from the lake after dawn, farmers were working in fields of cultivated crops which stretched as far as my eye could see from the roof of the boat. These were converted flooded forests and during the monsoon season would be entirely submerged. Our local guide mentioned that the fields produced mung beans, watermelons, and cucumbers or whatever crop was fetching a high seasonal price. One of the students inquired with the guide whether his family also planted crops. He replied that they only fish and that the farmers in these fields are from farther inland and not from Kampong Khleang. Apparently, the itinerant farmers showed up a few years ago to clear the land of trees and began planting crops. Another student asked why the townspeople did not stop them. I could sense the guide interpreted my question as an odd one. He explained how newcomers clearing flooded forest and encroaching on space around Kampong Khleang was commonplace.

On that last visit, I chatted with Sok Panha, a local fisherman in his early fifties who had spent his entire life in Kampong Khleang with exception to the time he joined the Cambodian National Army to fight against the Khmer Rouge. His family tree extended deep into Kampong Khleang's history, noting that while many of Kampong Khleang's residents settled there after the Pol Pot era, his great-grandparents were from Kampong Khleang. I mentioned to him how each time I visited, the townspeople were always busy fishing, and I voiced a concern about the lack of conservation efforts after Hun Sen ended commercial fishing on the lake 3 years ago. "There's no way we can make a living for ourselves using legal methods. All of the fishing you see on the lake is done with illegal nets and traps and to use these methods on the lake, all of the fishermen pay bribes to the local police. If you pay a bribe, you'll get word one day prior to police checks and know to stay away from the lake or hide your illegal nets." He took me down to the land beneath his home and showed me a net spindled neatly into a pile. "This net is more than 1 kilometer long. It's illegal. All of the gear here you see is illegal, and I bought it at a store near the Buddhist temple." He told me that the only way fishers in Kampong Khleang can compete with ethnic Vietnamese fishers living in the middle of the lake is to use illegal traps. "The Vietnamese have an advantage because they live on floating boats and can easily access the good fishing grounds. They have the most resources and can afford to pay the highest bribes. The police just close their eyes to what the Vietnamese do. I'm angry at the Vietnamese and the police. I pay bribes to the police, but they always ask for more money."

My conversation with Panha confirmed that despite the announcement of increased fish conservation efforts on the lake, no one in the town was engaged in such efforts, and no one was stopping locals from overfishing or using illegal nets. He told me,

"We are taking big fish and small fish out of the lake. We don't care what or how much we take. We know we shouldn't do this."

Although in the past, high-value fish like the Mekong Giant Catfish and the Mekong Giant Barb have been preferred catches for their market price and high nutritional value, the Tonle Sap has never been a selective fishery. Fishing gear used around the lake, dominated by large nets and traps, gives evidence to this. Over-fishing in a manner that does not discriminate which species of fish are pulled from the lake, such as that practiced with bag net fishing in the Tonle Sap, not only can impact the total population of fish, but also impact the total diversity of fish species. Large, high-value fish sit at the top of the food web and are typically predatory. Naturally, they are scarce in number when compared to the fish they consume. With indiscriminate net fishing, the population of large and high-value predators is reduced more quickly than lesser value fish ranked lower on the food web.

This kind of fishing is called "fishing down the food web" and eventually results in a total reduction of the spectrum of fish found in the system. With less diversity, the fish population of the Tonle Sap is less resilient and less adaptive to change. By most accounts, fish catches on the Tonle Sap are declining. The largest and most valuable species such as the Giant Mekong Catfish and the Giant Mekong Barb are rarely found these days. Fewer high-value predators mean the total value of the fish catch is also decreasing. Indiscriminate fishing also impacts biodiversity on land. As larger and medium-sized species of fish are removed from the ecosystem, land-based predators such as birds, mammals, and lizards that feed on these fish also lose their food sources.

Reducing fish diversity can actually *increase* the population of particular fish, such as cyprinids, in a system because of a reduction of natural predators. So it is possible that as the population of large predators decreases, fish harvests could increase. But this explosion of fish favors smaller fish with lower nutritional values. Fast-growth species are favored over slow-growth species, and the ecosystem ultimately moves toward a monoculture where culling can overwhelm the now dominant species and wipe out all productivity. Accurate accounts of annual fish harvest are rare in Cambodia, but fishers are reporting an increase in the number of cyprinids caught. Recently *dai* fishers in the Tonle Sap are reporting that up to 50 percent of their catch is composed of cyprinids, marking an increase.[18]

Kevin McAnn from the University of Guelph in Canada led a 2015 study of the impacts of fishing down the food web in the Tonle Sap fisheries. He thinks that as top predators are removed from the system, the ecosystem will lose its "community of stability."[19] Without top predators, the survival of this community is more vulnerable to shocks related to temperature rise such as that brought on by climate change and a change in flows such as that brought on by upstream dams. Overfishing not only poses high risks to the fish population but also to societies like Cambodia's that rely highly on fish as a main source of protein. McAnn's report calls fishing down the food web in the Tonle Sap both a social and ecological problem. In order to support the Tonle Sap's diverse fish population, smart conservation measures are needed immediately.

After Pheakdey and I helped push the rusty flatbed filled with tubs of *prahok* out of the muddy rut at Chhnok Tru, we boarded a speedboat and set out into the Tonle Sap. We traversed the part of the lake where it transitions into the Tonle Sap River, and off to the west I could see the Tonle Sap's famous bottleneck where the lake was less than 2 kilometers wide. Ahead of the boat, the trees of the flooded forests hovered on the horizon like distant oases. Pheakdey and I did not bring hats to protect our skin from the mid-morning sun, so he suggested I cover my head with a *kromma*, a traditional thin scarf knitted of cotton found almost ubiquitously across Cambodia. We were headed for Plov Tuok, a commune formed of six floating villages located near the opposite shore about 20 kilometers down the lake from Chhnok Tru.[20] Plov Tuok's commune chief Teou Sok accompanied us. In 2014, Pheakdey and other conservationists worked alongside local fishers like Sok to set up a fish conservation zone in Plov Tuok. Given the urgent need for stronger conservation measures in the Tonle Sap, I was curious to learn about its progress.

After 40 minutes on the lake, we pulled into one of the floating villages. As on my first visit to Kampong Khleang, I could not find a patch of dry land. Houses, roughly of the similar rectangular design as those in Kampong Khleang but comparatively smaller in size, were all positioned with their front porches facing the lake. Their clapboard walls were painted with a bright blue or green and, all houses had a rusting aluminum roof. The homes were either moored to each other or to tall trees, the bottom 2 meters of which were submerged in the lake. Unlike Kampong Khleang, no stilts supported these homes as they floated entirely on the water. The mobile flexibility provided by the floating homes allowed locals to change locations throughout the year, moving deep into the lake for fishing in the dry season or close to dry land for cash cropping. During the monsoon season, the flooded forest provided protection from winds and waves that menaced the lake during storms. This village had several hundred homes and, as expected, was busy with speedboat traffic. Two young girls no older than 10 wearing school uniforms piloted a small sampan past our boat. They were unaccompanied and dipped a long pole into the bottom of the lake to push their way to school. We pulled up to one of the houses to pick up one of the village's elders named Chuen Chim and buy a container of gasoline from his wife who greeted us with a smile as she fanned herself to keep cool.

Chim, Sok, and Pheakdey wanted to show me Plov Tuok's Ghost Forest, a large patch of old growth forest of local renown located across the way from the floating village. On our way, we passed one of the conservation zone's cement markers poking a high out of the water. "Without our IUCN project, the Ghost Forest would be gone," said Pheakdey as he explained how when the project's efforts began, villagers identified the Ghost Forest as an important cultural area to be protected. Chim pulled the boat into a copse of tall trees and pointed to a long box tucked into the Y of a tree. It was secured by smaller branches. Pheakdey said, "That's a coffin for one of the villagers. In the dry season, they bury their dead here. If someone dies in the wet season, their coffin is stored in the trees until the waters subside." I asked whether other parts of the lake had such intact patches of forest. "You'll still find some places like this around the lake," said Pheakdey, "but forest fire poses threats to the flooded forest, and cash crop farming makes farmers want to convert the flooded forest into farmland." Chim began to talk through a walkie-talkie. Pheakdey continued, "This forest is also an important habitat for monkeys, otters, and other mammals that are hard to find in other parts of the lake." Pointing toward Chim he said, "We should go. Chim is calling the commune council for our meeting."

We circled the boat around the entirety of the Ghost Forest to get a feel for its size and then headed back into the lake passing the other cement boundary marker for the commune's fish conservation zone. The zone protects a pool 9 meters deep in the dry season, apparently the deepest pool in all of the Tonle Sap, and covers an area of about 25 hectares. It is the smallest of the 3 conservation zones set up by IUCN with the participation of local communities since 2014. Pheakdey reminded me of a high value silverfish that we had eaten the previous night and noted that the fish is commonly found in this pool. I asked whether any of the lake's giants were found here, and Sok showed me a digital photo of a Mekong Giant Barb that he caught previously in another part of the lake and released into the pool three weeks earlier. "I've caught and released four Mekong Giant Barb this year," said Sok, obviously proud of his actions. "The water level this year is almost 2 meters higher than normal and with more water, we're likely to find more of these big fish."

It is known far and wide that many species of fish return to Plov Tuok's deep pool during the dry season. When Hun Sen banned commercial fishing lots on the lake in 2012, locals and outsiders descended on the pool to plunder its bounty. In 2013, local fishers told a scouting team from IUCN that they feared most of the fish had been removed from the pool. The IUCN team learned that half of the commune's households lived in poverty. Although all were involved in fishing, they typically only harvested 1 to 2 kilograms of fish per day.[21] Locals also noted that outsiders, half of whom were Vietnamese, fished the pool at night and used circle nets that dipped deep into the pool. Other outsiders used electro-shock to kill or stun fish. The outsiders harvested between 200 and 500 kilograms of fish per night. Some of this would happen in the dry season and deplete endemic stocks of fish.

IUCN suggested setting up the fish conservation zone under the condition that local fishers to self-governed their own conservation efforts. Detractors from the local fisheries authority and the community alike said that with villagers in charge, villagers will be more likely than government officials to take bribes from outsiders and fish stocks would reduce at a faster rate.[22] But these detractors failed to understand the regulatory power of a tight-knit community whose happiness and very survival depended on the conservation of its fishery.

Our boat docked at the commune council hall, a converted house floating in the middle of another of Plov Tuok's villages surrounded by scores of other floating houses homes. I entered another building beside the council hall bedecked by a large white sign bearing the IUCN logo, the starred flag of the European Union which funded the conservation zone. Below it read the title "Plov Tuok Fish and Cultural Forest Conservation Watch Booth." Members of the commune council began to arrive. As it is customary not to wear shoes inside of buildings in Cambodia, they left their shoes on the landing area, and came in to sit in a circle on the floor. Pheakdey distributed water and bananas and thanked the council's 7 members for coming.

From them I learned how Plov Tuok previously was the target of a handful of other programs funded by foreign organizations and governments. For instance, the UN Population Fund set up a program to improve women's affairs, sexual health, and decrease domestic violence. Japan's International Cooperation Agency bought the commune a boat, so children could attend school outside the commune. The UN Development Programme also tried to set up a commune committee for fish conservation in 2008. All of these projects failed. A commune official in his mid-fifties named Sen Try told me, "These programs all lacked engagement with the people in the village. And just focused on physical infra-structure – posters, boats, and other equipment. They focused on issues that villagers thought were not important. Those foreigners just focused on their studies us and then left us. Because of these failures, naturally there was some controversy and reluctance when IUCN showed up."

I asked the group how many times they had seen Pheakdey

over the last 4 years. All erupted in smiles. One commune elder exclaimed, "Many times! Countless. Whenever we have a problem, Pheakdey is here to help us."

Another elder continued, "Before IUCN came to manage the Ghost Forest, the amount of fish just declined from illegal fishing. That was before. But with the conservation zone, there are now many fish in the river. The people are now happy. They have an urge to protect fish. They are happy because the fish are abundant again."

Pheakdey told me, "They feel warm because of what has happened. Our team often meets with them, visits them. It builds their confidence and increases their commitment."

The elder jumped in, "We're not going to back down on this success. If we do nothing, we will not succeed. If we do something, then there will always be obstacles along the way."

To understand those obstacles, I asked whether keeping outsiders from fishing in the conservation zone had an easy start or invoked conflict. He replied, "We were worried at first because we had little help from the fisheries authority and government. But we quickly found patrolling the zone to be easy. When we see people coming in to fish illegally, we advise them once or twice and tell them not to do it. Gradually they started to understand. Some protested and some others gathered their friends and other people to come and threaten those who do the safeguarding. We continued to work with them through teaching them what IUCN has taught us. In the end, they understand."

Sen Try, the commune official, added, "Families here typically fish in the same traditional areas year after year. Once the people understood how conservation worked and saw the mutual benefits, even the outsiders participated."

Another man continued the conversation, "We've never levied a fine on anyone. We detained some people, educated them, and told them not to come back and fish here. We made them sign a contract with us. Those who signed the contract are now afraid to return."

Chim added, "This is our traditional home. We don't want to live anywhere else besides our village. The question comes down to conserving our resources and improving the livelihoods of fishers. When there were fewer fish before, a few people migrated to work in Thailand. But in the end, it turned out they didn't gain much and returned to the village."

I asked why life in Plov Tuok was more desirable than in urban areas. Chim continued, "It's not that it's difficult to live in the city. But there we need 'up front' money. Here we can make a good livelihood through fishing. We only need a small house and a small boat. That's why I often say that we are fishermen, and we have to protect this area. If not we will have to go upstream, and there we will lose the privileges of this area."

Pheakdey noted, "If the fish disappear here, the people will have bare hands for the city." He also noted how many villagers had taken on debt for dry season cash cropping, and recent fish catches were providing supplemental income to help service the debt. "Sustainable financing is also a trouble for the future of the fish protection here in the commune. Our program budget supported the compensation of rangers to patrol the conservation zone, the cost of meetings, and the upkeep of physical infrastructure, but this funding is ending this year." Pheakdey mentioned a temporary solution. The commune council previously agreed to save $5000 of the program budget into a micro-lending agency which promised to pay out a 10 percent return over the next 5 years. "This will be enough to support the zone through that time, but afterward we are not sure how to proceed. Also, what if the microlending agency fails? They are not protected by government guarantees."

As the conversation began to explore worries about the future, I could feel how the exuberance that initially pervaded the group was shifting to slight anxiety. Sok, the commune chief said, "I heard during some workshops I have attended about a plan to build a dam in Sambor. If this is the case, I think a big dam like that will affect the amount of fish even more than overfishing." As discussed previously, with only the Lower Sesan 2 in Cambodia, the fish that come from the Mekong are already affected. Laos and China will build more dams upstream, and this could lead to some serious impacts.

The only woman in the group added, "I've been worried about the dams from the very beginning. If more dams are to be built, I think it will have a tremendous effect on the community. Fish resources will be depleted which in turn will affect our fishery."

Both comments were not unfounded. While I was meeting with the commune council in Plov Tuok, the reservoir behind the Lower Sesan 2 Dam located near Stung Treng at the confluence of the Sesan and Srepok rivers was filling with water in preparation for a January 2018 commissioning.[23] As mentioned previously in this book, the 3S tributary system is a critical spawning ground for fish that live part of their lives in the Tonle Sap, but the dam and its untested fish ladders will severely neuter the ability of fish to find their spawning grounds. Even if a portion of fish make it past the ladders, when their eggs are swept from the headwaters in the monsoon season downstream, they will lose momentum and likely perish in the dam's massive reservoir. Very few if any would make it through the dam's turbines or spillway and then find their way into the lake.

Upstream dams will undoubtedly change the dynamics of water flow and in and out of the lake. China's mega-dams are already having some effect as they release more water during the dry season and store water during the monsoon season. Chinese engineers boast that they are doing the downstream a favor by regulating and reducing floods during the monsoons and provide drought relief during the dry season. But continued regulation of the river, which is compounded by adding more dams to the basin, will have a profound effect on the Tonle Sap's flood cycle. Upstream dams that release water in the dry season raise the river's water level and will prevent less water from draining out of the Tonle Sap. This will increase the amount of water held permanently in the lake. In turn, a portion of the flooded forest will be permanently inundated. But upstream dams will hold back more water in the monsoon season, lowering the river's average monsoon season water level. This will decrease the size of the flood zone and move the boundaries of the flooded forest and flooded grassland closer to the permanent lake. Ultimately, altering the seasonal flooding pattern will not only reduce the size of the flooded forest habitat for fish but it will impact the overall availability of food resources the vegetation that grows in the flooded forests. Moreover, with less floodwaters rushing through the entirety of the Mekong, fewer trees and bushes will be ripped away from the upstream portions of the river and sent into the Tonle Sap. This will result in a major net reduction of nutrients available to the river and lake's food web.[24]

A study carried out by a team of researchers led by water specialist Marko Keskinen on behalf of the Cambodian government, found that if the effects of upstream damming and climate change are considered cumulatively, the dry season water level in the Tonle Sap will rise between 0.5 and 0.9 meters. This could double or almost triple the amount of water in the lake during the dry season. This additional water will increase the lake's permanent area by 18–31 percent. During the monsoon season, the reduction of flood waters into the Tonle Sap would reduce the

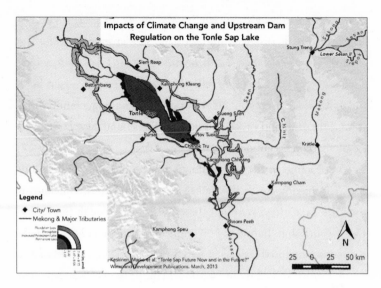

Model of climate change and upstream dam impacts to the Tonle Sap

current floodplain to 75 percent of its current area. Keskinen's modeling found that because of elevation differences, these impacts will affect different areas differently. The northwestern floodplain would experience the greatest reduction of around 77 percent of the floodplain while the more mountainous areas around the lake's bottleneck would have less impact.[25]

Keskinen surprisingly found that the effects of climate change will not have a significant impact on the size of the lake even though climate change is predicted to shorten the monsoon season. However, more intense rains and frequent storms brought on by climate change will, however, have a significant impact on communities. The flooded forests act as buffers to protect inland areas from storms and rough water on the lake. This is one reason why floating communities settle inside the flooded forest, tethering their homes to trees during the monsoon season. With the increase of severe weather events brought on by climate change and a reduction of flooded forest, floating communities and inland zones used for the planting of crops will become more vulnerable.[26] The fishers at Plov Tuok told me they had observed an increase of storms on the lake, and household surveys conducted in 2011 among communities around the lake and inside the flooded forest zone also confirmed the increased perception of weather variability.[27]

A reduction in the size of flooded forest can be modeled, but how will this impact the lake's fish population? So little is known about the lake's food web that these results are difficult to predict. The relationship between how nutrients and energy from the flooded forests and the rich sediments of the Mekong's system make it into the diets of Cambodians is still being explored. Nutrient-rich sediment carried into the Tonle Sap by the monsoons sits at the base of the food web. Plants fix sediments to their roots and extract nutrients. During the dry season, sunlight penetrates through the Tonle Sap Lake and the waters of the Mekong, and this allows permitting algae and other sediment fixing plants to grow. Fish and animals feed on these plants, phytoplankton, tiny microscopic plants suspended in the lake's and river's waters. Raising the level of a river during the dry season, as dams do, will decrease the amount of light that hits the river bottom and decrease plant and phytoplankton production.

Researchers Chouly Ou and Kirk O. Winemiller have discovered nutrient rich organisms found in the lake water such as plankton and algae are the most important for supporting the fish population in the dry season, whereas decomposing vegetation from alongside the lake and in flooded forests is most important during the monsoon season.[28] Without robust sediment flows into the river and lake, these plants will not thrive and thus their nutrients and energies cannot make their way up the food chain.

Importantly, 70 percent of the sediment in the Tonle Sap comes from the Mekong mainstream.[29] Since dams block and remove sediments from downstream stretches of the river, this makes maintaining river connectivity between the Mekong's main channel and the Tonle Sap floodplain extremely important. Sediment removal will not only reduce plant growth in the Mekong system but also lower the survival rate for fish eggs transported to the lake via the mainstream. High sediment loads increase the buoyancy of river water and keep eggs afloat. Without sediment, eggs and other small organisms transported in the river will sink to the bottom and perish.

Dams on the Upper Mekong in China are estimated to trap at least 50 percent of the river's sediment load.[30] Simply put, the mountains of Yunnan and Tibet are less settled, higher, steeper than those in the downstream countries and when it rains more of the mountainsides erode into the Mekong. These mountains are geologically richer in minerals as well. However, none of China's Upper Mekong dams is fit with sediment flushing mechanisms, so most of that sediment has already been removed from the Mekong system. Dams already constructed in the Lower Mekong like the Lower Sesan 2 and the Xayaburi will also have an inexorable impact on sediment flow in the Mekong. The Xayaburi Dam is fitted with state of the art sediment flushing gates, but experts estimate those gates will need to remain open a majority of the time in the monsoon season in order to allow enough sediment pass to come close to mimicking the natural flow of sediment. Sediment gates are opened at the expense of sending water through the dam's turbines. The longer the gates are opened, the less power is produced from the dam. Dam operators will have little incentive to open these gates. Each incremental addition of a dam compounds this problem, and the closer the dam is to the Tonle Sap, the worse the overall effect.

The 2600 megawatt Sambor Dam would be the farthest downstream dam on the Mekong mainstream. If built, it will block nearly 100 percent of the sediment coming from the Mekong upstream and also the 3S river system. To hold back that much sediment and water, engineers estimate the length of the dam to be more than 8 kilometers long. The Sambor Dam is currently listed on Cambodia's power development plan, but the project has many detractors inside and outside of government due to its known risks to the Tonle Sap. If constructed, the Sambor Dam would be the final nail in the Mekong's coffin.

A study produced by the Mekong River Commission in 2010 says that the lake's primary production of nutrients, that is the microscopic animals and plants that form the base of the lake's food chain, will be reduced by 50 percent under a scenario of 11 mainstream dams and a handful of tributary dams. Similar studies suggest that climate change will deliver a rise in lake temperature that will further reduce primary production by 8 percent.[31] How will removing more than half of the lake's basic food chain affect the fish further up the chain? Importantly how will Cambodia replace the loss in fish catch since the lake will produce fewer fish? The answers to these questions remain unknown, but the trend of nutrient loss is playing out as Cambodia's population, rural and urban alike, continues to grow.

As annual fish catches continue to decline, local and international organizations like IUCN are making strides in working with Tonle Sap communities to establish and manage fish conservations zones. Much more work still needs to be done. Moreover, Cambodia's progressively-minded Ministry of Environment has drafted a comprehensive set of environmental laws that will add further protections to the lake. However, it is uncertain whether these new laws, bundled together into an Environmental Code, the first of its kind among Mekong countries, will be passed by Parliament in 2018. The Environmental Code includes new laws to manage resources within more than half of the Tonle Sap's flooded forest. But even if passed, the laws are only effective if they can be enforced, and Cambodia's government agencies are woefully understaffed and underpaid. And the best conservation efforts will be laid to waste if upstream dams wipe out the underlying ecological recipe that produces the lake's fish population.

The Cambodian government is aware that upstream dams in Laos and any built within Cambodia's portion of the Mekong will reduce the yearly fish catch by cutting off important ecological flows such as fish, sediment, and water. To compensate, Cambodia's agricultural ministry is preparing to replace the amount of fish lost partially with farm-raised fish and the rest with protein from soybeans and other livestock. But there is wide variance between scientists and government officials over how much of the annual catch will be depleted by upstream dams. As discussed previously, government agencies tend to undercount the number of fishers engaged in Tonle Sap fishing which undervalues the total fish catch. Undervaluing the fish catch gives Cambodia's government agencies a false sense of confidence in its abilities to offset decreases to wild-caught fish harvests with farm-raised fish and protein derived from other sources. A miscalculation here will deliver a food gap that could result in famine.

Even if Cambodia made a concerted effort to replace most of its annual wild caught fish catch with other protein sources, what kind of infrastructure would be necessary to bring success to such an effort? In a region with decreasing water availability, how much water would need to be diverted from other uses to fill the fish ponds, irrigate soy fields, and provide drinking water for animals?

How much fish and animal feed would be imported or processed inside of Cambodia to feed that livestock? And importantly how much land must be converted to make way for this massive expansion of aquaculture and agriculture? One study carried out by researchers at the Australian National University concluded that in order to replace the protein derived from the Tonle Sap fish catch with farm-grown protein, Cambodia must increase its current agricultural land by up to 63 percent![32] Considering Cambodia's poor track-record on governance and limited access to resources to help achieve this result, the future of the Tonle Sap's fishery looks incredibly dim.

However, if the region shifts away from damming the river past the point of no return and generates electricity from other sources like solar and wind, perhaps the Tonle Sap, the beating heart of the Mekong, will continue to thrive. To achieve such a result, Cambodia's government would need to de-emphasize hydropower production within its borders and build no further dams between the Tonle Sap and the upstream. Also, Cambodia's government would need to convince Laos to build fewer upstream dams. Recently, Hun Sen has signaled the contrary by showing interest in buying more power from Laos. Buying power from Laos could be part of a sustainable way forward, as long as that power is generated from more solar and wind farms and fewer dams that have fewer impacts on the Tonle Sap's natural flood cycle and sediment flow. Such an approach would reduce the tremendous pressure on Cambodia to transition away from eating fresh-caught fish, which comes at a relatively low cost of conservation. The alternative is coping with the high-cost shift of setting aside new land and investing in infrastructure to replace fisheries losses. Doing nothing or miscalculating the protein needs of the country could bring about a food security crisis that shocks regional stability.

1 0

WHITHER THE
MEKONG DELTA

In April 2016 I flew to Can Tho, a large riverside city in the heart of
the Mekong Delta with a population of 1.2 million people located
90 kilometers upstream from where the Mekong meets Vietnam's
East Sea. In the final minutes of my flight, I looked down at one of
the most engineered landscapes on the planet, a flat and fertile agricultural plain crisscrossed with a network of 30,000 kilometers of
rivers and man-made canals. These waterways were carved out of
the land over the last two centuries by engineers from Vietnam and
the invading French and American colonial powers before them.
That spring the Mekong Delta, a piece of land roughly the size
of Denmark or West Virginia, was going through its most severe
drought in 100 years, but the rivers and canals below were all
filled with water. An El Niño weather pattern in the 2015 monsoon
season brought a severe shortage in rainfall, so without the normal
volume of freshwater rushing toward the ocean from upstream,
most of the water around Can Tho that spring was sea water.

I was in Can Tho to participate in a conference promoting
sustainable uses of the Mekong's water resources at Can Tho
University, the delta's first university and home to an active clique
of Mekong scholars and sustainability experts, all of whom vehemently and collectively oppose upstream dams on the Mekong. At
the conference, many of these scholars laid the blame for the delta's

current drought conditions on China's upstream dams located 2500 kilometers away. They claimed that without China's dams, which do hold back massive amounts of water,[1] more freshwater would be available in the dry season which in turn would reduce the levels of salinity intrusion and provide more freshwater for farming in the delta. There was some truth to their accusations, for during any given dry season, about half of the water in the Mekong comes from China. During the first 3 months of 2016's dry season, water releases from China's dams were at an all-time low. Then in mid-March, the Vietnamese government in Hanoi made an official plea to the Chinese government to release water from its upstream Mekong dams. Beijing answered by opening the spillways of the Jinghong Dam for more than 1 month. China's state-run media praised Beijing's actions with statements like, "While China and Vietnam face bitter relations due to the South China Sea dispute, the release of water will surely assuage tensions between the two nations."[2] Both China and Vietnam lay claim to overlapping parts of the South China Sea. Starting in 2014, the two countries were increasingly at odds with each other as the Chinese government had begun a massive campaign to convert atolls and reefs within the overlapping zone into military bases.

On the ground in the Mekong Delta, however, after more than a month of water releases from China, the local scholars attending the conference saw little evidence of relief. Some accused Thailand of pumping massive amounts of water out of the Mekong upstream to irrigate its parched northeast also affected by the drought. Others said the released water just was not enough to make a differ-ence. They all encouraged me to tour around the delta to see the drought conditions for myself. So after the conference concluded, to gain a deeper understanding of this 100 year drought, I jumped in a car with Van Pham Dang Tri, Head of Department of Water

Resources at Can Tho University and Terry Parnell, the director of Open Development Mekong, a regional environmental NGO.

In Vietnam, the Mekong is called the "Nine Dragons River" in reference to how the Mekong divides into 9 channels before its waters reach the ocean. Two major channels, the Hau and Tien, carry the most water after they enter Vietnam from Cambodia and then branch off into 7 other channels on a 200 kilometer run to the sea. In Cambodia, the Hau channel is called the Bassac, which splits off the Mekong mainstream in Phnom Penh. Hau means "back river" in Vietnamese. The Tien channel is the Mekong mainstream and translates to "front river" in Vietnamese. The "front" and "back" orientation makes little sense when looking at an aerial satellite map of the delta, but for the Vietnamese, the Mekong has always been viewed as the backyard of Ho Chi Minh City, formerly known as Saigon. When a traveler leaves Ho Chi Minh City for the delta, he or she comes to the front river first and the back river second.

Terry, Tri, and I drove southward from Can Tho toward the sea on a road running alongside the wide Hau channel of the Mekong. The riverside road was much higher than both the river to our left and farmers' fields to our right. It was built on a natural levee created when the river's annual floods deposited large amounts of sediment close to the riverbank. These natural levees or "garden strips" as they are called in Vietnamese form some of the highest and most fertile ground of the delta. The delta's largest cities such as Can Tho, My Tho, Vinh Long, and Long Xuyen sprung from early settlements on top of these garden strips by Khmer, Chinese, and Vietnamese who settled there. We passed fruit orchards that thrived on the sediments left on these natural levees but were visibly retarded in their growth this season due to the drought. Emerging from an orchard just 10 kilometers south of Can Tho, the road opened into a wide area marked for industrialization. "A few years ago this land was also orchards farmed by locals. Now it's been converted into an investment zone," said Terry. She pointed to a newly constructed paper mill and a thermal coal plant in mid-construction phase. Both were owned by Chinese investors. "This is the best agricultural land in the delta, and it's been auctioned off to foreign investors at the expense the local farmers."

Farther downstream, we made our first stop in Soc Trang province beside barren rice paddies. One year previous almost to the day, I visited this area, so I found a photo on my cell phone of the same location of thriving, green paddies with rice shoots more than a foot high to show Tri and Terry. Now in front of us was a desert of dry fields. Some were tilled in preparation for a season that had yet to come, and others laid unprepared covered with dried, leftover stalks of previous harvests. Far off on the horizon, a fence row of hardy palms trees formed the only living vegetation in sight. Small irrigation ditches filled with green, unmoving water aligned the fields, adding boundary lines to the patchwork. Tri said, "See, there's plenty of water here, but the farmers don't dare to pump it into the fields or open irrigation gates. It's too salty to grow rice. We're in the middle of a drought, but there's water all around us." We walked deeper into the field. The ground cracked beneath our feet. Tri pointed to an area of exposed, orange-yellow soil. At his suggestion, I picked up a handful and noted how it was sandy in its composition and left a dry, yellow stain on my hand. "This soil has a high level of acid-sulfate. It's of a low quality, basically toxic," he said.

"Even in normal conditions, how can this field produce rice if its soil is toxic?" I asked. Tri told me how more than a quarter of the delta's soil is unusable because of high acid sulphate levels. This was because the delta's land was formed only in the past several millennia by the retreat of the last major ice age and the deposition of sediment from the Mekong's flood cycles. Land previously underwater has naturally high levels of toxic acid sulphate.

"However in some parts of the delta, when the heavy rains or the Mekong's floods come, the toxicity will flush away," he added. "Then the soil is usable for agriculture. Another quarter of the delta's land is of this kind, and the field we're looking at fits this description. In times like this with no freshwater, soil quality worsens." The revelation that half of the delta's land had varying levels of toxicity caught me by surprise since my mental map marked the delta as one of the world's most fertile areas. The delta produces more than 40 percent of Vietnam's agricultural output on only twelve percent of the land[3]. And that output not only feeds Vietnam but also is sold to the rest of the world market. The delta produces 25 million tons of rice per year and a majority of that is exported to support food needs in China and Africa. Vietnam's income from rice exports is roughly $7 billion or 2 percent of the country's GDP. Additionally the delta also produces 70 percent of Vietnam's fruit and three-quarters of the country's farm-raised shrimp and fish.

We returned to the car to drive towards the river's outlet to the sea. For the next 30 minutes only dry rice fields occupied the land. We discussed the predicament of farmers who were not able to get effective relief from the drought because Vietnam's government had little resources stockpiled to assist individuals in times such as this. "How do you gather international support for drought relief?" Terry asked, mostly as a rhetorical question. "Droughts creep up slowly. They are not like hurricanes or sudden floods, the pictures of which can capture international attention and drive large amounts of humanitarian aid." She was making an important point that the

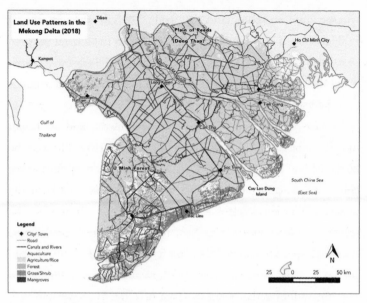

Map of land use patterns in Vietnam's Mekong Delta

2016 Mekong drought lacked international appeal despite the fact that it was affecting most of the delta's 18 million residents.

As we approached the mouth of the Hau river, the pattern of land use changed. Instead of fruit orchards and barren rice fields, we passed by shrimp farms which are noticeable for their shallow ponds. This was the most downstream part of the delta where the marriage of coastal salinity intrusion and the river's freshwater produced brackish water conditions perfect for shrimp farming. Over the last decade, agricultural industrialists and small farmers converted much of the delta's coastal zone into shrimp farms. Like rice, the delta's shrimp is sold all over the world. But unlike rice, some delta shrimp hits high-end markets in Europe and the United States. This high-value product fetches levels of income magnitudes higher than that of a rice farmer, bringing in a collective $5 billion per year for the delta. However, that day most of the shrimp ponds we passed were also bone dry. Tri said, "With the drought, there's just not enough freshwater around to mix with the coastal water to create the right brackish mix. These farmers will likely have to wait a few months until the monsoon season begins to fill their ponds and get operations going again."

The road took a long turn to the southwest, and we began moving along the delta's coastline, away from the river. This was the farthest I had ever been from Can Tho in my years of visiting the delta, and the drought-stricken surroundings made what normally was a lush Garden of Eden into a moonscape. Then ahead of us, the scenery changed once again. Neat rows of vegetables now dotted the landscape. We counted thriving fields of lettuce, cabbage, and cucumbers, and farmers were outside *en masse* tending to their crops – in the middle of the century's worst drought. We made our way down a small driveway toward the home of a farmer stood in the adjacent fields with his two teenage children. The three held on to the same hose as they walked forward in tandem, watering rows of vegetables. To communicate with the farmer, we had to speak loudly because of a noise coming from a loud generator in a nearby shed.

"What are you growing?" I asked.

"This is daikon," said the farmer. "I planted it a month ago."

"The drought had already set in a month ago," remarked Terry to the farmer. "And you still planted a cash crop knowing things could get worse?"

"Sure," said the farmer whose name we learned was Duc, "I don't worry about a lack of freshwater because I have plenty right here on my farm." Terry and I looked around the premises, not finding any irrigation canals. Behind Duc's home was a small boat and a dried-up pond. Duc gave over the hose for his children to manage and motioned us to the shed housing the generator. There he revealed his secret. "Using my boat's engine, I hooked one of the local irrigation pumps up to my well. So now I can use ground-water to water my crops. The drought doesn't hurt me." Millions of other farmers in the delta were facing significant economic losses during the spring 2016 drought, but Duc had found a way to keep himself and his family above board for time being.

After we left Duc's home, we saw that most other farmers in this coastal belt also used groundwater to irrigate their crops. Tri said this short-term solution comes at a long-term cost for the delta. "Intense groundwater extraction is causing the delta to sink or subside at an alarming rate. The need for irrigation has more than doubled in the last decade, and this increases pressure on available water resources," he said. "Most farmers are concerned about their personal livelihood first. They pay attention to which crop they can sell on the market and think about what crops will have a better price next year or in 3 months. They don't think about the next 10 years, what the environment will look like, that's not in their consideration."

With salinity intrusion penetrating deeper into the delta and a growing frequency of droughts, the delta's farmers are bringing up water from underground aquifers. Layers of underground water add buoyancy to the land above them, and when that water is removed, gravity causes the land to sink. The delta is now sinking at a rate of more than 1 centimeter per year. Some areas with the highest instances of groundwater extraction are sinking at a rate of 2.5 centimeters per year.[4] Melting ice caps and glaciers are causing the sea around the delta to rise at about 3 millimeters per year, but land subsidence rates now outpace sea level rise by 3 to 8 times.

Vietnam transitioned to a market-based economy in 1986 with its *Doi Moi* policy. As a result, intensive agriculture cultiva-tion, urbanization, and industrialization have increased pressure on the delta's groundwater resources. Studies show that in the early 1990s, the delta's aquifers were in an undisturbed state.[5] But by 1995, the rate of groundwater extraction was so high that it had already exceeded the aquifer's ability to naturally recharge. *Every day* 2.5 million cubic meters of water are now withdrawn from the delta's aquifers.[6] After 25 years, the delta has sunk 18 centimeters on average. Some hotspots in Soc Trang and Bac Lieu province to its west have sunk more than 30 centimeters. Ho Chi Minh City, which is relatively close to but not in the Mekong Delta has already sunk more than a meter, but this is now stabilizing due to increasing government regulation and treatment of runoff water for public use.

In the past millennia, the delta expanded at a rate of 16 square kilometers or about 3000 football fields per year. Now it is losing 430 football fields every year. As the delta sinks from groundwater extraction, naturally more seawater will penetrate deeper into delta's inland. This, in turn, will increase the need for groundwater extraction. The cycle will continue unabated until people are forced to abandon their land or provincial governments take measures to curb the pumping of water or farmers can gain access to freshwater. The delta has 13 provinces and achieving effective levels of regulation on any delta water management will require significant levels of coordination in a country with a woefully poor coordination track record.

Today the Mekong Delta ranks among the 3 most vulnerable river deltas in the world. The combined impacts of land subsidence and climate change threaten to undo the delta's robust agricultural productivity and centuries of engineering and resettlement policies that have recruited nearly 20 million people here to create Vietnam's farm belt. Farmers in the delta frequently report on climate change phenomena, talking of a shortened monsoon season and a longer dry season which brings higher temperatures. By 2050,

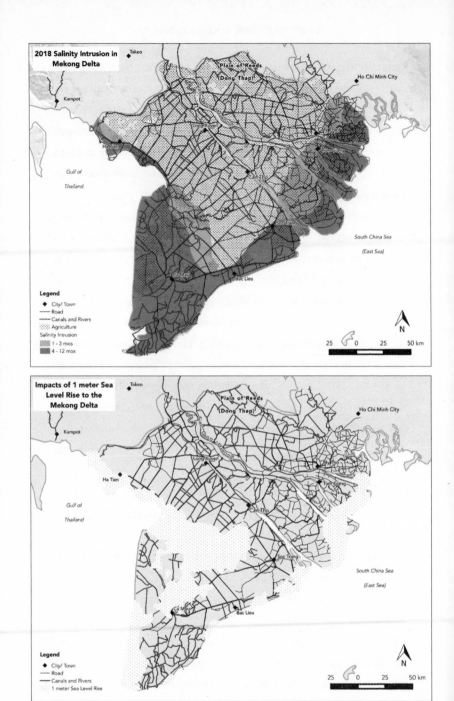

2018 Salinity Intrusion in Mekong Delta

Plain of Reeds
(Dong Thap)

Takeo

Ho Chi Minh City

Kampot

Ha Tien

Long Xuyen

Gulf of
Thailand

Can Tho

South China Sea

(East Sea)

Soc Trang

Cà Mau

Bac Lieu

Legend
◆ City/ Town
— Road
— Canals and Rivers
⋯ Agriculture
Salinity Intrusion
▦ 1 - 3 mos
▦ 4 - 12 mos

25 0 25 50 km

N

Impacts of 1 meter Sea Level Rise to the Mekong Delta

Takeo

Plain of Reeds
(Dong Thap)

Ho Chi Minh City

Kampot

Ha Tien

Long Xuyen

Gulf of
Thailand

Can Tho

South China Sea

(East Sea)

Soc Trang

Cà Mau

Bac Lieu

Legend
◆ City/ Town
— Road
— Canals and Rivers
⋯ 1 meter Sea Level Rise

25 0 25 50 km

N

*Diagrams showing salinity and sea level
intrusion impacts to Vietnam's Mekong Delta*

temperature increases in the delta are estimated to rise 0.8–1.4 degrees Celsius. Some parts of the delta are estimated to achieve a 4 degree increase, and some experts predict that up to almost half of the year will be above 35 degrees.[7] Longer dry seasons also drive the need for groundwater extraction especially in areas closer to the ocean where the surrounding water loses most of its freshwater content.

The delta's average elevation is around 1.5 meters, but its land elevation profile does not descend gradually from Cambodia to the sea. Much of the delta's uppermost provinces of An Giang, Dong Thap, and Long An are well below sea level. During the Mekong's monsoon season, these areas flood and serve as natural reservoirs which store water long into the dry season. In the Plain of Reeds, which spans much of Dong Thap and Long An provinces, tall reeds and wild rice varieties grow to heights of 3 or more meters to stay above the flood level during the monsoon season. Their heights demonstrate the depth of these large inland depressions. Throughout history, this swampy zone acted as a kind of "wet Zomia" giving shelter to pirates, heterodox religious sects, and rebel groups who avoided the expansion of states and colonial powers around them.[8] For example, in 1962, the South Vietnamese Army led by American military advisers were handed its first major defeat in the Plain of Reeds by rebel Viet Cong hiding out there. Moving downstream, the delta's central provinces are higher in elevation, and their garden strips have the best soil for agriculture. The lower, coastal provinces are most affected by salinity intrusion and most affected by drought.

If climate change activism at the global level cannot slow the rate of sea level rise and local policy cannot put an end to groundwater extraction, much of the delta could be underwater by the end of the century. Climate change experts are predicting a

30 centimeter rise by 2050 without consideration to effects of land subsidence. At this rate of sea level rise, which could come well before 2050 when accounting for groundwater extraction, the Asian Development Bank believes impacts will still be moderate and manageable. Some low-lying roads will need to be raised, and farmers whose land is inundated or too saline will have to move into other industries. With a 50 centimeter rise, things start to get difficult. Cities, towns, and industrial zones will need to be raised or completely surrounded by dykes. Currently, to fend off the encroaching sea, Vietnam's government plans to add 450 kilometers of sea dykes, 1290 kilometers of river dykes, and an additional 7000 kilometers of canal embankments to its existing battery of 7000 kilometers of raised embankments along rivers and canals.[9] The cost of maintaining these dykes will increase as tidal pulses and intense flooding press harder against them and work to undercut their foundations. At 50 centimeters rise, the loss of land from inundation and erosion will cripple the delta's economy, massively decreasing the annual production of rice, shrimp, crabs, and fruit. Much of the dry season crop will fail from salinity intrusion. The Asian Development Bank predicts a 20 percent reduction of economic productivity.[10] Beyond this is difficult to say – some suggest a 1 meter rise by the end of the century, and if that happens, the delta will likely lose about half of its land.

Ky Quang Vinh is the recently retired director of Can Tho's Climate Change Coordination Office. He has tracked the impacts of climate change in the Mekong Delta for the last 15 years. Vinh first observed a gradual increase in temperatures when observing the delta's meteorological charts and alerted local officials of the need to understand how climate change could impact the delta. In 2007 he made a funding appeal to the Rockefeller Foundation to establish the country's first climate change coordination office. "At first, Vietnam's government didn't think my observations suggested any major problem. Officials said it was unnecessary to do anything radical. They thought this was just a way to get support from foreign governments and organizations," he said. "Then in 2010, we had an 80 year drought followed by record floods. I continued to collect temperature statistics. In 2014, we recorded the hottest year of the earth in history. And then in 2015 and 2016, we had a 100 year drought. Now officials are very well aware that these effects are real, but our response might be too little, too late." Scientists predict what previously were labeled as 100 year drought and flood events will now occur every 15 to 40 years; 20 year events will now occur every 5 to 10.[11] The cumulative effect of these sudden extreme weather events could have a greater impact than the slow onset of sea level rise.

The Paris Agreement signed in 2015 by 196 countries is oriented to keep global temperatures well below a 2 degree (Celsius) rise compared to pre-industrial levels. Vietnam is a signatory country. Vinh believes that if a 2 degree rise happens, most of the Mekong Delta is likely to disappear. "Even if we keep temperature levels within a rise of 1.5 degrees, the most ambitious target of the Paris Agreement, I think we will have two scenarios play out in the delta. One, if we do nothing different from how we currently manage the delta, it will be broken into islands because of land subsidence, upstream hydropower impacts, and climate change effects. But if we can shift course and apply a smart water management system, the Mekong Delta will still be alive." I noted some hesitance in Vinh's voice. "But making this transition will be difficult. The current approach is tooled to protect agricultural yields, so this means keeping flood waters off the lands and preventing salinity intrusion during droughts. What we should be doing is finding ways to store water during the monsoon season so that water could be used in the dry season," said Vinh. He mentioned how the below-sea-level-areas upstream in An Giang, Dong Thap, and Long An provinces are now entirely encircled by dykes to prevent flooding, so farmers could grow up to 3 yields of rice per year. Most of the natural storage capacity of the Plain of Reeds is gone. "This is a big problem for us. When the monsoon season comes, instead of naturally storing water upstream, the waters rush downstream into the sea more intensely than ever before. Today we lose too much of our freshwater too fast. It's such a waste."

Parts of downtown Can Tho now flood during the daily high tides in autumn of every year. When the monsoon floods, the speeds and heights of which are increased because of too many dykes upstream, meet the high tide pulse at Can Tho in the middle of the delta, parts of the city flood for 4 to 5 hours each day. The city's low-lying areas, where the poorest people live, are those most affected by these daily floods. In October 2015, I walked through one of these neighborhoods behind Can Tho University with one of Vinh's colleagues and saw how some of the wealthier residents built structures around their homes or raised their foundations to keep water out. This only pushed more water into the surrounding homes whose owners could not afford such preventative measures. Matters were made worse when a national road was built without ample drainage pipes on the northern periphery of the neighbor-hood. This made the daily floods, which exceeded levels higher than 1 meter in some areas, stick around even longer. In urban Can Tho, the costs of being poor are high.

As I wrapped up my conversation with Vinh, he noted that the current approach to coping with climate change impacts relies too much on construction and engineering projects. "The current strategy is not working well to manage crises like floods and droughts. We really lack an integrated vision for making communities more resilient to climate change hence the problems like intense groundwater extraction."

Early Chinese historians and cartographers who visited the Mekong Delta area in the third century called it the Funan Kingdom. Specifically which ethnic grouping comprised the population of Funan is unknown, but most evidence points to these people as related to the modern Khmer people. Today the Khmer ethnicity makes up about one-tenth of the delta's population. And Cambodian politicians still make irredentist claims to the Mekong Delta, citing it as part of the former Khmer Empire. Over the centuries, many Chinese fled collapsing Chinese empires in droves to set up enclaves throughout coastal and maritime Southeast Asia.[12] In the 18th century these Chinese immigrants gained concessions from Vietnam's Nguyen Dynasty located at Hue to establish and oversee city-states in the delta such as My Tho and Saigon.[13] At this time the delta was seen as a wild frontier unable to be tamed by the expanding southern Vietnamese Empire. The delta's swamps, coastal zones, and few mountainous areas were the hideouts of menacing pirates and bandits. Rooting out these "unruly" populations was a shared challenge of whichever state showed up, be it the Vietnamese, French, or American, to "civilize" the delta.

In 1859, the French invaded Saigon and established the colony of Cochinchina to serve as the key administrative center of its ostensible mission to civilize Indochina. In reality, the French chose Saigon due to its proximity to the mouth of the Mekong, believing the Mekong could provide a backdoor entrance to the markets and resources of China. Early on, the French were so bogged down by wet terrain and Vietnamese military pushback that their hold on Saigon did not expand for several years. The French gradually expanded its *mission civilisatrice* into the delta area as a way to generate agricultural crops such as rubber, cotton, and rice to feed into bourgeoning Indochinese colonies. First the French had to clear land in the delta and pacify or co-opt local resistance. But in the early decades of French occupation, much of the delta was off limits for growing crops and thus proved a challenge for settlement. The soil around the delta's coastline was too saline for farming, and inland areas of the west coast had deep forests and impenetrable wetlands. To illustrate just how difficult the terrain was, the Ca Mau peninsula on the delta's southwest corner is named from a Khmer word that translates to "black water" in reference to the peat-filled waters that pervade this area.[14]

Since many parts of the delta couldn't be converted into areas suitable for French-led farming and resettlement programs, the local Vietnamese resistance retreated away from French-built canals and settlements to live off the delta's robust endowment of natural resources. Here they carried out traditional ways of cultivating the land, using the forests and swamps as a place to hunt and gather food and other valuable non-timber forest products. These efforts, combined with those of the Khmer and Chinese that lived there centuries and millennia before the Vietnamese, resulted in the cultivation techniques of 500 different rice varieties. The Vietnamese resistance used these impenetrable zones to launch counterattacks and antagonize the French invaders. This pattern continued well after the 1954 French defeat in Vietnam and into the American war. The delta's rich cultural history contains the songs and stories of the rebels, pirates, and religious leaders that drove out these foreign invaders.

The first French maps of the delta envisioned a system of canals, waterways, and telegraph lines to link administrative centers in the delta to Saigon for the purpose of control and pacification of the local population.[15] The French sought to build canals for brown-water gunboat patrols and also to conduct commercial activities with Chinese merchants who acted as middlemen in the delta's expanding agricultural networks. At the turn of the century, the French, who were at the global forefront of engineering, science, and architecture, saw their colony in southern Vietnam as the perfect zone to marry these technological advances with its civilizing mission. The delta presented a blank slate for the building of large agricultural estates, schools, hospitals, and other public works. French engineers needed to move land to create dykes and irrigation dams to prevent floods and divert water for agricultural purposes. Where it cost too much to hire or train local laborers, imported steam dredgers could dig new canals and deepen and widen former ones. Steel girders coming from Gustav Eiffel's factories in France supported numerous bridges and a new railway from Saigon to My Tho.[16] These innovations lifted wheeled transport high above the swamps and greatly increased the pace of commerce and colonial penetration into the delta. Where bridges could not reach across the wide expanses of the Mekong's major channels, imported steamboats could solve the problem. The once-wild delta was becoming harnessed under the yoke of French engineers.

This injection of modern technology and water and land use management techniques facilitated new population flows of Vietnamese and Europeans into the delta. By the turn of the century, most settlements throughout the delta were occupied by colonial administrators and the French Legion which recruited soldiers from French colonies around the globe. Tourist groups from Europe arrived on a daily basis. The roots of Vietnam's current agricultural approaches to the delta formed when the French introduced irrigation pumps and sluice gates to control water flow in the early 1900s. This opened more land for agricultural settlement and motivated the conditions for hundreds of thousands and then millions later in the 20th century to come from the central and northern parts of Vietnam to work on agricultural plantations. Sales taxes on agricultural goods and revenue gained from taxing opium consumption paid for the costs of these public works.

The new machines and their capabilities were so powerful that they took politics out of the process.[17] No one could resist, no one could deny that this was not the wave of the future. Nor could anyone foresee the short-term and long-term problems the application of foreign technology on such a dynamic ecological landscape would deliver. To ensure the delta's agricultural jugger-naut could move ahead, the French administration kept the iron dredges working 19 hours a day and pumped untold amounts of financial resources into maintaining the delta. But the machines were constantly breaking down and in need of repair with parts from Europe. Many would sit idle for months as they waited for maintenance. Water and nature itself were seen by the French as a menace, something to be tamed and controlled. Colonial engineers wanted to eliminate the ebb and flow of the delta – the impact of floods and tides – and create static waterways because nature threatened the French investment in public works.[18]

Because the French could not keep dredges maintained and had a poor understanding of the delta's ecological forces, new canals often silted up shortly after completion. Sometimes floods wrecked areas on one side of a canal because the canal's levee blocked the natural flow of floodwaters. More resources were constantly being plowed into maintaining canals and waterways. In his excellent environmental history of the Mekong Delta, *Quagmire*, David Biggs, an academic at University of California, Riverside, describes this perpetual cycle of investment and upkeep as a "Penelope problem" in reference to the wife of Odysseus in Homer's *Odyssey* who dutifully awaits her husband's return and fends off potential suitors by unravelling a robe every night only to begin weaving it again the next day.[19] The French engineers, like Penelope, gained great benefit from keeping their unending cycle of creation and destruction going.

By 1929, the French cleared 2.4 million hectares for culti-vated land, about two-thirds the amount of arable land in today's delta. They also created 1500 kilometers of navigable waterways and 3500 kilometers of secondary canals.[20] By that time, most of the delta's primary forests were gone and with them disap-peared an incredible bounty of fauna – the panthers, crocodiles, and elephants, and other large animals – that were once found throughout the delta. When the Great Depression hit, the global demand for rice exports bottomed out, and much of the delta was abandoned. Without anyone to manage the complex system of sluice gates and canals, the monsoons caused unpredictable floods because water sloshed around to parts of the delta never penetrated by canals before. Agricultural productivity declined and systemic breakdown of the delta into the Second World War period contrib-uted to a famine in northern Vietnam. An estimated 2 million people perished.[21] All the while the delta harbored Vietnamese nationalists who chipped away at the French hold on the south through raids and guerrilla tactics encouraged by an ascendant Ho Chi Minh and his army in the north.

In 1954, the French army suffered a complete and utter loss at Diem Bien Phu in Vietnam's northwestern corner to Ho Chi Minh's national army, the Viet Minh. A peace treaty signed at the 1954 Geneva Conference divided the country into a northern half administered by Ho Chi Minh who was popular throughout the country and a southern half administered by a new southern government backed by the Americans and the French. The treaty promised national elections which would eventually lead to reunification in 1956. American advisers plotted to ensure the national elections would never happen because their newly installed president of the southern Republic of Vietnam, Ngo Dinh Diem would surely lose to Ho Chi Minh. A few years earlier, the US began to pay for the French war in Vietnam providing more than $70 million per year in support. The Truman administration and later the Eisenhower administration saw Vietnam as a critical domino in the expansion of global communism. The US government began to plow more resources into propping up anti-Communist governments in Vietnam and the Mekong region at large.

American engineers and some remaining French engineers now regained control of managing land and water in the delta. Millions of Vietnamese, many of them Catholics, were resettled to the delta from the Red River Delta near Hanoi after the 1954 division between the north and south. To underpin the success of the newly formed Vietnamese state in the south, the Mekong Delta once again was prioritized for agricultural production. This time around, the close historical memory of floods and famine from the Great Depression through the Second World War inspired the American engineers to look upstream and envision a grand design to harness floods and reduce droughts by building large dams in Laos and Cambodia. Arguably, this mid-20th century vision, discussed in greater detail in Chapter 7, set the entire basin on the path of ecological destruction that it faces today.

The American War in Vietnam lasted from 1955 to 1975 and during this time the French pattern of canalization, resettlement, and pacification intensified in the delta. To root rebel Viet Cong out of the jungles and swamps, the US brought its water engineering apparatus to expand and build more canals. Americans also used toxic defoliants such as dioxin, infamously known as Agent Orange, on these landscapes to clear the trees of leaves and land of vegetation, so no one could hide there. The legacy from this debilitating strategy still produces disabling birth defects among portions of the delta's population and throughout the rest of Vietnam today. Some of the war's fiercest battles were fought in the delta and much of the ground won by the Americans during the day was retaken as night fell by the Viet Cong who moved swiftly through the delta's waterways and gained much loyalty from the people in the delta.

In parts of the delta that the Americans pacified, they introduced innovations of the Green Revolution. This moved the delta's farmers and planners away from traditional agricultural practices toward the use of chemical fertilizers, pesticides, tractors, and industrial farming methods to produce increasingly higher yields.[22] American salesmen brought in Kohler speedboat engines which the locals converted into pumps to provide water to their farms during the dry season. By 1974 a Dutch study estimated that the 1 million pumps in operation held influence over the direction and movement of water in the delta.[23] Despite the prevalence of conflict, toward the mid-1970s, the delta emerged as a standard bearer for agricultural production in Southeast Asia.

The American War ended in 1975 when North Vietnamese troops occupied Saigon. Vietnam was finally unified and independent after more than a century of foreign occupation. In the US, veterans and their families continue to mourn the 58,000 soldiers killed in a failed conflict marked by the folly and hubris of American presidents and defense policy planners. But in Vietnam the war took a much greater toll, killing more than 3.5 million Vietnamese soldiers and civilians on both the north and south sides.[24] The conflict set the country's economic development back nearly half a century. The legacy of war and the memory of famine created deep insecurities within the Vietnamese leadership. After the war, to help unify the country, Vietnamese planners shunned the market-based agricultural practices of former South Vietnam and transferred highly centralized methods of agricultural production from the Red River Delta in the north to the Mekong Delta in the south. Similar to planned economy experiments in agriculture worldwide, Vietnam's efforts produced zero results through the next decade. In 1988, less than 2 years after the government introduced a market-based transition, more than 3 million Vietnamese were once again on the brink of famine.

Nguyen Huu Thien, a conservation biologist and sustainable development expert, attributes the fate of the delta to the legacies of the American War and Hanoi's subsequent designation of the delta as a zone prioritized for food security. "Somehow the delta was responsible for providing food from the beginning of historical memory. In the early 1990s the government set up the 'Rice First Policy', a plan to set aside 1.8 million hectares of land for rice production." Thien, who was born in 1968, remembers the delta as having a highly functioning ecology. The war had little effect on his hometown, a village just a few kilometers outside of Can Tho. "I was a real farmer. I knew everything about farming in a village and catching fish from the surrounding rivers. I still have vivid memories of those days," he said. "I remember how the natural system worked – how the delta was. In the old days, we ate wild vegetables collected from fields and riversides. We had clean rivers, and everybody took a bath in the river. Now nobody dares to bathe in the water anymore. The water now drains from the fields polluted with pesticides, and you itch."

Thien spent the early 1990s earning a graduate degree from the University of Wisconsin. When he returned to Vietnam, he saw the delta's ecology take a turn for the worse as the rice-first policy took hold. At first, settlers cleared land for rice production, and then once land was cleared, top-down directives demanded the intensification of production. Yield targets grew, and more engineering infrastructure in the form of sluice gates and irrigation pumps was built into the land. Foreign assistance programs paid for these investments. "The mentality was like the man hiking through the snow in Jack London's 'To Build a Fire.' After 1975 we were starving. We had a food shortage. So the delta became the food production center for all of Vietnam, regardless of the costs," he said.

Annual rice production targets rose, and meeting those targets paved political pathways for provincial governors and officials. Some farmers in An Giang and Dong Thap started to build high dykes around their fields so they could plant a second and third crop of rice each year. Rice harvests in the delta rose from just 5 million tons per year in 1986 to more than 25 million tons in 2017.[25] By 2000, rice production stabilized, and Vietnam began to export its bumper crop of rice. Some farmers began to explore diversification into higher value crops, but rice remained king. A mania of producing a third crop of rice spread throughout the delta.

"When villagers in Dong Thap saw how their neighbors built dykes and made some profit, they asked the local government for money to build their own dykes. Since increasing rice yields help local officials meet economic development targets, the local government responded, and now the province has 130,000 hectares surrounded by small dykes. The state budget paid for the cost of dykes which was never internalized into the production costs of rice," said Thien. With more levees, the dry ground on the other side is believed to be safer, and thus more development in the form of housing, agriculture and industrial investment are drawn to these "safe zones." Thien continued, "The fish gradually disappeared, and the people blamed overfishing and climate change, and then water quality started to degrade. Now once you're inside the high dykes, you're in there with five hundred other households. You build your house low, beneath the level of the river, and you bury your ancestors on the low ground.[26] Even though profits are falling, no one will agree to let river water back into the fields because it would mean an instant flood for you. So you're trapped."

Building dykes is seen by many in the delta as a way to increase productivity. After all, more rice is coming out of the same plot of land. Today achieving that third crop of rice is resulting in increasingly smaller gains for farmers. To produce a third rice crop, farmers typically reduce the yield of the first and second crops so fewer nutrients are removed from the soil. They then end up paying a lot for fertilizer, the price of which is increasing, since outsized demand means fertilizer must be imported from abroad. Sediments that could replenish the land from floodwaters, never reach the land inside the dykes.[27] Without the annual floodwaters, this stagnant system increases the likelihood of disease and provides no opportunity to flush the toxicity out of soil with high levels of acid sulphate. In 2010 more than a quarter of the delta's residents were getting water from canals and rivers contaminated by human and animal waste.

As soil quality decreases year on year inside the dykes, rice yields continue to fall. Rice productivity in fields outside of dykes, those that are irrigated by floods, remains stable. Falling yields and the increased costs of fertilizers and pesticides translates into lower income levels for the delta's rice farmers. Incomes in the Mekong Delta are now 10 percent lower than the rest of the country. In 1999 the average delta income was 10 percent higher than the national average. A few years ago Thien conducted a situation analysis on triple rice cropping. He discovered that 10 years previous, a family of 5 in Dong Thap province could live off of 1 hectare of land producing 2 crops of rice per year. Today, the same family on the same hectare of land producing 3 crops of rice has no other choice but to migrate and find wage labor in urban areas. The cost of farming and associated living costs are simply too high.

Triple rice cropping has caused a chain reaction where provinces build more levees downstream to prevent flooding that would typically occur upstream if the high dykes were not constructed there. Most urban areas in the delta are already surrounded by high ring dykes to prevent flooding. Because of the importance of An Giang province and the Plain of Reeds to rice production, Vietnamese engineers now plan to encircle the entirety of this area to prevent extreme flooding as climate change promises to deliver higher peak floods. Just a few years ago, this part of the delta was originally zoned as a partially protected area to allow for floods to replenish the land and recharge aquifers close to the surface. Thien also claims the ecological costs of excessive dyking and triple rice cropping outweigh any benefits. "Now the whole delta is compartmentalized by dykes, and the rivers act merely as gutters. With the exception of the Hau and Tien channels, most other rivers are entirely imprisoned by their banks for much of their course to the sea. The water and the floodplains are not connected anymore so they are robbed of sediment deposits."

In 2017, the Mekong River Commission calculated annual costs (damage) of flooding in the delta to be between $60–70 million dollars and the benefits of natural floods between $8–10 billion![28] Sediment delivered by the river's annual floods is the basic building block of the Mekong Delta. Without it, the delta's land begins to fall apart under natural conditions, and with intense groundwater extraction and sea level rise, the situation quickly worsens. Sediment flow to the delta is also really important for the maintenance of river banks and coastal areas. When the speed of water slows as the river approaches the sea, the heaviest sediments are deposited along river banks and coastal estuary areas, building up the integrity of the land mass. For the past 3000 years, the Mekong carried about 150 million tons of sediment in its system to the delta each year. Chapter 2 of this book discussed how China's dams on the Upper Mekong hold back more than half of all the sediment in the Mekong system.[29] But dams do not treat all particles of sediment equally. They trap the heavier sediments, those which act as the delta's building blocks, and allow the finer particles of sediment to pass through. Since the finer sediments tend to be suspended all the way out into the ocean, a 50 percent reduction in sediment load will have a greater than 50 percent reduction in what is deposited on the delta's plain.[30] If all 11 dams on the Mekong mainstream are built, along with a handful of tributary dams, 96 percent of the Mekong's sediment will be trapped behind reservoir walls.[31]

The previous chapter on the Tonle Sap explained how the removal of sediment from the Mekong's flow decreases the total fish population in the Mekong ecosystem. Sediment removal also creates a situation known to hydrologists as "hungry water" which induces erosion in the river's bed and along its banks. To illustrate the hungry water phenomenon, imagine the river in a state of harmony with a normal sediment load suspended in its stream. By removing a portion of that sediment, the harmony is upset, so the river will seek to restore balance by robbing soil from banks and cutting deeper into the riverbed. With a deeper riverbed, the level of the river lowers. This decreases the frequency and height of floods which are important for the health of the delta and the Tonle Sap's ecosystem. Dams already regulate water flow which lowers the river's level during the monsoon seasons, so with the added removal of sediment, dams deliver a double whammy against promoting connectivity across the delta's floodplains.

Hungry rivers induce riverbank erosion which pulls riverside structures into the river and rips away vegetation that would otherwise hold a riverbank together. As an avid researcher of Mekong issues, I am a regular reader of newspapers from Cambodia and Vietnam. By far the stories most frequently reported in these newspapers is the loss of property – homes, livestock, farm equipment – from riverbank erosion. By the end of 2017, 1200 families were already relocated in the delta, and the Vietnamese government estimates more than 500,000 people will need to be moved away from landslide zones in the coming years.[32]

Thien believes the experience so far is defined by aggressive intervention into nature. "Now that kind of intervention is coming back to haunt us with erosion, land subsidence from groundwater extraction, and a depletion of our natural resources. There's been a lag time of about 20 to 25 years for people to wake up and realize that there's a major problem here," he said. "Now with dams going up and sand mining happening all over the place, people are talking about the important role of sediment, but before, we took it for granted that the soil of the delta would be fertile forever."

Sand mining also threatens the delta's integrity. People throughout the Mekong Basin should value sediment for its incredible contribution to supporting life throughout the Mekong's ecosystem, but in the last decade, river sand has gained value as a commodity used to meet the demands of Southeast Asia's construction boom. Between 2000–2016 Cambodia sold 80 million tons of sand to Singapore, despite a ban on sand exports since 2009. The value of that export was significant at $778 million. High-quality sand, such as that found in the Mekong Delta is becoming scarce as the region uses more sand to form the foundations of large urban areas and raised road networks. Sand miners can receive between $5–10 a ton, and prices continue to rise, making the business a very lucrative venture. In 2016 Vietnamese police caught more than three thousand people dredging sand without permits or in protected areas. In Vietnam, sand miners can earn well over $10,000 per year – nearly 50 times the national average.[33]

Conservative estimates suggest the rate of sand removal from the Mekong is 50 million tons per year. These numbers are based on sales from sand to other countries which are logged into a global commodities tracking system. No one really knows how much sand is used for construction and infrastructure projects inside of countries like Laos, Thailand, Cambodia, and Vietnam. Cambodia and Vietnam have both banned the export of sand, but mining for domestic use continues unabated. Sites in Laos and Thailand individually extract less from the river, but they are greater in number and entirely unregulated. In Vietnam each provincial department of environmental resources will issue licenses for sand mining within their respective jurisdictions. Thien suggests this is done with zero consideration of downstream impacts. "They think simply that erosion will only take place where you extract the sand. They ignore the fact that the river is one system, that when you take sand out at one place, the whole system, including the coast, is imbalanced," commented Thien.

"You can see from all of this unregulated and uncoordinated upstream activity that we really need a regional vision for development, but here in Vietnam a delta-wide vision is needed as well," said Thien. "At the outset, we needed an overarching body to set the development vision for the delta. Unfortunately, that role was left to the engineers who only saw three things: rice production, freshwater management, and the uses of land," he said. "It seems as if the coastal water belonged to someone else – it's not in their vision. They don't see brackish water and saline water as resources.

From their perspective, salinity intrusion is anathema for the delta. So they build whatever infrastructure to keep freshwater for rice production." He also mentioned how it is common for engineers to benefit personally from the projects they design and manage. "The engineers think this way because they are taught that humans are superior. They are led to believe in having the technology which can change nature and make nature serve us. What they want is so narrow. They do not respect the rules of nature and do not cherish the variety of the delta's resources. What they want is more rice, and more rice will make us richer. That's the logic."

Engineers in Vietnam argue that the boundary between freshwater and saline water needs to be controlled by dykes and sluice gates, otherwise it will fluctuate and cause damages to freshwater agriculture inside.   But engineers and even most development partner governments, who assist the Vietnamese government with planning processes, exclude the contribution of coastal water to the delta's dynamic ecosystem. This means wild capture fisheries, which total between 500,000 and 730,000 tons per year in the delta are at risk since sluice gates prevent fish from entering critical habitats – and when the sluice gates are opened, pollutants from intense rice and shrimp farming is released into the coastal zone.

Promoting connectivity is a way to think about maintaining and conserving the complexity of the Mekong Delta's ecosystem. Chapter 9 discussed the importance of keeping the length of the river connected so that the river's abundant fish population can reproduce and find habitats to mature and so sediment can be delivered alongside those fish to support their growth. Another way to consider connectivity is to look across the land laterally and consider how floods that run across the land are necessary for flushing the acidity out of the soil, for depositing sediment to replenish soil and nutrients lost during the previous year. Without this lateral connectivity, the delta's soil quality worsens, and there is less of it, so the ground level lowers relative to the level of the river and ocean. Finally, a third dimension of connectivity is that between the river and the aquifers that store groundwater as a kind of vertical connectivity.[34]

Built structures like dykes, sluice gates, and dams ruin this three-dimensional connectivity. They also cost a lot to build and maintain. After the 2016 drought, Vietnam's national government began to talk of the drought conditions as a new normal, and the delta's engineers responded with plans for $150 million worth of additional built structures farther upstream and deeper into the delta. "We told them the 2016 El Niño drought was an extreme event," said Thien, referring to the advocacy he conducts with ministries in Hanoi. "It might happen more frequently, but it won't happen every year." Thien noted that the political rhetoric of food security still trumps most arguments. "We're told the delta is now responsible for food security for Vietnam. During the 2016 drought, we still exported almost 5 million tons of rice. If we're doing that, then there is no food security issue here. Every year we produce 25 million tons of rice, and we export more than half of it. Forty five percent of the export goes to China. So that's not food security. Food security needs to be long-term, and you don't have to be responsible for the rest of the world. Nobody asked you to be responsible for *their* food security, and nobody thanked you for that."

I asked Thien how he drives change toward more appropriate solutions to challenges in the delta. "You have to test limits and be constructive when you deliver messages to government officials," he said. "There was not much room for discussion before, but the space is opening. The key is to translate hard-core science into easy to understand messages – and to be persistent. It could take years for the public and decision-makers to understand an issue."

"Can you tell me an approach that worked?" I asked.

"Ten years ago it was taboo to be critical of triple rice cropping. Nobody would listen. We first talked about smaller issues and built an argument against triple rice cropping. The media began to take on an important role when we started taking reporters out for 5 day tours to different parts of the delta. We showed them how the natural system of the delta works. We'd ask the reporters to look for issues on the ground and ask them to write 10 articles about what they saw. We did that twice a year, and now many journalists are well informed about the delta," he said. Vietnam's news agencies, although controlled by state censors, are known to be an effective force for disseminating information about environmental impacts throughout the country. "Before, everyone would talk about sea level rise as the biggest threat, as if the delta would be inundated tomorrow. Now you rarely see that any more. You tell them to calm down, if anything it's 100 years from now, and it's a gradual process. And the worst scenario is not the most likely scenario. What we need to worry about is how fast the delta is sinking and destroying our rivers because of chemicals, because of stagnant waters. This is all because the food security concept has been abused for so long," said Thien.

"We have reached a point that the delta is in danger. You have to change it, otherwise we will lose the whole thing," warned Thien. If he could set priorities, Thien would put rice in the number three spot. "First, we should prioritize maximizing economic value coming out of a unit of land, not maximizing the yield of a crop. And choose the crops or fish or shrimp that best fit that unit of land. Second, we need to improve the quality of our products and move up the value chain," he said. Previously Thien told me how wealthy families in the delta now choose to import rice from Cambodia because the quality of delta rice is so low. "Third, we should continue to produce some rice, but move away from multiple crops of rice per year. Increasing income for individual farmers should matter, but now people are talking about high technology and applying advanced agricultural techniques like what is being done in Israel, but this is not realistic for the delta. You have to learn to walk before you run," he concluded.

I asked Thien whether it is too late to transition away from rice. "It will not be easy. People have become passive. They've lived inside the system for too long. But now Hanoi could be taking things in the right direction with Resolution 120 which is calling for respecting the rules of nature." Thien referred to a recent pronouncement from Vietnam's Prime Minister Nguyen Xuan Phuc that looks to transition the delta away from being the world's rice basket through promoting high-quality agriculture and flexible patterns of land use. "With Resolution 120, we are now setting the right strategic direction. The captain has agreed to shift course of the massive ship. But it is too big to move. It will take 10 years to get this ship on course, and there are vested interest groups who will put up a tough fight along the way."

At the end of November 2017, I took a day trip to Cuu Lao Dung, an island at the end of the Mekong's Hau channel. I traveled there from Can Tho on the back of a motorbike driven by Nguyen Minh Quang, an assistant professor and conservationist in his early thirties from Can Tho University's Faculty of Education. A few days earlier, I asked Quang to take me to a part of the delta where people were moving away from rice and adjusting to a livelihood in settings with high levels of salinity intrusion. I wanted to understand how locals were coping with change. By midmorning we reached the ferry to Cuu Lao Dung. Here the river was more than 3 kilometers wide – the widest I had ever seen, and the ferry, which traversed the river more than 20 times a day, took about 15 minutes to reach the island's shore. Quang told me our destination was the community of An Thanh, located near the end of the island that buttresses against Vietnam's East Sea. I reminded Quang that I was particularly interested in talking to farmers who had transitioned into shrimp production and asked him to stop along the way if he saw anyone who fit the bill.

The road to An Thanh, like most roads in the Mekong Delta, is wide enough for two-way motorcycle traffic. An irrigation ditch, not deep enough for navigation even by the smallest of boats, runs parallel on the road's western side for its 30 kilometer length. Coconut palms shaded the road, and as we sped farther southward, Quang pointed out sugar cane and taro plantations that lined the road's opposite side. About 30 minutes later we stopped alongside small shrimp farm comprised of 4 ponds, each roughly the size of an Olympic-size swimming pool. Parking the motorcycle behind a new Lexus SUV, we approached a makeshift lean-to nearby where we expected to find the Lexus's owner who we assumed to own and manage the shrimp farm. A middle-aged woman stepped out of the lean-to to deliver an unenthusiastic greeting. She was wearing high-heels and what looked like two large diamond rings on her hands. The heels and the jewelry and the Lexus felt out of place for this remote island at the end of the Mekong. Quang approached her asking whether she and her husband, who we saw smoking a cigarette and sitting shirtless under the shade of the lean-to, could spare a few minutes to talk about the opportunities and challenges of managing a small shrimp farm. I could tell by the reaction that she was politely refusing. After an additional comment from her husband, Quang turned to me and said, "Sorry, they aren't interested in talking. Her husband said having strangers like you and me around might bring bad luck to the shrimp. People here are very superstitious and overly protective."

I paid a smile to the couple, and we returned to the motorcycle. Quang then explained how a variety of factors such as a sudden temperature spike or a garbage spill could ruin an entire shrimp harvest. He also noted how feuding families in the delta were known to sabotage each other's shrimp farms. "Farmers are known to invite monks to bless their ponds and engage in all kinds of superstitious protection rituals because so much is on the line. They probably were extra concerned since you're a foreigner." We continued on down the road, and just outside of An Thanh, we stopped at the gate of a large two-story residence made of grey and beige brick surrounded by large shrimp ponds on three sides. The house's defining feature was an archway supported by tall Doric columns that surrounded the front three sides of the home. Here, the owner had created several spaces to receive guests and dine outside. Quang and I heard laughter from a small gathering of people coming from behind the home, and since the gate was open, we entered to search out the lucky shrimp farmer, hoping to discover the secret to his success.

A young man named Linh greeted us, and after a brief introduction from Quang, whose Can Tho University credentials carry much currency in the Mekong Delta, Linh invited us to sit at a table with the young man's father, a farmer in his fifties named Hoang, and six other members of his family. Seated next to me was Hoang's brother Vu who proudly boasted that the equally large and identical residence next to this one – also surrounded on three sides by large shrimp pond – belonged to him. It was lunchtime, and the two brothers and Linh had finished off most of a case of Beer 333. At Hoang's insistence, Quang and I joined in the merriment.

Through the next hour, we learned how Hoang and his brother moved to Cuu Lao Dung from Tra Vinh province more than a decade ago to set up the area's most successful small-scale shrimp farm. At first, they tried other crops, but after a few subpar seasons, they decided to transition into shrimping. "The soil was too saline and getting worse every year, so we had to do something else," said Hoang. I inquired whether he and Vu took on debt to start the operation. He answered, "We paid for it by ourselves with our life savings – around $6500. Shrimp farmers are not welcomed by the banks now because shrimp farming is now seen as a risky venture."

"Have you had friends whose farms failed?" I asked.

"So many," he replied. I continued my line of inquiry, asking why their shrimp farm succeeded where others failed. The two brothers conferred for a few minutes and then gave me a brief lecture on what they believed to be the three elements of success: maintaining water quality and an overall healthy environment, the quality of shrimp larvae purchased on the market, and being disciplined in managing the farm. "We learned these techniques by ourselves through trial and error. No one taught us, and we will teach no one else. This is a very competitive market."

Hoang gave Quang and me some deep-fried fish as long and thin as a plastic straw to go with our Beer 333. Quang noted these were a local wild-caught delicacy. Hoang also demanded we try another snack fresh out of the frying pan which at first I thought were large grasshoppers, but after closer inspection, I realized that not much is left over after you deep fry a frog. Hoang slapped me on the back, offered a garrulous toast, and said, "You should come here and do a shrimp farm! It's a good life. We are all happy here! The price of shrimp is very stable now." Since it is common to openly talk about income and profits in Vietnam, I inquired into the family's annual harvest. "We raise three cycles of shrimp per year. We could do four, but we need to take a break and so does the farm. In total, we harvest between 30,000 and 36,000 kilograms of shrimp," he said. Shrimp from the Mekong Delta sell at about $5 per kilogram (100,000 VND), so with that harvest, Hoang and his brother are jointly earning more than $150,000 per year. Vu added, "We're household farmers. We can do everything by ourselves and don't need to hire workers. So the cost of production is low. We keep more than half of our earnings."

Clearly the two brothers had hit the jackpot with their invest-ment. Hoang told me he planned a new business venture to introduce ecotourism on the island. He was impressed by other ecotourism services he experienced while traveling to other parts of Vietnam over the years. Hoang too also hopes to travel abroad soon and see the rest of the world. Before leaving, I mentioned that I often buy shrimp from the delta in American supermarkets. Hoang offered to keep in touch so that someday perhaps I could give him a personal tour of America's supermarkets to see his shrimp.

After saying goodbye to Hoang and Vu and their families, Quang and I rode into An Thanh commune. We stopped at a roadside café near the village's main intersection to exchange notes and obser-vations from the morning. We sat down in the shade of a large fig tree at a low-lying table with its seats facing the road. The chairs at many roadside cafés are oriented this way throughout Vietnam so friends can sit and converse while watching traffic go by. Seated at the end of the table was a man in his sixties wearing sunglasses and a worn, button-down white shirt and grey slacks. Quang struck up a conversation and quickly learned the man, whose name was Nguyen Vung Diep, was a sugar cane farmer. When asked about the farming on Cuu Lao Dung island. Diep added "We used to grow rice here in the past but do so no longer. The land around here is young and used to be underwater, so it has a high sulphur content. Rice just won't grow. People on Cuu Lao Dung have shifted to other crops like sugar cane, taro, chili or pumpkins. And for those who are rich, who have money, they can dig out shrimp farms. But many people here are poor so they don't have the ability to do that."

I asked Diep what he did for a living, "Like most people here on the island, I plant sugar cane, but it's hard to find workers to come and harvest the fields since the young generation tends to move to Ho Chi Minh City to work in factories. There's a huge shortage of workers here. Low number of workers means wages are high, that's the problem," he said with a voice of despair. "The price of sugar cane this year is very low. I have no income. Many of the farmers here have no income because we get less than what we invested into the farm. We are very disappointed."

Diep continued to tell us how 5 years ago farmers could earn twice as much harvesting sugar cane because the price of sugar globally was quite high, and the quality of sugar cane coming out of the island was also high. When the money was coming in, farmers plowed more income into their fields and acquired more land for farming. Then things changed quickly when salinity intrusion seeped deeper into the island's fields, and the sugar cane growing in the affected soil lost its quality. "I've heard about climate change, but I don't know what that is really," he said, "All I know is sugar companies don't want to pay market price for this cane, and I can't find anyone to cut it down."

I asked whether he thought about transitioning into another crop, but all of his money was tied up in his fields filled with sugar cane that would never be harvested. Trying his luck on shrimp also was not an option he was willing to explore. "I'm too old. Anyway to become a shrimp farmer, I'd have to surrender my land use certificate over to the bank to get a loan. Half of my friends who have gone into shrimping have failed. After that they lose their land and have no choice but to work in factories. This is a gamble I'm not willing to take. So now I drive a motorcycle taxi. That's why I'm waiting here at the intersection," he said.

We learned that Diep moved to Cuu Lao Dung in 2000 from An Giang province, far upstream near the border with Cambodia. His wife, a native of the island, was given a deal for 180 hectares of land, a huge parcel considering most households in the Mekong Delta live on less than 1 hectare. But having access to a large plot of land brought little benefit when the soil was no good. He and his wife now earn about 1000 dollars per year, a number well below a quarter of Vietnam's average income for two people. Since sticking around the island to plant crops is a losing bet, he and his wife encouraged his four children, all in their twenties and thirties, to move to Ho Chi Minh City.

"What do your children do in Ho Chi Minh City?" I asked.

"Three of my daughters work in garment factories making shoes, and my son works in an electronics factory. The youngest still lives with us," said Diep. I asked whether his children come home often. "It's not a long trip for them, but they return once a year at Tet Holiday. They earn little income, so they can't come home often."

For the past 25 years, 1.7 million people have left the delta. In 2016, 300,000 people left.[35] Nearby in Ho Chi Minh City where wages are 5 times the average farmer's income in the delta, more than a third of the city's 8.6 million inhabitants is migrant. Women under the age of 30 make up a majority of Ho Chi Minh's migrants.[36] Vietnam's government has tried to curb this flow of outmigration by denying benefits to new arrivals in Ho Chi Minh City and instituting laws to increase access to the delta's natural resources, but these efforts produce little fruit. Most migrants arriving in Ho Chi Minh City work in low wage manufacturing jobs in the city's industrial zones or in hotels and restaurants that cater to the service industry. New arrivals have no social safety net.

Can Tho University's Professor Duong Van Ni, one of the delta's most fervent conservationists, says with the imbalances of wages between the delta and the rest of the country, migration is inevitable. "More should be done here in the delta to prepare people before they migrate. We can give them a level of higher education so they can become skilled before they migrate and earn higher wages," said Dr. Ni. He has long observed the delta's outmigration and noted how most young parents head off to the city, leaving their children home with only grandparents to take care of them. "This creates a breakdown in cultural flow from one generation to the other. Grandparents aren't as diligent in raising children as their parents are, and this will create risks to both social development and nature further into the future. Without parents at home, a child's education suffers." Dr. Ni believes the government and the private sector in Ho Chi Minh City can work together to provide public services to the migrant workers that fuel the city's ballooning economic growth. "The government could tax industry to provide low-income housing for the workers for rent or to buy. If the government subsidizes health care and education then I believe the parents will bring their children with them. If they do that, they will not worry about children skipping school or how their children will be affected if there's a typhoon or flood here in the delta. They can watch their children grow up, share culture, and build social relations."

In 2007, the Intergovernmental Panel on Climate Change (IPCC) identified Vietnam's Mekong Delta as one of three extreme global hotspots in terms of potential population displacement, and certainly, Mekong watchers wonder what will happen to the delta's economy if its population drains significantly. But Dr. Ni has a controversial opinion toward migration out of the delta. "Let them go," he says. "The drive for agricultural production and economic growth is what brought so many people here in the first place. The delta's population almost doubled after Vietnam transitioned to a market economy in 1986. Sustainable growth relies on a long-term balance between nature and economic return. So now one of our biggest challenges is that the population is too high. On average people have less than 1 hectare of land. With such a small area, it is believed that the fastest way to a higher income is through intensive production. And when you do intensive production, you ignore conservation. With too much intensive production – either rice, fish, vegetables, or whatever – you push the environment to work very hard. The landscape doesn't have enough room for recovery."

Dr. Ni has worked with farmers for the past two decades to transition away from rice production into activities that build resiliency to both climate change and economic shocks as well as generate comparatively higher levels of income. He is a big proponent of shrimp farming in the brackish zones, but warns that like intensive rice production, overdoing shrimp farming has its dangers. "You should never put all of your eggs in one basket. Shrimp are very vulnerable to shocks. The global price might be low, disease could affect your ponds, or a temperature spike might wipe out your entire farm," he said. Indeed these risks mark a big difference between raising aquaculture versus other kinds of livestock both in the delta and globally. Insurance companies in the United States, where the aquaculture sector is relatively mature, struggle with issuing coverage plans to farmers since the likelihood of losing an entire harvest is somewhat high. It is rare for the entire stock of a farmer's cows or pigs to die at once, but not so with aquaculture. Some farmers alongside the Mekong raise aquaculture in large cages or nets and lose the entire stock when an unexpected storm or landslide whisks the nets into the river system. If those fish or shrimp species that escape are invasive to the river, they often wreak havoc on local biodiversity.

Dr. Ni also warns against shrimping's effects on the delta's natural landscape. "The delta used to have a thick band of mangrove forests along the coastline and bordering rivers. These mangroves provided protection from incoming typhoons and storm surges and helped keep the shorelines and banks intact. Unfortunately, today shrimp farmers have cleared most of the mangroves to make way for shrimp ponds," he said. Mangroves also form a cornerstone for biodiversity since numerous mammals, birds, and reptiles are known to make their homes in exposed bushy parts of trees. Fish and other aquatic species find habitat and nutrition among mangroves' knotty underwater root systems. For the last two decades Dr. Ni has trained farmers and an up-and-coming generation of delta conservation experts on techniques to make aquaculture work in a sustainable way. Professor Nguyen Minh Quang, who accompanied me on the tour of Cuu Lao Dung island, is one of his protégés.

Quang grew up in the U Minh Forest, one of the delta's remaining jungles on the southwest coast in Ca Mau province. The U Minh Forest is well-known for its biodiversity and high-quality honey, but it is also one of the most impoverished areas in the delta. Quang's grandparents were Viet Cong rebels and sought refuge in U Minh Forest. This put them in contact with Agent Orange sprayed out of American planes during the war. Today many of Quang's immediate family members struggle with congenital disabilities. Quang considers himself lucky to have his health intact, and today he is on the road to becoming a major advocate for sustainability in the delta. "When I was a student in primary school, I had to wake up at 4 am to have breakfast and walk 6 kilometers through muddy rice fields to school," he said. "I had to take off my trousers when I got to school because I was so muddy and had a plastic bag for my books and pencils. I was afraid of the ghosts and monsters. It was so dark outside, and we only had a flashlight to guide us along narrow paths. There were snakes and insects and all of those scary things. My friends were too afraid to walk to school, so they stopped going. Now they have many children and are farmers in U Minh. But I persisted, and now I'm bringing what I've learned at Can Tho University and at university in Europe back to my community."

In 2017 he founded the Mekong Environment Forum, an NGO focused on combining traditional and cutting-edge sustainability practices and sharing them among farmers in the delta. "We need to shift farmers into a more climate-resilient mode of livelihood where they are less reliant on costly, damaging external inputs such as fertilizers and pesticides," he said. Quang's magic bullet is to educate local farmers about a technique called mangrove-based polyculture, a small-scale agricultural system where many aquacultural and agricultural crops such as shrimp, fish, crabs, vegetables, and fruits are raised within close proximity of each other by a single household. "We create ponds for fish and shrimp, but instead of clearing them away, we plant mangroves to act as a habitat for aquaculture. The mangroves naturally filter the water, provide nutrients, and keep the land intact in the event of extreme weather," he told me. "What we do won't make a farmer extremely wealthy, but on average if they get their farms up and running, they will do much better than a rice farmer and not be put at risk for indebtedness or migration to the city for wage labor." In early 2018, Quang received a small grant from the public affairs section of the United States Consulate in Ho Chi Minh City to set up demonstration sites and train farmers in the U Minh Forest – a fitting gesture of diplomacy coming nearly a half-century after the US military forces laid waste to the forest.[37]

On a recent trip to the delta, Quang showed me polyculture at work on a small farm operated by Le Hoang Thanh, a few kilometers outside of Can Tho University. Thanh converted his half-hectare of land into a polyculture project nearly two decades ago, and alongside Quang, he trains other farmers on making the transition. Thanh is one of the proudest and most ingenious farmers I have met in all of my journeys through the Mekong region. He started our conversation with a bit of English he learned from American GIs during the war, and then began to describe his pathway to sustainability. "In terms of income, I have a stable income year by year from polyculture farming. Compared to those who just raise shrimp or rice, sometimes they have higher income, but there are also times when they bring in little income. Their success entirely depends on the market for one crop. Sometimes the price for what they raise is high, but they don't have a lot to show. And sometimes they produce a bumper crop but the price is low," he told us. "I'm lucky because I sell many things from my farm all year long. When the price is high I can take advantage of it, and the different animals and plants on the farm support each other. It's a very stable system."

He took us behind his home to give us a tour of the farm which had two ponds surrounded by mangroves filled with carp, tilapia, snails, and floating plants called water lettuce. Surrounding the ponds and his house are 80 fruit trees bearing grapefruit, durian, and menteng fruit – a tart, lychee-like fruit found in the hotter climes of Southeast Asia. Every product from the farm would qualify as organic and his system is entirely closed, meaning he brings in nothing from outside of his farm, no pesticides, fertilizers, or antibiotics to maintain its productivity. "The fish and snails eat the lettuce for nutrition – all of the fish are herbivores so they will not eat the snails. My snails are top quality and highly sought after by restaurants in Can Tho," he said as he pulled a few snails the size of golf balls off a water lettuce plant he removed from the pond. Thanh piled more water lettuce into a wheelbarrow and hauled it over to a 3 meter long concrete tube closed at one end. "This is my biodigester. It provides all the gas we need for cooking heat and covers our air conditioning bill during the dry season," he told us as he pushed the water lettuce into the mouth of the biodigester with a long pole. Inside the biogasser, micro-organisms break down the water lettuce or any other organic matter put inside. This produces methane which is then collected in a bladder. When the bladder is full, the gas can be consumed. "I used to raise pigs and used their waste to feed the biogasser, but now the price of pork is low, so the water lettuce and grass clippings from around the house are good enough." When the decomposition process is finished, Thanh removes the leftover organic matter from the biogasser and tosses it in the pond to serve as a nutritional base for the floating water lettuce. This closes the nutritional loop for the pond. "Every year, college students from the University of Minnesota come here to learn my methods. I teach them how to build a biodigester," he said.

Quang added, "Thanh's fruit grows at different times of the year, and his fish and snails can be harvested at any time, so he's not like rice or shrimp farmers who only collect income a few times a year. On average he earns between 5000 and 6000 dollars a year." This number is particularly impressive compared to Mr. Diep the sugar cane farmer on Cuu Lao Dung who earned 1000 dollars per year using 180 hectares of land.

"You seem to enjoy this, but maintaining the system looks like a lot of work," I suggested to Thanh after he showed us how he raised snail and fish eggs that he removed from snails and fish in the pond.

Thanh answered with a proud smile, "I really enjoy this, and it's not a lot of work. Now the system can take care of itself. Sometimes I don't have to tend to it for a few weeks."

"That's how he has time to go around the delta with me and teach other farmers how to start polyculture farms. He gets paid to do that too," said Quang. "Thanh is well-known throughout the delta." Thanh is 1 of 300 farmers in the Can Tho suburbs who have transitioned away from monoculture to polyculture farms. Quang's vision is to transfer this closed-loop system to other parts of the delta. "There are many different ways to do polyculture. What works for Thanh here around Can Tho, might not be replicable in Ca Mau or other parts of the delta. I design systems to adapt to the land and water around it." If he and other promoters of polyculture are successful at a greater scale, a significant portion of farmers could move out of rice and other monocrops and sell their high-value, organic quality polyculture products on the regional and global market. However, an expansion of this kind faces a major obstacle in the delta: there are not enough roads to get these perishable goods to far-flung markets.

When compared to other parts of Vietnam, the delta has a significantly lower number of roads. This should come as no surprise when considering most of the delta's infrastructure investment has been poured into building dykes and sluice gates to promote rice production. The existing network of waterways is underutilized and lacks a network of ports to ship goods from the delta to the rest of the region. Roads and water networks combined are 72 percent of Vietnam's national average. Like incomes, transportation infrastructure is falling behind, and these two figures are interrelated.[38] Many of the delta's existing roads are flooded over or impassable during the monsoon season. Even in the dry season, a 150 kilometer trip from Can Tho to the U Minh forest in Ca Mau province could take up to 6 hours. To date, only 4 bridges span the Hau and the Tien rivers. All were built with foreign assistance funding from Japan and Australia in the last decade. This lack of transportation connectivity keeps wealthy Vietnamese and foreign investors who might want to invest in high-value agriculture or other industries away from the delta.

But all of this could be changing soon as the aforementioned Resolution 120 issued late in 2017, which de-emphasizes rice production and calls for the radical solutions to shift the delta onto a more sustainable development pathway, begins to take shape. Some of the resolution's official language is very much encouraging and in tune with needs in the delta and the region at large. For example, that economic development should "serve the people" and focus on "quality versus quantity." Importantly, the resolution calls for a development model based on "an ecological system, in harmony with natural conditions, biodiversity, culture and people, and natural rules." It calls for a combination of "modern, advanced technology and local indigenous knowledge" – an inspiriting change for a region where the state typically views indigenous traditions as backward and uncivilized.[39] However, a specific pathway for implementing the vision has yet to manifest itself.

This shift comes at a particularly difficult time when the country has reached its limit in borrowing loans from multinational banks like the World Bank or the Asian Development Bank. Creative thinking that can show planners in the delta how to do more with less is very much needed. Pouring concrete into dykes, building sluice gates, and creating a complex set of regulatory arrangements to manage how water flows throughout the delta will only increase risks in a time when the competition for water resources, both in the delta and the region at large, is heating up. Placing trust in an engineered system assumes a country can continue to cope with increased climate change risks and costs of maintenance, retiring, or failure of those projects. Clearly the delta must move away from the "Penelope problem" of building and maintaining more dykes and sluice gates even if the purpose is to make a defiant stand against sea level rise.

To find a smart pathway forward for the delta, Vietnam could turn to the success of the Netherlands' development model. Most of the Netherlands is below sea level and sits on the delta of the Rhine-Meuse-Scheldt rivers. The Netherlands is known for its extensive network of sea dykes that has allowed the Dutch delta to be transformed into one of the world's most valuable zones of agro-economy. The Dutch are globally the number two exporter of agro-products and have achieved one of the world's highest income levels partially by choosing this path. In 2013, the Dutch produced a Mekong Delta Plan for Vietnam which recommended for the delta's economy to transition into the production of high-value agro-products produced, processed, and packaged in the delta and then shipped to the rest of Vietnam and the region at large.

The Dutch plan recommends avoiding a strategy that maintains the delta solely as a food production hub because as such the delta's talented youth will continue to migrate out and much of the delta's resources would remain underutilized. A prioritization of food production will also continue overinvestment in dykes, canals, and sluice gates that will continue to fragment the delta's ecosystem. Also, agriculture alone will not generate enough economic growth to support urbanization in the delta's cities.[40] Comparatively, prioritizing agribusiness will continue to make good use of the delta's abundance in natural resources and drive locals and outsiders to invest in ways add that value and create innovative products. Instead of demarcating land for rice production, applying flexible land use systems will let the market decide what products will generate the most value for farmers. This pathway would be more cost effective and benefits will spill over into dividends for industrialization and urbanization in the delta. A wealthier income base in the delta can then provide more resources to fend off the threats of climate change.[41]

In the coming century, how much of what happens in the Mekong Delta's environmental and economic future is the responsibility of the rest of the world to solve? After all, the excessive fossil fuel consumption that has delivered climate change threats to the delta came from the developed West. These practices are now transferred to major carbon emitters such as India and China, the most upstream country in the Mekong. Moreover, a portion of the delta's fish, shrimp, and rice are sold all over the world. When consumers in the United States, Europe, Africa, and China buy these products, they are buying a portion of the Mekong's water and sediment – the two most critically important environmental flows now under threat throughout the Mekong. If at the global and regional scale, a connection is made between the delta food we as consumers eat and a drive to keep the delta alive, then solutions for sustainable growth and the conservation of its natural resources could pour in to assist Vietnam as its farmers, planners, and academics orient the delta onto a smarter and more resilient development pathway.

In my conversation with Nguyen Huu Thien, the Mekong Delta ecologist, he made a comparison between the mentality of delta engineers and the ill-fated protagonist in Jack London's 1908

short story "To Build a Fire."[42] In the story, the main character fumbles ahead in the freezing temperatures of Alaska's Yukon territory despite several warnings from wiser people around him against such a journey out into the cold. He moves forward in his hubris with absolutely no respect, understanding, or empathy for the natural setting around him. It is the classic narrative of man vs. nature, and in the end, despite several attempts to build a fire and warm his body, the main character dies of hypothermia. This mentality not only applies to delta engineers but also to the network of officials, investors, and political élite in the Mekong Basin who are driving the Mekong toward ecological ruin despite more than 15 years of warnings from trained scientists, policy experts, and community leaders. Now the Mekong's ecosystem itself is giving off warning signs. Unlike London's main character, however the cast of characters currently ruling over the Mekong's future is unlikely to feel the pain of their decisions. These instead are being borne by the Mekong's bountiful ecosystem and the vulnerable communities that live among it.

In a recent warning, the Mekong River Commission Secretariat issued the findings of its "Council Study" a 4 year analysis of the impacts of hydropower development on the Mekong mainstream and tributaries. It is the first study of its kind paid for by the governments of the Lower Mekong and development partners to quantify in dollars the economic, social, and environmental losses delivered by dams. As expected, and consistent with most other peer-reviewed studies on these impacts, the study's results predict a dire future for the river system and the people who rely on its resources. It emphatically urges the exploration of alternatives to avoid these shocks. To date, Vietnam, the Mekong's most downstream country is the only country to fold the results of the "Council Study" into its planning processes.

Despite the warning call, Laos continues to dam the Mekong mainstream, issuing a June 2018 announcement of the Pak Lay Dam, the fourth dam to be built on the mainstream of the Mekong. Additionally, also in June, the government of Laos announced two dams for construction by Thai companies on the Sekong mainstream, the last of the undammed 3S rivers, despite efforts of conservationists to keep the Sekong River running free. Sand continues to come out of the Mekong to fill in wetlands for urban development in all of the countries of the Mekong. Riverside homes keep falling into the Mekong and fish catches continue to decline. China continues to suggest its upstream dams cause little downstream ecological damage. Business as usual proceeds toward ecological peril in the Mekong Basin.

To borrow another literary allusion from more than a century ago, the various stages of the Mekong Delta's history are like the ghosts of the past, present, and future for the rest of the Mekong Basin. Starting with the past, the beginning of this book described the upland people of the Mekong as Zomian, those who can easily avoid the state and define their livelihood on their own terms given the abundance of natural resources around them. Leafing through the delta's historical record, one will inevitably draw comparisons to the delta's swamp pirates and maroon rebels and the Mekong's ethnic groups. But today, with the exception of the Khmer Khrom who originally inhabited the delta, they are entirely gone. The domineering state-building apparatus of engineers, canal dredgers, and sluice gate managers fully cover the extent of the delta. Gone too, by and large, is the delta's once abundant biodiversity. The people of the delta aged 50 and older still remember a time when the swamps and wetlands served as their "supermarket" in the same way that Khru Tee in the Golden Triangle today reminds communities there that their forests still have much to offer.

Moving to the present, the delta faces the same effects from upstream dams, poor planning, and climate change as most of the rest of the Mekong Basin. Since Vietnam's delta is located the farthest downstream, the interactions of upstream impacts and climate change are the most profound and complex. It does not help that the delta is the most densely populated portion of the Mekong. However, growing populations in Laos, Cambodia, and Thailand will continue to put pressure on natural resources and water use. Since the problem set is strikingly similar for all countries in the Mekong, it makes the most sense for their governments and other stakeholders to work together to derive common solutions. But instead they choose to compete and reduce resource access to each other. Only a shared crisis such as a severe drought, military conflict, or economic recession will expose their common vulnerabilities and drive them toward each other, but this suggestion, of course, is speculation.

The delta's present also represents a kind of ghost of the future of the rest of the Mekong. Laos's damming spree, what many call a poorly conceptualized idea, really kicked off with the Xayaburi Dam in the mid-2000s. Vietnam's Rice First Policy, another poorly conceptualized idea, took off in the mid-1980s two decades earlier. Both of these development initiatives rely heavily on the plans of engineers and poorly set economic targets. The Rice First Policy is wrecking livelihoods and the natural resource base of the delta. Laos's plans will inevitably wreck livelihoods and the natural resource base of those downstream. Millions of people are now leaving the delta as a result of the depletion of resources and fragmentation of core environmental flows. Now three decades later, Vietnam's leadership is trying to rectify the mistakes of the past with Resolution 120. Will it take Laos three decades to realize its "Battery of Southeast Asia" plans are unachievable and call for a course correction? At that point in time, will Laos, or Cambodia in a similar position, have enough resources and know-how to wrench itself into an entirely different direction? And with a solution set currently on the horizon for the delta, is it really worth going through the pains of wrecking Mekong's amazing ecosystem by overdamming the upstream and cutting off connectivity through key stretches of the mainstream, tributaries, and the Tonle Sap?

Technologies such as solar and wind power and battery storage will soon provide alternative solutions to damming the Mekong and meeting regional energy needs. Renewables can both replace dams and also reduce the need for countries like Thailand to look for energy generation sources outside their borders. These major transitions in energy generation and distribution might be coming sooner than expected. In March 2018, Thailand's government shocked Laos's dreams of becoming the "Battery of Southeast Asia" when it announced the temporary suspension of the Pak Beng Dam, the third dam scheduled for the Mekong mainstream in Laos. The Pak Beng Dam had gone through the MRC notification and consultation process in 2017 and was ready to break ground when the suspension was announced.

Thailand's national electricity agency EGAT attributed the Pak Beng pause to a review of Thailand's power development plan. Thailand's energy ministry cited a need to integrate electricity generated from inside Thailand's before drawing energy from dams in Laos and Myanmar. An excess of biogas, solar, and wind power already ballooning inside of Thailand's borders is driving this conversation. Also, a new look at demand for electricity in Thailand suggests less power is needed into the future. Since Laos has no use for power generated from mainstream dams other than exporting to its neighborhood, with no other power market in the region making an appeal to buy Mekong mainstream hydropower, the rate of dam building could possibly come to a grinding halt. How countries in the region respond to the dynamic technological innovations and power demand shifts over the course of the next 5 years will determine the fate of the Mekong River's ecology. So there is no better time than now to join the chorus that simultaneously sings of the wonders of the Mekong, renewable energy technologies, and ways to reduce electricity consumption across the region.

But two trends showing no sign of subsiding are China's increasing encroachment in the Mekong region and the total assimilation of Zomian cultures into a lifestyle and economic milieu entirely determined by lowland states. These trends are interrelated because Chinese investors continue to double down on bringing the technological innovations – the dams, roads, rails, advanced markets, and now drones and artificial intelligence – that will depopulate the hills or tie the people who choose to remain there further into lowland economic system. The flow of Chinese infrastructure investment, market penetration, laborers, and tourists is changing economic, social, and environmental landscapes in the Mekong at a pace never brought before by any foreign power. If the quality of change is to be altered, it can only be done by Chinese stakeholders themselves becoming more responsible and more attuned to the unique qualities of the Mekong region. Alternatively, downstream stakeholders can collectively and constructively engage with China on a course for change. Development partners from the West can assist on both sides of this equation. Otherwise, barring a sudden domestic downturn, the externalities delivered by China's economic march into Southeast Asia will not subside.

Of the many things I have learned while talking to hundreds of stakeholders working at the community, government, and academic level is that communities in the Mekong can solve their own local problems if their members have the right tools and approaches in hand. Throughout the region, individuals in communities are working together, sometimes with assistance from universities, local government, international development partners, and the private sector, to constructively conserve the natural resources base around them while they preserve the unique cultural milieu of their own corner of the Mekong. The Akha in Yunnan are doing this. Communities in the Golden Triangle continue to not only culturally thrive in Chiang Rai province, but Kru Tee and his peers teach these lessons to communities all over Thailand. Success stories are also to be found in the fishing villages in the Tonle Sap and among polyculture farmers in the Mekong Delta. The same cannot be said for ethnic communities alongside the Nam Ou river in Northern Laos or in the Erhai Valley in China's Yunnan province where a top-down system of governance has removed almost all sense of agency from individuals to improve their own lot and the quality of the environment around them. The successful cases all share a similar context: democratic and transparent processes that empower change and strong, consistent leadership to guide forward a vision. However, while communities can cope with local change, into the future their resilience will be tested by actions upstream thousands of kilometers away from them as well as the effects of climate change. If most of the sediment is gone and the river is turned into a series of still reservoirs or their land disappears, the best alternative for communities depending on the river's resources might be to leave.

Among the numerous ways this book explains how the Mekong's ecological system works, I hope that the concept of connectivity has the most sticking power with readers. Connectivity is a way to think about the river as a system linked from its tributaries to its mainstream to the land surrounding it and to the ocean. With connectivity as a starting point for thinking about how to manage and conserve a river system, environmental flows come to the forefront of any discussion. Connectivity is not just a way to think about the Mekong but also a highly effective paradigm for thinking about conserving the world's rivers regardless of their size. A parting comment in my conversation with Mekong Delta ecologist Duong Van Ni reminded me of the importance of connectivity and seeing the Mekong as a connected system.

Dr. Ni said, "The river itself doesn't have an Upper or Lower Mekong. The system is one. Without the upper part of the Mekong River, there is no delta. Without activity along the channel, through Laos, through Thailand, to Cambodia there is no rich biodiversity of the Mekong. I like to compare the river to a tree. The stem itself doesn't grow alone. It grows because of the canopy, the leaves, the roots. When you think about the Mekong River, you should think of it like a tree. If it's just a stem, then the people in China, Laos, Thailand, Cambodia or Vietnam think that the part that belongs to them is the most important. But the part that belongs to them is not at all the most important. If you cut all the branches of the tree, the stem will die. If you cut the roots of the tree, the stem will die. So, if we are to preserve this mighty Mekong, we have to look at the all the parts of the river as connected to one system," he concluded. Unless we begin today to see the river and the landscapes around it as a connected system and act jointly for its conservation, the Mighty Mekong's last days are here and now.

NOTES

Introduction

1 To be sure, the name Zomia was coined by historian Willem van Schendel in 2002, but Scott's work has done much to popularize and disseminate the geographic conceptualization of Zomia. Scott, James C. The Art of Not Being Governed. Yale, New Haven. 2009.

2 Hortle, Kent. (2009). "Fishes of the Mekong – How Many Species are There?" *Catch and Culture*. 15. 4–12.

3 Mekong River at Risk. World Wide Fund for Nature. 2012. mobil. wwf.de/fileadmin/fm-wwf/Publikationen-PDF/WWF_factsheet_ The_Mekong_River_at_Risk.pdf

4 Osborne, Milton. The Mekong: Turbulent Past, Uncertain Future. Grove press. 2001.

5 www.mekongeye.com/2017/03/03/mrc-ceo-hydropower-development-will-not-kill-the-mekong-river/

Chapter 1

1 Hilton, James. Lost Horizn. Macmillan. 1933.

2 www.revolvy.com/main/index.php?s=Kawagarbo

3 Osburg, John. Anxious Wealth: Money and Morality Among China's New Rich. Stanford. 2013. sinosphere.blogs.nytimes.com/ 2014/12/16/q-and-a-john-osburg-on-the-angst-found-among-chinas-newly-rich/

4 Jenne, Jermiah. Interview in March 6, 2017. Jeremiah Jenne teaches history in Beijing for various university programs and is a frequent writer for publications such as ChiaFile, World of Chinese, and Radii China.

5 Yu, Dan Smyer. The Spread of Tibetan Buddhism in China. Routledge, 2011.

6 sinosphere.blogs.nytimes.com/2014/12/16/q-and-a-john-osburg-on-the-angst-found-among-chinas-newly-rich/

7   www.nature.org/ourinitiatives/regions/asiaandthepacific/china/
    placesweprotect/china-meili-snow-mountain.xml?redirect=https-
    301

8   Ibid.

9   www.chinadialogue.net/article/show/single/en/4518-Vanishing-
    Shangri-La-1-

10 Bo, Wang. Interview with Wang Bo on March 19, 2018.

11 www.npr.org/templates/story/story.php?storyId=17200108

12 Allison, Elizabeth (2015). "The Spiritual Significance of Glaciers in
    the Age of Climate Change." *Wires Climate Change*. 6. 5. Wiley.

Chapter 2

1   www.icimod.org/?q=18647

2   World Energy Outlook 2015. International Energy Agency.

3   Eels, Mark. "China's Delicate Pursuit of Natural Gas." *The Diplomat*.
    April 15, 2014.

4   www.eia.gov/todayinenergy/detail.php?id=15531

5   bigstory.ap.org/article/f5f4735a01234f3aaa6c1ac0d41db961/coal-
    not-going-away-anytime-soon-despite-renewables-push

6   www.wri.org/blog/2015/07/closer-look-chinas-new-climate-plan-
    indc

7   news.nationalgeographic.com/2016/05/160512-china-nu-river-
    dams-environment/

8   www.chinadialogue.net/article/show/single/en/9760-Hydropower-
    boom-in-China-and-along-Asia-s-rivers-outpaces-electricity-demand

Chapter 3

1   Jon Yong's most successful series is the *Condor Trilogy* (Hong Kong
    Commercial Press, Hong Kong) published between 1957 and 1961.
    The trilogy is a fictional kung-fu sga spanning the rise of the Mongols
    during the late Southern Song dynasty through ther establishment
    of the Mong era. Dali history is highlighted in Jon Yong's 1963
    novel Demi-Gods and Semi-Devils (Hong Kong Commercial Press,
    Hong Kong).

2   Thant Myint, U. Where China Meets India: Burma and the New
    Crossroads of Asia. Farrar, Strauss and Giroux. New York. 2012, p 148.

3   He, Liyi and Chix, Claire Anne. Mr China's Son: A Villager's Life.
    Westview. 2002.

4   Flahive, Colin. Great Leaps: Finding Home in a Changing China. Hudson River Press. 2015, p 46.

5   Siekman, Dan. "Kunming Deploying Invasive Species to Clean Up Dianchi." *GoKunming*. February 3, 2010. www.gokunming.com/en/blog/item/1354/kunming_deploying_invasive_species_to_clean_up_dianchi

6   Tang et al. (2013). "Status and historical changes in the fish community of Erhai Lake." *Chinese Journal of Oceanology and Limnology*. 31: 712. doi.org/10.1007/s00343-013-2324-7

7   Scally, Patrick. "Erhai Lake Quality Steadily Improving." *GoKunming*. June 16, 2015. www.gokunming.com/en/blog/item/3506/report_erhai_lake_water_quality_steadily_improving

Chapter 4

1   www.theguardian.com/world/2013/may/03/china-arrests-fake-meat-scandal

2   www.gokunming.com/en/blog/item/3517/chinas_national_meat_scandal_hits_yunnan

3   Pelley, Patricia M. Post-Colonial Vietnam: New Histories of the National Past. Duke University Press, Durham. 2002.

4   Wang Jianhua (2013). *Sacred and Contested Landscapes: Dynamics of Natural Resource Management by Akha People in Xishuangbanna, Southwest China*. (Unpublished doctoral dissertation.) University of California, Riverside. California, p 55.

5   Scott, James C. The Art of Not Being Governed. Yale, New Haven. 2009, p 116.

6   Von Geusau, Leo Alting, "Akha Internal History: Marginalization and Ethnic Alliance System," chapter 6 in Turton, Andrew (ed). *Civility and Savagery*. Routledge. 2000.

7   Wang Jianhua (2013). *Sacred and Contested Landscapes: Dynamics of Natural Resource Management by Akha People in Xishuangbanna, Southwest China*. (Unpublished doctoral dissertation.) University of California, Riverside. California, p 119.

8   Scott, James C. The Art of Not Being Governed. Yale, New Haven. 2009, p 192.

9   Ibid. p 278.

10 Von Gesau, Leo Alting. "Akha Internal History: Marginalization and Ethnic Alliance System," in Tuton, Andrew (ed). *Civility and Savagery*. Routledge. 2000, p 130.

11 James Scott develops the concent of "weapons of the weak" in his seminal work Weapons of the Weak: Everyday Forms of Peasant Resistance. Scott, James C. Weapons of the Weak: Everyday Forms of Peasant Resistance. Yale. 1987.

12 Wang Jianhua (2013). *Sacred and Contested Landscapes: Dynamics of Natural Resource Management by Akha People in Xishuangbanna, Southwest China.* (Unpublished doctoral dissertation.) University of California, Riverside, California, p 177.

13 Chen, Huafang et al. "Pushing the limits: Patterns and Dynamics of Rubber Monoculture Expansion in Southwest China." *PLoSOne.* 11. 2. e0150062. journals.plos.org/plosone/article?id=10.1371/journal.pone.0150062

14 Wang Jianhua (2013). *Sacred and Contested Landscapes: Dynamics of Natural Resource Management by Akha People in Xishuangbanna, Southwest China.* (Unpublished doctoral dissertation.) University of California, Riverside. California, p 229.

15 www.sjonhauser.nl/akha-swing-festival.html

16 Li Haiying (2013). *Neo-Traditionalist Movements and the Practice of Aqkaoqzanr in a Multi-Religious Community in Northern Thailand.* (Unpublished masters dissertation.) Chiang Mai University, Chiang Mai, Thailand. p 3.

17 Li Haiying (2013). *Neo-Traditionalist Movements and the Practice of Aqkaqzanr in a Multi-Religious Community in Northern Thailand.* (Unpublished masters dissertation.) Chiang Mai University, Chiang Mai, Thailand, p 147.

18 Ibid. p 149.

19 Ibid. p 7.

20 Wang Jianhua (2013). *Sacred and Contested Landscapes: Dynamics of Natural Resource Management by Akha People in Xishuangbanna, Southwest China.* (Unpublished doctoral dissertation.) University of California, Riverside. California, p 229.

21 Ibid. 235.

22 Li Haiying (2013). *Neo-Traditionalist Movements and The Practice of Aqkaqzanr in a Multi-Religious Community in Northern Thailand.* (Unpublished masters dissertation.) Chiang Mai University, Chiang Mai, Thailand, p 115.

23 Scott, James C. The Art of Not Being Governed. Yale, New Haven. 2009, p 177.

24 Morton, M. F. (2013). "If you come often, we are like relatives; if you

come rarely, we are like strangers": Reformations of Akhaness in the Upper Mekong Region. *ASEAS – Austrian Journal of South-East Asian Studies, 6.* 1. 29–59, p 5.

25 Tooker, Deborah (2004). "Modular Modern: Shifting Forms of Collective Identity among the Akha of Northern Thailand". *Anthropological Quarterly.* 77. 2. 243–88.

Chapter 5

1 "Turning battlefields into marketplaces" was a slogan popularized by Thai Prime Minister Chatichai Choonhavan, a democratically elected leader who served from 1988 to 1991.

2 Howe, Jeff (2013). "Murder on the Mekong." *Atavist Magazine.* 30. magazine.atavist.com/murderonthemekong

3 Ibid.

4 Ibid.

5 Sin City: Illegal Wildlife Trade in Laos' Golden Triangle Economic Zone. Environmental Investigation Agency (EIA). March, 2015.

6 Tivasuradej, Areeya. "Unexpected Waters: How Sudden Water Changes in the Mekong are Affecting Local Thai Livelihoods." May 29, 2014. Eastbysoutheast.com. www.eastbysoutheast.com/ unexpected-waters-sudden-water-changes-mekong-affecting-local-thai-livelihoods/#more-2030

7 news.nationalgeographic.com/news/2005/06/photogalleries/ giantcatfish/index.html

Chapter 6

1 www.rfa.org/english/news/laos/former-lao-deputy-pm-joins-monastery-07132016155004.html

2 www.globalconstructionreview.com/sectors/fears-little-laos-under-chinas-kunming-singapore-r/

3 Phothisane, Souneth et al. History of Laos (From Ancient Times to the Contemporary Period). Lao PDR Ministry of Information and Culture. 2000. p 551.

4 The Lao people pronounce the name of their country without an s sound at the end. The French continued this pronunciation given that the plural s sound is unspoken in French language.

5 Mayoury Ngaosyvanth and Pheuipanh Ngaosayvanth. Paths to Conflagration: Fifty Years of Diplomacy and Warfare in Laos,

Thailand, and Vietnam 1778–1828. Southeast Asia Program Publications, Ithaca. 1998, p 50.

6   Ivarsson, Soren. Creating Laos. NIAS Press, Copenhagen. 2008, p 18.

7   Ibid. 43

8   Ibid. 167.

9   Pietrantoni, Eric (1953). "La population du Laos de 1921 a 1945." *Bulletin de la Société des Études Indochinoises*. 28. 1. 1953, p 34. As cited in Ivarsson, Soren. Creating Laos. NIS Press. Copenhagen. 2008.

10 Tuck, P. The French Wolf and the Siamese Lamb, p 63. As cited in Ivarsson, Soren. Creating Laos. NIS Press, Copenhagen. 2008.).

11 Ibid. 98.

12 Dwyer, Michael B. "The 'New' New Battlefield: Capitalizing Security in Laos's Agribusiness Landscape." p 196 in *Changing Lives in Laos: Society, Politics, and Culture in a Post Socialist State*. NUS Press, 2017.

13 www.rfa.org/english/news/laos/governor-11222017133554.html

14 Evrard, Olivier and Ian Baird. "The Political Ecology of Upland/ Lowland Relationships in Laos since 1975," p 172. in *Changing Lives in Laos: Society, Politics, and Culture in a Post Socialist State*. NUS Press. 2017.

15 Ibid. p 174.

16 Ibid. p 178.

Chapter 7

1   We will see this pattern repeated in much greater extent on the Tonle Sap Lake in the following chapter.

2   Osborne, Milton (2014). "Mekong States Speak Out Against the Don Sahong Dam." *The Lowy Interpreter*. January 22. www.lowyinstitute.org/the-interpreter/mekong-states-speak-out-don-sahong-dam

3   www.worldwildlife.org/stories/say-no-to-don-sahong-dam

4   laoenergy.la/admin/upload_free/cb0bfaff9558d1d767476c ca252b287d0dad5c39a1b262b8ce97b4c963686fefa7e c9d5704d9d2686823d68b5a2f9360don_sahong_made_simple 2%20 Q&A.pdf

5   No such documentation was reference in the fact sheet. This response came after a blanket denial that noise from underwater blasting would affect the dolphin population, since no underwater blasting would occur. No question was raised related to above ground blasting or blasting near the dam site.

6 The other channels that might have promoted fish passage in the dry season were small streams. No "extensive" studies were referenced in the document. Mega First has not produced or made transparent a study of this nature.

7 These were Thailand, Laos, Cambodia, and South Vietnam. North Vietnam was excluded from UN committees until after its successful reunification of the country in 1975.

8 www.youtube.com/watch?v=NSWQztZPMdg

9 Lilienthal, David E. The Journals of David E. Lilienthal Vol 6: Creativity and Conflict. Harper Collins, 1976, p 377.

10 Ecology and the Mekong Project. United Nations Economic Commission for Asian and the Far East, December 1972, p 4.

11 icem.com.au/portfolio-items/sea-of-hydropower-on-the-mekong-mainstream-summary-of-the-final-report/

12 Assuming a 3 percent discount rate for net present value calculations. Three percent is a commonly accepted discount rate standard for natural resources in cost benefit analysis. Costanza, Robert et al. Planning Approaches for Water Resources Development in the Lower Mekong Basin. Portland State University. 2011.

13 A large dam here qualifies as larger than 15 megawatts. This is the standard used by the Lao government for differentiating large dams and micro-hydropower projects.

14 Ziv et al. (2002). "Trading-off Fish Biodiversity, Food Security, and Hydropower in the Mekong River Basin." *Proceedings of the National Academy of Science*, p 2.

15 Orr et al. (2012). "Dams on the Mekong River: Lost Fish Protein and the Implications for Land and Water Resources." *Journal of Global Environmental Change*.

16 Norway, Belgium, France, China, USA, Thailand, Vietnam, Russia, Korea, Malaysia, and Laos.

17 Baird, Ian G and Quastel, Noah. (2015) "Rescaling and Reordering Nature–Society Relations: The Nam Theun 2 Hydropower Dam and Laos–Thailand Electricity Networks." *Annals of the Association of American Geographers*. August.

18 Intralawan, A., Frankel, R., and Wood, D. Economic Evaluation of Hydropower Projects in the Lower Mekong Basin. Mae Fah Luang University. 2017.

19 Cronin, R., Eyler, B., Weatherby, C. A Call for Strategic Basin-Wide Energy Planning in Laos. Stimson. 2016.

20 Mekong Effort Fails after Year of Lavish Foreign Funding. Associated Press. 2016.

21 Ibid.

22 Lichtefeld, J., Haque, M., Guen-Murray, J. "Mekong River Commission at a Turning Point: Perspectives From Inside the Region." (Unpublished.) Stimpson. 2017, p 18.

23 Ibid. p 22.

24 Opperman, Dr. Jeff, Grill, Dr. Gunther, and Hartman, Dr. Joergg. The Power of Rivers: Finding Balance Between Energy and Conservation in Hydropower Development, *The Nature Conservancy*. 2015. p 21.

25 China's Debt Surpasses 300 percent of its GDP. CNBC (TV channel). June 28. 2017. www.cnbc.com/2017/06/28/chinas-debt-surpasses-300-percent-of-gdp-iif-says-raising-doubts-over-yellens-crisis-remarks.html

26 A run of the river scheme constantly allows the flow of water either through the dam's powerhouse or through its spillways. Its flow cannot be turned off to increase storage in its reservoir. These dams produce a smaller reservoir but water is only stored for a period of a few days or weeks depending on the size of the dam. Run of the river dams are promoted as a more sustainable dam construction than storage dams since the overall hydrology of the river is not affected. However, run of the river dams pose the same threats to fish migration and sediment trapping as storage dams and still turn the reservoir behind the dam wall into a pool with minimal flow, thus the local hydrology of the river around the dam is affected.

27 For more information on how non-hydropower renewables will likely take the place of hydropower and other forms of fossil fuel generation in Southeast Asia see Mekong Power Shift: Emerging Trends in the GMS Power Sector, by Courtney Weatherby and Brian Eyler. Stimson. May 2017.

28 Interview with Franz Gerner, World Bank, March 2016.

Chapter 8

1 Eimer, David (2014). "Vann Molyvann: The Unsung Hero of Phnom Penh Architecture." *South China Morning Post*. February 8.

2 www.nytimes.com/2018/01/09/business/cambodia-real-estate.html

3   Ibid.

4   Kry, Suyheang (2014). "The Boeung Kak Lake Development Project: For Whom, For What? Poor Land Development Practices as a Challenge for Sustainable Peace in Cambodia." *Cambodia Law and Policy Journal*. 3. December, p 11.

5   Ibid. p 11.

6   Ibid. p 20.

7   Sahmakum Teang Tnaut (2010). "A Home No More: Stories from Boeung Kak Lake." *Facts and Figures*. 18. December, p 6.

8   Suyheang Kry (2015). "The Boeung Kak Development Project: For Whom for What?" *Cambodia Law and Policy Journal*. July 2015, p 38.

9   Otis, Daniel (2013). "Phnom Penh's most famous planner sees a city on the verge of collapse." *Next City*. December 31. nextcity.org/daily/entry/phnom-penhs-famous-urban-planner-sees-a-city-on-the-verge-of-collapse

10 Kuch, Naren (2017). "Hun Sen goes on tirade against opponents." *Cambodia Daily*. May 26. www.cambodiadaily.com/second/hun-sen-goes-tirade-opponents-130441/

11 phnompenhpost.com/national/man-held-after-calling-government-authoritarian-facebook

Chapter 9

1   thingsasian.com/story/got-fish-its-prahok-season-cambodia

2   Baran, E. Cambodia Inland Fisheries: Facts, Figures and Context. WorldFish Center and Inland Fisheries Research and Development Institute, Phnom Penh, Cambodia. 2005, p 4.

3   Cambodia's official records state the annual Tonle Sap production as 350,000 tons, but this is underestimated for reasons discussed later in this chapter.

4   Fukushima, M., Jutagate, T., Grudpan, C., Phomikong, P., Nohara, S. (2014). "Potential Effects of Hydroelectric Dam Development in the Mekong River Basin on the Migration of Siamese Mud Carp (Henicorhynchus siamensis and H. lobatus) Elucidated by Otolith Microchemistry." *PLoSONE*. 9. 8. e103722. doi:10.1371/journal.pone.0103722

5   Baird, Ian, et al. (2003). "Rhythms of The River: Lunar Phases and Migrations of Small Carps (Cyprinidae) in The Mekong River." *National Historic Bulletin of Siam Society*. 51. 1. 5–36, p 5.

6 Ibid. p 23.

7 Sarkkula, J., Baran, E., Chheng P., Keskinen, M., Koponen, J., Kummu, M. Tonle Sap Pulsing System and Fisheries Productivity. (2004). *Contribution to the XXIXe International Congress of Limnology (SIL 2004)*, Lahti, Finland, 8–14 August, p 12.

8 Baran, E. Cambodia inland fisheries: facts, figures and context. WorldFish Center and Inland Fisheries Research and Development Institute, Phnom Penh, Cambodia. 2005, p 4.

9 Evans, Patrick, T. et al. Flood Forests, Fish, Fishing Villages: Tonle Sap Cambodia. Asia Forest Network. 2004, 18.

10 Food and Nutrition Security Vulnerability to Mainstream Hydropower Dam Development in Cambodia. Inland Fisheries Development Research Institute. 2012.

11 Baran, E. Cambodia Inland Fisheries: Facts, Figures and Context. WorldFish Center and Inland Fisheries Research and Development Institute. Phnom Penh, Cambodia. 2005.

12 Keskinen, Marko, et al. (2013). "Tonle Sap Future Now and in the Future?" *Water and Development Publications*. March, p 13.

13 Ibid. p 21.

14 Baran, E. Cambodia Inland Fisheries: Facts, Figures and Context. WorldFish Center and Inland Fisheries Research and Development Institute. Phnom Penh, Cambodia. 2005.

15 Ibid. p 8.

16 Evans, Patrick, T. et al. Flood Forests, Fish, Fishing Villages: Tonle Sap Cambodia. Asia Forest Network. 2004, p 6.

17 Cooperman, M. S., So, N., Arias, M., Cochrane, T. A., Elliott , V., Hand, T., Hannah, L., Holtgrieve, G. W., Kaufman, L., Koning, A. A., Koponen, J., Kum V., McCann, K. S., McIntyre, P. B., Min, B., Ou, C., Rooney, N., Rose, K. A., Sabo, J. L. and Winemiller, K. O. (2012) "A Watershed Moment for the Mekong: Newly Announced Community Use and Conservation Areas for the Tonle Sap Lake may Boost Sustainability of the World's Largest Inland Fishery." *Cambodian Journal of Natural History*. 101–6, p 102.

18 Fukushima, M., Jutagate, T., Grudpan, C., Phomikong, P., Nohara, S. (2014). "Potential Effects of Hydroelectric Dam Development in the Mekong River Basin on the Migration of Siamese Mud Carp (Henicorhynchus siamensis and H. lobatus) Elucidated by Otolith

Microchemistry." *PLoSONE*. 9. 8. e103722. doi:10.1371/journal. pone.0103722

19 McAnn, Kevin et al. Food Webs and Sustainability of Indiscriminate Fisheries. NRC Research Press. 2015, p 7.

20 Plov rhymes with the English language word "'low."

21 Milne, Sarah. Situation Analysis at Three Project Sites on the Tonle Sap in Cambodia. IUCN. 2013, p 14.

22 Ibid. p 24.

23 Impacts of the Lower Sesan 2 Dam are discussed in Chapter 7.

24 Ou, Chouly and Winemiller, Kirk. Seasonal Hydrology Shifts Production Sources Supporting Fishes in Rivers of the Lower Mekong Basin. NRC Research Press, March. 2016, p 2.

25 Keskinen, Marko et al. Tonle Sap Future Now and in the Future? Water and Development Publications. March. 2013, p 27.

26 Baran, E. et al. Influence of Built Structures on Tonle Sap Fisheries. Cambodia National Mekong Committee and the WorldFish Center. Phnom Penh, Cambodia. 2007, p 23.

27 Keskinen, Marko et al. Tonle Sap Future Now and in the Future? Water and Development Publications. March. 2013, p 35.

28 Ou, Chouly and Winemiller, Kirk. Seasonal Hydrology Shifts Production Sources Supporting Fishes in Rivers of the Lower Mekong Basin. NRC Research Press. March 2016, p 2.

29 Sarkkula, Juha et al. "Ecosystem processes of the Tonle Sap Lake." Full paper for 1st Workshop of Ecotone Phase II, 2003 in Phnom Penh and Siem Reap, Cambodia, p 3.

30 Matti Kummu and Olli Varis. 2007. "Sediment-related impacts due to upstream reservoir trapping, the Lower Mekong River." *Geomorphology*. 85. 3–4, pp 275–93.

31 Keskinen, Marko et al. Tonle Sap Future Now and in the Future? Water and Development Publications. March. 2013, p 30.

32 Orr et al. (2002). "Dams on the Mekong River: Lost Fish Protein and the Implications for Land and Water Resources." *Journal of Global Environmental Change*, p 930.

Chapter 10

1 In 2016, China's six upstream dams, the only dams operating on the mainstream of the Mekong at that time, stored 45.4 cubic kilometers of water.

2   www.globaltimes.cn/content/974022.shtml
3   Implementation Completion and Results Report on Integrated Water Management Program for the Mekong Delta. World Bank. March 12. 2018, p 5.
4   Minderhoud, P. S. J. et al. (2017). "Impacts of 25 Years of Groundwater Extraction on Subsidence in the Mekong Delta, Vietnam." *Environmental Research Letters.* 12, p 1.
5   Ibid. p 1.
6   Ibid. p 3.
7   MacKay, Peter et al. Climate Risks in the Mekong Delta. Asian Development Bank. 2013, p 8.
8   In later writings and public lectures, James C. Scott brought the concept of Zomia out of the mountains and into wetlands and swamps citing these areas as equally difficult for the state to penetrate. He has listed examples of "wet Zomias" in the pre-Saddam Hussein Tigris/ Euphrates Delta, the Great Dismal Swamp during the American slavery era, and the Mississippi Delta in its early European settlement era.
9   Mekong Delta Central Connectivity Project on Rapid Climate Change Threat Vulnerability Assessment. International Center for Environmental Management. September 2012, p 10.
10 MacKay, Peter et al. Climate Risks in the Mekong Delta. Asian Development Bank, 2013, p 20.
11 Mekong Delta Central Connectivity Project on Rapid Climate Change Threat Vulnerability Assessment. International Center for Environmental Management. September 2012, p 61.
12 For most of the first millennia AD, Vietnam was ruled over by Chinese empires as a province. Vietnam achieved independence from China in 938 AD; however until the early 19th century, the land of the Mekong Delta was attributed to the territory neither China nor Vietnam, but rather to the Khmer Empire.
13 Biggs, David. Quagmire. Silkworm Books, Chiang Mai. 2010, p 16.
14 Ibid. p 18.
15 Ibid. p 30.
16 The railway operated from 1885 to 1958, closing due to a lack of use and poor maintenance under the government of South Vietnam.
17 Ibid. p 43.
18 Ibid. p 57.

19 Ibid. p 36.

20 Ibid. p 71.

21 apjjf.org/2011/9/5/Geoffrey-Gunn/3483/article.html

22 Biggs, David. Quagmire. Silkworm Books, Chiang Mai. 2010, p 207.

23 Ibid. p 209.

24 Obermeyer, Ziad, Murray, Christopher J. L., Gakidou, Emmanuela
    (2008). "Fifty Years of Violent War Deaths from Vietnam to Bosnia:
    Analysis of Data from the World Health Survey Programme". *British
    Medical Journal* 336. 7659. 1482–86.

25 Kontgis, C., Schneider, A., Ozdogan, M.. (2015). "Mapping Rice
    Paddy Extent and Intensification in the Vietnamese Mekong River
    Delta with Dense Time Stacks of Landsat Data." *Remote Sensing
    Environment*. 169. 255–69. doi.org/10.1016/j.rse.2015.08.004

26 Traditionally the Vietnamese bury ancestors on or near property they
    tend to.

27 The delta's natural sediments are estimated to provide one third
    of the total nutrient base for growing rice in the delta. Manh, N.
    V., Dung, N. V., Hung, N. N., Merz, B., Apel, H. (2014). "Large-
    scale suspended sediment transport and sediment deposition in the
    Mekong Delta". *Hydrology Earth Systems Sciences*. 18. 3033–53. doi.
    org/10.5194/hess-18-3033-2014

28 www.mrcmekong.org/topics/flood-and-drought/, accessed August
    1, 2017, p 11.

29 Prior to those dams being built, records from the measuring station at
    Chiang Saen, Thailand in the Golden Triangle just south of China's
    border with Southeast Asia showed an average of 84.7 million tons
    per year of sediment in the Mekong. By 2014, the sediment load had
    decreased to 10.8 million tons – half of the total load.

30 Kondolf, G. Mathias (2018). "Changing the Sediment Budget of
    the Mekong: Cumulative Threats and Management Strategies for a
    Large River Basin." *Science of the Total Environment*. 625, p 121.

31 Piman, Thanapon and Shrestha, Manish. Case Study on Sediment
    in the Mekong River Basin: Current State and Future Trends.
    Stockholm Environment Institute. November 2017, p 2.

32 news.nationalgeographic.com/2018/03/vietnam-mekong-illegal-
    sand-mining/

33 news.nationalgeographic.com/2018/03/vietnam-mekong-illegal-
    sand-mining/

34 For an in-depth discussion of this multi-dimensional connectivity see Kondolf, G. M., Boulton, A. J., O'Daniel, S., Poole, G. C., Rahel, F. J., Stanley, E. H.,Wohl, E., Bang, A., Carlstrom, J., Cristoni, C., et al. (2006). "Process-based Ecological River Restoration: Visualizing Three-dimensional Connectivity and Dynamic Vectors to Recover Lost Linkages." *Ecology and Society.* 11. 5.

35 Interview with Nguyen Huu Thien on May 26, 2018.

36 Migration, Resettlement and Climate Change in Viet Nam. United Nations. March 2014, p 2.

37 Since US relations with Vietnam resumed in 1995, the US government has supported Vietnam with more than $1 billion in development assistance.

38 Mekong Delta Plan: Long-term Vision and Strategy for a Safe, Prosperous and Sustainable Delta. Government of the Netherlands. 2013, p 22.

39 For more information on Resolution 120, see www.mekongdeltaplan.com/pm-resolution-120/

40 Ibid. p 45.

41 Ibid. p 45.

42 London, Jack. "To Build a Fire," in *The Century.* The Century Company. August 2018.

INDEX

ZED

Zed is a platform for marginalised voices across the globe.

It is the world's largest publishing collective and a world leading example of alternative, non-hierarchical business practice.

It has no CEO, no MD and no bosses and is owned and managed by its workers who are all on equal pay.

It makes its content available in as many languages as possible.

It publishes content critical of oppressive power structures and regimes.

It publishes content that changes its readers' thinking.

It publishes content that other publishers won't and that the establishment finds threatening.

It has been subject to repeated acts of censorship by states and corporations.

It fights all forms of censorship.

It is financially and ideologically independent of any party, corporation, state or individual.

Its books are shared all over the world.

www.zedbooks.net
@ZedBooks